An Introduction to the Study of
Wisdom Literature

Other titles in the T&T Clark Approaches to Biblical Studies series include:

An Introduction to the Study of Wisdom Literature

by

STUART WEEKS

t&t clark

Published by T&T Clark
A Continuum imprint
The Tower Building, 11 York Road, London SE1 7NX
80 Maiden Lane, Suite 704, New York, NY 10038

www.continuumbooks.com

British Library Cataloguing-in-Publication Data
A catalogue record for this book is available from the British Library

ISBN: 978-0-567-13582-7 (hardback)
ISBN: 978-0-567-18443-6 (paperback)

Typeset by Pindar NZ, Auckland, New Zealand
Printed and bound in Great Britain by CPI Antony Rowe Ltd, Chippenham, Wiltshire

Contents

For Charity Weeks

Abbreviations

AB	The Anchor Bible
AJSL	*American Journal of Semitic Languages and Literatures*
BETL	Bibliotheca Ephemeridum Theologicarum Lovaniensium
BZAW	Beihefte zur Zeitschrift für die alttestamentliche Wissenschaft
CBQMS	Catholic Biblical Quarterly Monograph Series
CBR	*Currents in Biblical Research*
ConBOT	Coniectanea Biblica, Old Testament Series
DJD	Discoveries in the Judean Desert
ET	English translation
FAT	Forschungen zum Alten Testament
HUCA	*Hebrew Union College Annual*
JAAR	*Journal of the American Academy of Religion*
JANESCU	*Journal of the Ancient Near Eastern Society of Columbia University*
JAOS	*Journal of the American Oriental Society*
JBL	*Journal of Biblical Literature*
JSJ	*Journal for the Study of Judaism in the Persian, Hellenistic and Roman Periods*
JSOT	*Journal for the Study of the Old Testament*
JSOTSup	*Journal for the Study of the Old Testament* Supplement Series
JTS	*Journal of Theological Studies*
NICOT	The New International Commentary on the Old Testament
OBO	Orbis Biblicus et Orientalis
SPAW	*Sitzungsberichte der Preussischen Akademie der Wissenschaften*
TLZ	*Theologische Literaturzeitung*
UF	*Ugarit-Forschungen*
VT	*Vetus Testamentum*
VTSup	Supplements to *Vetus Testamentum*
WBC	Word Biblical Commentary
WMANT	Wissenschaftliche Monographien zum Alten und Neuen Testament
WUNT	Wissenschaftliche Untersuchungen zum Neuen Testament
ZTK	*Zeitschrift für Theologie und Kirche*

Preface

The study of wisdom literature is an untidy business. The three biblical books that are usually classed as wisdom each present serious problems of interpretation, and the category 'wisdom literature' is itself understood in many different ways. For most of the last century, furthermore, scholars have recognized links between wisdom literature and a large body of other compositions from other countries, whilst the Qumran discoveries have added yet further texts to an existing stack of biblical and apocryphal works that can reasonably claim to be wisdom literature themselves. There is a mass of texts and interrelationships to deal with, therefore, but little consensus about the nature of the tradition which is supposed to link them. With an added pinch of historical speculation and a sprinkling of methodological uncertainty, we have all the ingredients for a fine stew.

It would be a lengthy and very complicated undertaking to outline the many theories and viewpoints that have been expressed about each text or question, or even to address all the issues in detail. Although we shall look at many of them, this introduction does not attempt, therefore, either to survey all the scholarship on wisdom literature, or to present a detailed examination of every text. Rather, my main purpose has been to equip the reader with an understanding of the materials, the methodological issues, and the limits of our knowledge: although, inevitably, my own views will everywhere be apparent (especially in the summaries of individual texts, where limited space forbids lengthy discussion), this is intended to be more an introduction to the ways we should approach the evidence, than a guide to the conclusions we should draw.

From that point of view, I hope that it will be of no less interest to scholars of wisdom literature than to the students and general readers at whom this book is aimed. As a compromise between the expectations of two such different audiences, I have restricted my suggestions for further reading to works in English only, provided only indicative citations of secondary literature, and refrained from detailed discussion of textual and linguistic questions, but I have also attempted to indicate, as far as possible, the basis of any statements which might be considered controversial, and to argue a case for my suggestions about the nature of wisdom literature. I am grateful to my students and colleagues at Durham for their helpful comments and conversations, to Esther Hamori for some valuable suggestions about Qohelet and the Satan, and to my children for occasional peace and quiet.

Introduction

Certain books of the Bible – Proverbs, Job and Ecclesiastes – have tradition-ally all been described as 'wisdom literature', a category which is widely accepted to be useful, but which is not the product of modern scholarship, and is based on no simple, agreed definition. On the face of it, in fact, these books are very different from each other (and all are very different from the Song of Songs, which is sometimes also included in the category, but which will not be discussed here; cf. Dell 2005). Proverbs is an anthology of various materials, mostly offering advice either through long collections of short sayings, or through more elaborate units of teaching. Job uses the framework of a story, in which God permits the destruction of almost every-thing its hero holds dear, to encompass a long, poetic conversation about divine justice. Ecclesiastes, finally, offers advice reminiscent of Proverbs, but in the context of a monologue that seems to dismiss the usefulness of such advice, and even to question the possibility of any lasting human achievement. All three, to be sure, lack the emphasis on God's relation-ship with Israel which dominates many other books in the Hebrew Bible; instead, they focus on issues that are relevant to all humans, ranging from good manners through to the purpose of living. Accordingly, they are all more interested, it seems, in the world as it is, than in analyzing the past or looking to the future, while their concern is much more with the individual than with any nation or group. It is less obvious, however, that they all take a common attitude or approach to any of these issues, so to begin with, at least, it is simpler to speak of wisdom literature's interests than of its views, and to save questions about any distinctive 'wisdom thought' for later discussion.

For practical purposes, then, let us use 'wisdom literature' in the first place as a loose designation of subject matter, not of origin or standpoint, just as, say, 'crime fiction' is a literature *about* crime, not a literature com-posed to promote crime, or written by criminals. It is beyond doubt that all of the biblical wisdom books – along with the apocryphal books of Ben Sira (also known as Ecclesiasticus) and Wisdom of Solomon – are inter-ested in the very concept of 'wisdom', and that the concept itself, variously understood, embraces many of their central concerns. Whatever else it may prove to be, wisdom literature is at least a literature about wisdom, and to understand the concept is to understand a great deal about the literature. Before we turn to a more detailed examination in the following chapters, therefore, it is important not only to say something about that concept, but also to look at the way in which it shapes the self-presentation of the texts. As I hope will become clear, the interest in wisdom has consequences in itself for the various forms that the material takes, so that the subject matter is not easily divorced from other generic considerations.

1. The concept of wisdom

Although the English word 'wisdom' is loaded with overtones of thought-fulness and experience, the underlying Hebrew word *hokma* (pronounced with a rough *h*) means something rather simpler, and is actually closer in sense to the English 'skill' or 'know-how'. So in Exod. 28.3, for example, *hokma* is used to describe skill in sewing, just as in Exod. 35.26 it is used to describe the ability to spin wool, or in 1 Kgs 7.14 to describe Hiram's ability to work bronze. Elsewhere we find the noun used to describe political judgement (1 Kgs 2.6), business acumen (Ezek. 28.5), and military skill (Isa. 10.13), while the related adjective *hakam* is used to describe, amongst others, magicians, skilled craftsmen, boatmen and professional mourners (see. Exod. 7.11; 2 Chron. 2.6 [ET 2.7]; Ezek. 27.8; Jer. 9.16 [ET 9.17]). In such contexts, the terms are commonly used alongside other words for knowledge and skill, and they imply nothing beyond the intellectual or practical ability to which they refer. This may even be true when it is God, rather than a human, who possesses such skill (as in, for example, Ps. 104.24; Prov. 3.19; Jer. 10.12).

Sometimes, when the type of skill is unspecified, the reference may be to some broader competence, just as we can call someone 'able' without specifying precisely what it is that they are able to do; that is probably the case in, for example, Deut. 1.15. More often than not, however, *hokma* is used to refer to an ability or skill which is more general in another way: a person may possess not merely 'know-how' in construction, say, but the 'know-how' of living their life. It is this type of wisdom that principally concerns wisdom literature. To achieve it, of course, is to live better, which is to say, longer and more successfully. So, according to Prov. 24.14, wisdom offers a certain future, and Prov. 8 famously has wisdom, personified as a woman, boasting not only of her roles in government and creation, but of her ability to make her adherents wealthy and prosperous (vv. 17–20). Naturally, this is perceived as highly desirable ('better than gold', as Prov. 16.16 puts it), and it corresponds to other aspects of living life, such as righteousness or proper behaviour (e.g. Ps. 37.30; Prov. 29.3). Like more specific skills, however, it can be acquired through learning (Prov. 29.15), and terms like 'knowledge' or 'understanding' continue to be used as syno-nyms for it. This general wisdom, therefore, is still an intellectual ability or attainment, but it functions not in the accomplishment of specific tasks, so much as in the shaping and perpetuation of one's life.

Whether the biblical writers took this skill to be solely an intellectual one, of course, is another matter. The linking of wisdom with righteousness in many places hints at a religious dimension: if one believes that long life and prosperity are a reward from God, then wisdom becomes associated with pleasing God – that is, the skill lies not so much in understanding life itself as in discerning the divine will. It is also important to appreciate that not every potential decision in life can be foreseen, and so wisdom cannot be purely a matter of knowing what to do in advance. It is not a list of answers, but an aptitude for making the right decision – honed perhaps by knowledge and experience, but as much to do with having a character shaped in the right way. The literature correspondingly talks often of wisdom or of the 'wise man', in an absolute way: the world is not filled, as one might expect, with those who possess a modicum of wisdom, but with those who are wise and those who are not. In our terms, therefore, to be wise is something more than simply being knowledgeable, but if the basic nature and purpose of wisdom is clear, how one acquires it is less so.

2. Wisdom and genre

The claim that one can be taught to be wise involves a practical issue about authority. If somebody claims that they can provide the key, or part of the key, to a long and successful life, it is reasonable to examine their credentials. Where the offer of teaching is made through written literature, moreover, which can present no author directly for interrogation and evaluation, then this literature has to find a way of accrediting itself in the eyes of its audience. To understand the conventions that came to govern this in the Jewish literature, it is helpful first to look further afield.

Although other countries in the ancient Near East did not encapsulate the idea in any concept precisely equivalent to *hokma*, texts offering advice about living are amongst some of the earliest literature known from both Egypt and Mesopotamia. Such advice literature, indeed, was being composed more than a thousand years before the biblical wisdom literature, and, as we shall see, there is little reason to doubt that the biblical writers drew, to some extent at least, on traditions of composition which had long been established in the region. What shaped the earlier literature also, therefore, indirectly shaped the biblical texts, and is important for understanding the particular forms that they adopt. This may be especially true when it comes to the claims made by the texts about their own value, which are often stated explicitly, but are also implicit in aspects of the presentation and genre. Indeed, the two main types of advice literature that we find in the ancient world are each, broadly speaking, based on a different type of authority.

In order to appreciate the first, we must recognize the important role that proverbs play in many societies, although this role is difficult to define, and is itself the subject of much discussion. A few proverbs arguably offer established 'truths', like 'an apple a day keeps the doctor away'. More generally, though, they serve as analogies which establish common ground between the participants in a discussion, and so address specific contexts. A speaker suggests that some particular phenomenon or case may be understood in terms of an established proverb, and seeks the assent of others to that understanding (see especially Fontaine 1982). I might say, for example, that it is easy to forget about work when I'm on holiday – 'out of sight, out of mind' – but that I also miss my friends, even the difficult ones – 'absence makes the heart grow fonder'. In doing so, I am effectively citing an accepted authority to characterize and legitimize my feelings, and the proverbs become such authorities by virtue of the very fact of their currency. If they do not have that currency, they are merely my own, more or less convincing turns of phrase; when they do have it, or the listener can be persuaded that they have it, they show that my experiences correspond to an experience shared more generally.

By using a saying so much that everyone comes to recognize it as a proverb, a society effectively accepts the claims of that saying to embody or exemplify a recognized cultural norm. Of course, to gain such circulation in the first place, sayings need not only possess some recognition of their inherent ability to express common experience, but also both brevity and an appealing, memorable turn of phrase. Their effectiveness derives not only from what they say, therefore, but from the way in which they say it. In the biblical literature, and also elsewhere in the ancient world, most notably Mesopotamia, we find numerous examples of sayings which employ the pithiness of proverbs, and these aphorisms, when not actually proverbs themselves, are apparently looking to borrow the status and authority of proverbs. Commonly presented in collections of varying lengths, these sayings constitute a type of composition often called 'sentence literature'.

We also find, however, a second type of claim to authority in advice literature, which is based not on acceptance by society, but on the credentials of an individual with whom the advice is associated. Most particularly, if an individual is recognized as having enjoyed a long and successful life, then that fact in itself lends authority to their advice about living. The individual concerned is often depicted as the author of that advice, but it may also be stated or assumed that they have themselves received the advice from earlier generations, and prospered merely by heeding it. Primarily in Egypt, although also in Mesopotamia and elsewhere, a great deal of advice literature is presented, correspondingly, as speeches by famous individuals, passing on their know-how to the next generation (usually their sons). These speeches are sometimes set within a narrative context, explaining the circumstances in which they were delivered, and this style of composition is known as 'instruction'.

By aligning itself, then, with the real-life phenomena of proverbial sayings, or of advice passed on by fathers, ancient advice literature grounds itself in familiar sources of authority. It is important, however, not to confuse the literature itself with those sources. In Egypt, for example, it is unlikely that the many texts portraying fathers advising their sons were actually written by those fathers, or are records of their words (in at least one case, indeed, the father is already dead when he speaks!). Rather, the father-son setting in each work is a literary convention, which draws ultimately on the idea of paternal advice to children, but more immediately associates the work with other works that employ the same convention. It is, in other words, a mark of genre, not an account of actual circumstances.

Likewise, it is by no means certain that all of the many sayings presented to us in collections from Mesopotamia actually circulated as popular proverbs, and some later writers certainly sought to create new aphorisms which sounded like proverbs. The presentation of advice literature in the ancient world, therefore, is shaped not only by the desire to draw on familiar sources of authority to validate its content, but also by subsequent literary conventions of form and setting.

This should put us on our guard when it comes to the Jewish literature. Much of the material in Proverbs, especially, tends to fall into the same categories we find in the foreign literature, and appeals to the same sources of authority: it is aphoristic in style, presenting itself as proverbial, or else it is admonitory, associating itself with parental teaching from the wise and successful. To some extent those sources compel the styles, and it is conceivable, although unlikely, that advice literature developed quite separately in Israel, but in a way parallel to the developments elsewhere. If it did not, as seems more probable, then it may have inherited these generic self-presentations from foreign literature. In neither case, however, should we assume that the types of authority on which the literature rests are actually clues to the origin of particular texts, any more than they were in Egypt or Mesopotamia.

For the moment, though, the key point is not that we should look beyond folk proverbs and family lectures for the creation of Jewish advice literature, but that the need for such literature to commend itself has shaped the way in which it presents itself. Advice on living, in other words, is associated both in Israel and elsewhere with particular types of composition, which enable it to draw on the authority of proverbs or of individuals, but which have consequently become conventional vehicles for advice. If we can say that wisdom literature has a particular subject matter, then we can also say that some wisdom literature uses traditional styles of presentation linked to that subject matter. Of the three biblical books, it is Proverbs to which these considerations most obviously apply, although Ecclesiastes also makes extensive use of the aphoristic, proverbial style. Job is shaped by its subject matter in another way, using the voices of different characters to present different points of view. That is not itself without precedent elsewhere, as we shall see, but it is also important to observe that Job and Ecclesiastes, in particular, each draw on other traditions of composition. If there are certain literary genres that play an important role in wisdom writing, it is also true that the writers did not confine themselves to those genres.

From all this, it may be apparent both that we need some understanding of the literary conventions it used if we are to understand what wisdom literature was all about, and that the analogous literature from other countries has a role to play in achieving that understanding. Indeed, this foreign literature has been crucial to scholarly discussion of the biblical texts for most of the last century, and we can hardly ignore it in any case. Before we turn to the individual Jewish works, therefore, the first chapter will look in more detail at the nature and development of related texts outside Israel, and at their implications for our literature.

3. Wisdom thought

If the subject matter of wisdom literature is important for understanding the ways in which it is presented, then it is even more obviously linked to the content. In their individual ways, our texts offer or examine advice, and deal with a wide range of issues associated with the value or limitations of wisdom. It will be clear when we discuss them each, of course, that they do not share a common opinion: Proverbs is sometimes described as 'optimistic', in that it tends to view wisdom as achievable, effective and desirable, while the more critical ideas in Job and Ecclesiastes lead them to be labelled 'sceptical' or 'pessimistic'. That they hold different opinions, however, does not necessarily imply that they are operating with different assumptions, and modern scholars generally suppose that there is an identifiable way of looking at the world which can be especially associated with the wisdom literature.

As we have already observed, the biblical wisdom books lack any self-evident interest in certain of the themes or ideas that dominate much other biblical literature. To some extent this is undeniably just a function of their subject matter: they are simply not talking about the same things as those other books, which affects what they say and the way that they say it. Their emphasis on individual living, though, is not always easily reconciled with ideas found elsewhere. How can someone secure their own future through their own actions, for example, when the behaviour of others might lead God to abandon or destroy the whole nation? Where in the wisdom literature are the many actions which Deuteronomy, say, or Leviticus regard as crucial for survival and success? The biblical wisdom books, furthermore, seem oriented to issues which affect every human, while other texts see a special status, and special rules for Israel: their views seem grounded in ideas about the world, and God's relationship with the world, rather than in notions of covenant, election or law.

As we shall see, some of the contrasts may not be as sharp as they first seem, but the differences are real enough. One consequence, of course, is that a focus on the historical and prophetic books has frequently led scholars in the past to marginalize wisdom texts. That tendency has been replaced more recently by a growing interest in the literature and its ideas, reinforced by a perception that wisdom literature was a significant influence on the development of later Judaism. This involves, of course, attempts to understand the literature in a more positive way, rather than defining it by what it is not. In chapter six, we shall look more closely at some of the aspects of 'wisdom thought' that have been identified, and return to the questions of classification with which we began here. A further, related consequence of wisdom literature's distinctiveness is that many scholars have surmised that wisdom literature must have arisen in circles distinct from those that produced much of the other biblical literature; for a number of reasons, moreover, those circles have often been associated specifically with the scribal, bureaucratic class in Israel. Of course, there are a lot of problems involved even in the notion of specific circles, let alone in the identification of such circles, and we shall examine the evidence in the last chapter. We shall also take the opportunity then to assess how far the assumptions of the wisdom books are confined to those books. The issues cannot easily be quarantined, however, and the theory of wisdom circles has become entwined with questions about the influence of foreign thought and literature, so we shall deal with some initial considerations in the course of the first two chapters as well.

Chapter 1

Wisdom Literature and its Foreign Counterparts

It would be difficult to overestimate the importance of the role played by earlier, non-Israelite texts in much of the modern scholarship on wisdom literature. Their direct influence on the biblical texts may have been overstated in some discussions, but they do, at the very least, provide a useful analogy, and they probably offer insights also into the basic conventions which governed some types of composition. In this chapter, we shall begin by looking at the main types of advice literature and their development. It is these sayings collections and instructions which have most commonly been linked to the book of Proverbs, and we shall touch briefly on questions about their direct influence before moving on to discuss the development of styles and ideas more comparable to those in Job and Ecclesiastes.

The danger of a brief review like this is that it necessarily isolates the texts to some extent from the broader cultures within which they each emerged. By juggling texts from different periods and places, moreover, we can easily end up with a false impression of some compact and coherent body of work, which might all have sat at once on someone's bookshelf. It is important to be clear then, that the texts discussed here come from a very wide area – the north-eastern tip of Africa through to the borders of modern Iran – and from many different eras: the interval between the earliest and the latest, indeed, is greater than that between the latest and our own time. Although it is convenient to speak of them as a corpus, therefore, it is also necessary to understand that each is historically linked more strongly to the other literature and ideas of its own time and culture than it is to most of the other texts. This is a crucial point, which we shall pick up again in the last section of the chapter.

1. Sayings collections in Mesopotamia

Proverbs and aphorisms were often used in other types of composition, and are sometimes preserved singly. From a very early period, however, around the middle of the third millennium BCE, they were also being collected together to form anthologies in Mesopotamia (the region which corresponds largely to modern Iraq). Most of our sources are somewhat later, dating from the first half of the second millennium, but they attest to a literary tradition that was well established by that time, and Bendt Alster's recent edition of the Sumerian works identifies twenty-eight major collections in that language (Alster 1997; see also the useful comments on the work in Veldhuis 2000). Some clearly continued to be read and copied for many centuries, and we later find both bilingual Sumerian/Akkadian texts, and a few collections which may have been composed in Akkadian, although they are less obviously a key component of Akkadian literature.[1] It would be going beyond the evidence to suggest that the active creation of such works took place in every period of Mesopotamian history, but we are dealing, at least, with a type of literature that established itself as classic from an early time, and continued to exercise an important influence.

The content of the collections is very diverse, and they range across many topics. Although they tend toward aphoristic brevity, furthermore, the sayings themselves share no single form, and they include short fables or anecdotes, direct admonitions, blessings, and much else beside more straightforwardly 'proverbial' or proverb-like sayings such as 'He who possesses many things is constantly on guard' (Alster 1997: coll. 1.16). Sometimes, indeed, the 'sayings' are really just witty or familiar descriptions, like 'A pig sprinkled with mud' (Alster 1997: coll. 8 sec. A5), or 'A donkey eating its own bedding' (Alster 1997: coll. 2.77). Equally, they may perhaps be humorous things to say in unusual situations, like 'Something which has never occurred since time immemorial: didn't the young girl fart in her husband's lap?' (Alster 1997: coll. 1.12; see also Lambert 1960: 260). It seems probable that many of the sayings really were popular proverbs or expressions, culled from everyday speech, but also that some were jokes or witticisms, insults or compliments, written down for reasons other than the preservation of some profound truth. They were intended, perhaps, to be sprinkled in the speech of the educated, through citation or allusion, like the later *sententiae* of classical rhetoric (Lambert 1960: 280–2, gives several examples of such use from letters).

Although the creators of the collections were working largely with the words of others (and perhaps borrowing from each other – some sayings appear in several collections), it is important to recognize that they were not mere archivists, and that some skill went into the arrangement of their materials. Sometimes the underlying principles are self-evident: the Sumerian Collection 5, for instance, assembles animal sayings and fables, grouping together the sayings about each type of animal in turn, so that sayings about lions are followed by sayings about wolves, then about dogs and finally bitches. The links may be more subtle, though, as in Collection 11, when saying 69 is linked to the previous saying by the mention of water in each, and to the following saying by the mention of mountains:

+ Your evildoer, like the floodings of the river, let him return to his city.
+ Those who live near the water look into the mountains, they don't look in their own direction.

* Adapa knows no loss. He walks in the inner mountains.
(Alster 1997: coll. 11.68–70)

Elsewhere we find other methods at work: Collection 1 commonly groups sayings with the same initial cuneiform sign, for example, whilst Collections 12 and 13 group sayings which begin with the same word. Although their methods are not always obvious, it is apparent that the writers are seeking not merely to collect, but to compose and arrange the sayings, so that it is legitimate to see in all this a genuine literary endeavour.

Whatever the initial motives for the composition of these collections, they quickly came to be used extensively in the education of the literate, scribal class, not just providing material for writing practise, but supplying a key part of the shared cultural awareness that marked someone as 'educated'. To be sure, the many sayings provided some practical advice about human relationships or the way of the world, but they were not obviously intended to provide any more specific sort of training, except possibly in Sumerian language and writing (Veldhuis 2000): these are far from being handbooks of etiquette or career guidance. Indeed, it might well be wrong to lay too much emphasis at all on the role of these collections as 'advice literature': whilst keen to present proverbial truths, they seem no less interested in the expression of those truths, and in clever speech more generally. As Niek Veldhuis puts it, 'Many proverbs do not seem to have any moral implication at all. They simply describe a situation or a mental state in a particularly vivid way' (2000: 385). To varying degrees, this was to prove true of advice literature more generally across the ancient world.

The distinction between authority rooted in 'proverbial', cultural experience and that derived from individual experience is an important one, but in practice the two are not mutually exclusive – a fact demonstrated by another early Mesopotamian work, the *Instructions of Šuruppak*. This work, a version of which existed in the mid-third millennium BCE, comprises a collection of sayings very similar to the Sumerian collections already discussed, but it presents them as a speech made by Šuruppak to his son Ziusudra, the hero in some versions of the Sumerian flood story. It is possible that this identification picks up a tradition of knowledge being preserved from the period before the flood, but it more immediately associates the advice with the only man able to survive, and so offers an affirmation of its value. In the classical version of the text, attested from the early second millennium, we are told that:

In those days, in those far remote days,
In those nights, in those far-away nights,
In those years, in those far remote years –
In those days, the intelligent one, who made the elaborate words, who knew the
     (proper) words, and was living in Sumer,
Šuruppak – the intelligent one, who made the elaborate words, who knew the
     (proper) words, and was living in Sumer –
Šuruppak gave instructions to his son,
Šuruppak, son of Ubartutu, gave instructions to his son Ziusudra:

My son, let me give you instructions, may you take my instructions!
Ziusudra, let me speak a word to you, may you pay attention to it!
Do not neglect my instructions!
Do not transgress the word I speak!
The instructions of an old man are precious, may you submit to them!

(Alster 1974: 35)

The advice then begins with a series of sayings in the form 'Do not . . .
(because) . . . ', and this form of advice is common throughout the work,
often appearing in shorter series, but also intermingled with more basic
statements and other types of saying. In this version, the advice is also
broken into sections, with Šuruppak instructing his son a second and third
time, and appealing for his attention and obedience on each occasion. The
narrative framework of the sayings is constantly reiterated through these
introductions, therefore, but also emphasized by shorter appeals to 'my
son' at the beginning of some sayings. It is not a mere formality, then, but
something integral to the composition, which distinguishes it from the
strictly anonymous collections of sayings, and gives it a personal flavour.
The advice can seek to persuade by its aphoristic, proverbial qualities,
but in this way is also given authority as words of great antiquity, used to
educate a man of legendary qualities.

2. Instructions in Egypt

The *Instructions of Šuruppak* was transmitted over many centuries, and
we possess part of a later translation into Akkadian (Lambert 1960:
92–5), but its self-presentation as parental advice is unusual in the surviving Mesopotamian literature, where only a few other texts seem explicitly
to identify themselves as the words of a father to his son. This setting, in
fact, is much more common in Egypt, where simple collections of sayings,
conversely, are much rarer than in Mesopotamia. It seems doubtful, in
fact, that we can see any very early connection between the development
of advice literature in the two areas. Much later, as we shall see, Egyptian
texts were strongly influenced by conventions which probably originated
in the Mesopotamian tradition of collecting sayings, but the early Egyptian
examples can be understood more readily as a result of wider developments
in Egyptian literature than as imports from abroad.

Here it is important to observe that writing came to be used very quickly
in Egypt to advertise the accomplishments of the dead, through inscriptions in their tombs. Autobiographical speeches, addressed to the living,
provided a vehicle not only for narratives about the specific accomplishments of individuals, but for claims about the ways in which they had
lived, and probably provided much of the impetus for the development of
literary compositions after the Old Kingdom (Assmann 1983).[2] The classic Egyptian advice literature, therefore, shares with much other Egyptian
literature the general format of a speech, or monologue, delivered by an
individual; it also has, however, a testamentary quality: the advice is passed

on by one generation as it gives way to the next, in the face of inevitable death. In fact, we can see a continuing relationship between Egyptian advice literature and tomb inscriptions, with the latter sometimes describing themselves in the terms used of such literature, or even adopting material from didactic texts (cf. Weeks 1994: 178; 2007: 5).

There is some controversy about the date of the earliest instructional texts in Egypt, which are called *sbayt* (seb-a-eet, 'teaching' or 'instruction'). Many of these portray themselves as speeches delivered by eminent men living in the Old Kingdom, and those claims were taken seriously by earlier generations of Egyptologists, with a few still continuing to defend them. It is widely accepted now, however, that the works were actually composed some centuries later, in the Middle Kingdom, and were backdated to enhance their authority, rather in the way that the *Instructions of Šuruppak* had been backdated to the time before the flood (see, Parkinson 2002: 45–50). Instructions probably emerged as a major literary genre, therefore, around the end of the third millennium BCE, and a significant proportion of the surviving works can be dated to the very early second millennium. As was the case with sayings collections in Mesopotamia, the instruction established itself as a classic style of literature quite early on, with texts continuing to be copied for many centuries, but the number of new compositions after this initial burst of writing may have been quite limited, at least until the Graeco-Roman period.

Amongst the earliest instructions, that attributed to a 5th-dynasty vizier Ptahhotep is probably the best known, and it has much to say about the nature and origin of the advice it offers. (There is a translation in Lichtheim 1973: 61–80). The advice follows a brief story, in which Ptahhotep, coming to the end of his own life and career (in the early 24th century BCE, more than four hundred years before the work was probably composed), obtains royal permission to educate his son. His teaching is not directed specifically toward that son, however, with the various admonitions covering a wide range of situations in which individuals might find themselves, and offering general advice for each. This conforms to an idea, expressed in the work's prologue, that Ptahhotep is passing on not a distillation of his own experience, but a body of teaching, taught to human ancestors by the gods. After the advice itself, Ptahhotep commends obedience to it, as a source of long life and prosperity, urging that it be passed on to future generations, and pointing to his own success.

We possess similar instructions offering quite general advice about life, but the format was also adopted for other purposes in the Middle Kingdom. The *Instruction of Amenemhet*, for example, has the assassinated king describe what happened to him, outline his previous achievements, and commend his son Senwosret, who succeeded him: it offers little advice, except that the son should trust nobody (see Posener 1956 on the historical context; Lichtheim 1973: 135–9 for the translation). Another work, addressed to the more obscure King Merikare, and set in the difficult period before the Middle Kingdom unification of Egypt, uses its advice to explore the nature and duties of kingship, often with explicit reference to the religious and ideological framework within which Egyptians understood the institution (Lichtheim 1973: 97–109). The *Instruction of Khety*, on the other hand, precedes its short section of practical advice by a lengthy commendation of the scribal profession, which spells out, often humorously, the trials and tribulations of other trades (Lichtheim 1973: 184–92).

These compositions share no single content, and vary considerably in form. They are linked, however, not only by their own descriptions of themselves as 'instruction', but also by the father-son presentation, and by their poetic character. The last point is important, but often overlooked: just as the Mesopotamian collections showed a keen interest in language and expression, so too the Egyptian instructions employ an elevated, literary style for their advice. Egyptian, indeed, has a term which is important for understanding the very nature of this literature: *mdt nfrt* (medet neferet – 'perfect speech') sums up the attitude that fine ideas deserve fine expression. There was little inclination in the ancient world to view truth as something that should be plain and self-evident. Correspondingly, instructions are quite sophisticated literary works, and they reflect important Egyptian concerns about the proper behaviour of individuals. Much Egyptian literature reflects, or reflects on *maat* (ma-at), the term used to conceptualize truth, order and correctness, to which individuals and society should conform (see especially Assmann 2006). Behaviour in harmony with *maat* would bring personal benefits, but also contribute to strengthening order against chaos.

In the later New Kingdom, the Middle Kingdom instructions enjoyed high prestige, and some of them were widely used in schools, alongside other classic literature. Again, like the Sumerian collections, their role was not specifically to offer practical advice, and works like *Amenemhet* were widely read and copied despite offering virtually no advice directly relevant to commoners. Young scribes also read stories like *Sinuhe*, the fictional autobiography of an Egyptian exiled abroad, or the *Tale of the Eloquent Peasant*, in which a poor man overcomes injustice by the eloquence of his pleas, and this use of literature was more about inculcating Egyptian culture and values (along with a knowledge of the classical Middle Egyptian tongue), than about practical training, for which other texts were employed.

Only a few instructions have survived that were actually composed in the New Kingdom, and most are fragmentary. It is not clear that many instructions were actually being composed in this period, but the two main works which we know, *Any* and *Amenemope*, both show some development in the genre (translations in Lichtheim 1976: 135–63). In each case, the instruction is attributed to a more minor official than was typically true of the earlier texts, and both are concerned much more with matters that might have characterized the lives of such officials. To that extent, both may reflect the changed social circumstances of their era, with its much-enlarged scribal class. *Amenemope* also displays a strong interest in personal piety and in divine control of events, which mirrors the growing preoccupation with such matters in Egyptian thought (see e.g. Assmann 1979; Baines 1991: 194–8).

3. Ahiqar and the Demotic instructions

The greatest shifts in the character of Egyptian instructions come, how-ever, in the Graeco-Roman period. Up to this point, sayings collections in Mesopotamia and instructions in Egypt were each distinct traditions of classic literature. Although some minor collections of sayings have been found in Egypt, and although Mesopotamia had instructions of its own, there is no reason to suppose that either region substantially influenced the other. In the last few centuries BCE, however, the composition of new instructions seems to have enjoyed a tremendous resurgence in Egypt, the initial impetus for which probably came from a foreign work, *Ahiqar*.

This text, like *Šuruppak* long before it, takes the takes the sort of sayings, admonitions and other materials typical of Mesopotamian collections, and places them within a narrative framework, as the words of a man instruct-ing his son (or rather, in this case, his nephew, whom he has adopted as his son). The framework, however, is much more sophisticated than anything found in earlier instructions, embracing a tale in which a royal counsellor at the Assyrian court, Ahiqar, is betrayed by that nephew, Nadin, saved from execution by a soldier whom he had earlier helped, and eventually restored to his former station, enabling him to exact revenge on Nadin. The story, then, is much more than a mere introduction to the advice, and, indeed, the two parts may have developed separately before being brought together. In any case, the combination proved irresistible to ancient readers: although the earliest copy which we have dates from the fifth century BCE, the work, originally written in Aramaic, was adapted and translated into many versions over the following centuries (see Conybeare *et al.* 1913), and the name of the hero was known in many different cultures – Ahiqar even plays a role in the apocryphal book of Tobit, where he is portrayed as Jewish.

The place and date of the original composition are not known for cer-tain, but the evidence points to Syria at some time around the seventh or eighth century BCE (Lindenberger 1983: 19–20. This work also offers an edition and translation of the sayings). Mesopotamian culture had long influenced that area, and an Akkadian sayings collection, along with a version of an Akkadian instruction, were amongst the many texts found at Ras Shamra on the Syrian coast (Lambert 1960: 116; Nougayrol 1968: 779–84). It is not surprising, therefore, that we should find a Syrian sayings collection, or that it should be attributed to an official in the Assyrian court. Given the great popularity of the work, furthermore, it is also unsurpris-ing that Ahiqar's name should have been found in Egyptian sources, and our earliest copy of the text was, in fact, found in Egypt – although it was an Aramaic text, in the possession of Jewish mercenaries stationed there. What is more unexpected, however, is that *Ahiqar* seems to have inspired, as Miriam Lichtheim (1983) has suggested, a deliberate imitation which rejuvenated, but also transformed the Egyptian tradition of instructions.

Most obviously, the many new works that were created in the late Demotic script, probably from about the late fourth century BCE onward, show a standardization of form which is lacking in earlier instructions:

they use short sayings, almost always just a single line in length, which are often carefully arranged. This standardization does not extend to all aspects of form: the contents may still be statements, admonitions, conditions, or other types of saying. There is a strong emphasis on aphoristic brevity, however, which is largely lacking in earlier Egyptian instructions, and goes beyond what we usually find even in the Mesopotamian collections or in *Ahiqar*. One major work, the *Instruction of Ankhsheshonq*, owes a clear debt to the latter, presenting its own long story about its protagonist as a preface to his sayings, but it also alludes to motifs in existing Egyptian literature. (Translation in Lichtheim 1980: 159–84). Another important composition, most fully preserved on Papyrus Insinger (Lichtheim 1980: 184–217), groups its sayings to produce contradictions, so that the instruction essentially undermines itself, and proves the author's point, regularly stated, that the fate of individuals lies ultimately in the hands of God, outside their control. If, then, we can certainly see the influence of *Ahiqar*, and ultimately of Mesopotamia, it is also important to stress that the Demotic instructions have a character of their own.

4. Israel and the ancient Near Eastern advice literature

Even before we turn to a closer examination of the biblical texts, anyone familiar with the book of Proverbs will appreciate already that it contains materials similar to both the sayings collections and the father-son instructions found in other countries. Since, as we have seen, these types of literature are shaped in part by the ways in which they try to lend authority to their advice, it would not be astonishing, in principle, if the biblical examples evolved independently, governed by the same constraints. In practice, however, Israel emerged in a region where literature had already been composed for well over a thousand years, and it lay on a major route between Egypt and Mesopotamia. It was not a primitive backwater, struggling to develop its own literary culture from scratch, and the biblical literature was not created in a vacuum.

In fact, it seems probable that foreign compositions exerted some direct influence on the Hebrew literature. This has been a significant issue in the study of wisdom literature for many decades now, since Adolf Erman pointed out in 1924 that Prov. 22.17–23.10 contains a series of sayings which appear to be based on the Egyptian *Instruction of Amenemope*. Despite various attacks, that observation has been affirmed by subsequent studies, and the influence of *Amenemope* is probably visible elsewhere in Proverbs, not least in the initial statement of purpose at 1.2-6, which seems to be modelled on a similar statement in the Egyptian work. It is not clear, however, in what form *Amenemope* was actually available to the biblical writers, and the extent of its influence may suggest that it had already been translated into some language more accessible than Late Egyptian.

No other single text has been identified as a definite source, although it is likely that *Ahiqar* was known in Israel as elsewhere, and some links with that work have been suggested. Many commentaries on Proverbs, however, have devoted significant effort to identifying specific parallels between particular sayings in the book, and sayings found in other ancient advice literature. There are some obvious problems with this: the parallels they identify are often very vague, and there is great scope for coincidence. Moreover, many of the texts in which purported parallels are found may have enjoyed only very limited circulation, or might have been inaccessible in other ways. Such works as the Demotic instructions, for instance, were probably not composed early enough to have exercised any influence on Proverbs, and we cannot presume that the sayings they contain had some independent existence beforehand. In the case of older works, language is a significant issue, since there is no reason to suppose that the Jewish writers could easily have read or understood texts in archaic languages such as Sumerian or Middle Egyptian, or even in Akkadian and the later forms of Egyptian.

More generally, we know little about the composition of advice literature in the countries and city-states closer to Israel, or in Palestine itself before the emergence of Israel, and such literature, if it existed, might well have been a more immediate influence upon the biblical works. It is by no means impossible, then, that individual sayings found their way from Egypt or Mesopotamia into Proverbs less directly, via oral use or intermediary texts. If it tries to identify specific dependence rather than a more general resemblance, however, the quest for parallels can very quickly run into problems of method, and it is easy to overstate the evidence for a reliance of Proverbs on foreign sources.

The potential influence of those sources cannot, on the other hand, be ignored altogether. The probability that the biblical writers were aware of these literary traditions makes it difficult to suppose, for instance, that the composition of sayings collections was solely motivated in Israel by some new-found desire to collect folk proverbs, or that the presentation of advice as parental is anything more than a literary convention. The poetic character of the foreign literature, moreover, and its high prestige, suggest that we might expect some stylistic ambition in its Hebrew counterparts as well. The foreign literature, in other words, prevents us from attributing certain key characteristics of the biblical material to entirely local circumstances or concerns, while it also obliges us to take seriously the poetic and literary aspects of that material.

Mention should also be made of one further area in which the foreign advice literature is important, and that is the question of formal development within such literature. It used to be supposed quite commonly – and is sometimes still suggested – that there was an evolution within Israel from the basic proverbial form toward more complicated forms of teaching, with admonitions building upon observations. This is improbable, and it was argued many years ago that Israel most likely inherited different types of saying from different types of composition: short aphorisms from sayings collections, longer admonitions from instructional works (see McKane 1970; Kayatz 1966). This seems to be broadly correct, if a little oversimplified. It is important to emphasize both that different styles of saying are not confined to particular types of composition, and that the differences are not, in any case, a matter of evolution or formal development. On the first point, as we have seen, instructions can consist of short sayings, be they admonitions or observations, whilst sayings collections can contain much longer units: neither genre places such specific limitations on content. On the second, we should observe that different backgrounds and ideas are at work. James Crenshaw expressed quite a common view of the time when he claimed that 'Early brief maxims and sayings give way to instructions which in turn are eclipsed by dialogue' (Crenshaw 1981: 18). In no country, however, do we have any particular reason to suppose that styles of composition succeeded each other in that, or any other specific order; in Egypt, indeed, aphorisms become far more common in later literature.

5. Antecedents to the 'sceptical' literature

Those considerations apply primarily, of course, to the book of Proverbs, although they are also relevant to those parts of Ecclesiastes that present themselves as direct advice. The book of Job, in contrast, quite clearly does not depend, to any perceptible extent, on the conventions of earlier advice literature, and Ecclesiastes also incorporates much that seems very different. For these works, it is less straightforward to identify any particular literary genre to which each might clearly be assigned, although they both have affinities with various other works, and Ecclesiastes (as we shall see) is often believed to cite material drawn from the Mesopotamian *Epic of Gilgamesh*. Without pre-empting our detailed examination of the two, however, it is important to indicate that more pessimistic literature was to be found in other countries as well, even if it did not constitute a specific genre of writing.

Advice literature was shaped and presented with a view to validation of its authority, but authority is not the only issue which arises in connection with advice: any teaching is open to challenge also on the grounds of its effectiveness. Proverbs can contradict each other, and this fact was certainly known to ancient writers – Prov. 26.4-5, indeed, sets two contradictory sayings side-by-side. The implication, that apparent truths may not always be absolute, is drawn out, as we have seen, in the late Demotic instruction on Papyrus Insinger, where such contradictions point to the ultimate futility of human action and advice in the face of divine activity. The same sort of idea can be found in other types of literature, however, and often much earlier. One of the most striking examples is the Babylonian *Dialogue of Pessimism* (Lambert 1960: 139–49; 1995: 36–7), where a master keeps changing his mind about what he will do, and his servant offers a persuasive affirmation of each contradictory choice, in terms reminiscent of the sayings collections:

'Slave, listen to me.'
    'Here I am sir, here I am.'
    'I am going to love a woman.'
    'So love, sir, love. The man who loves a woman forgets sorrow and fear.'

'No, slave, I will by no means love a woman.'
'[Do not] love sir, do not love. Woman is a pitfall – a pitfall, a hole, a ditch, woman is a sharp iron dagger that cuts a man's throat.'

(adapted from Lambert 1960: 147)

The text is probably humorous, culminating in a certain exasperation on both sides, but its point is a serious one: it is possible to find a compelling argument (and perhaps a proverbial saying) for almost any course of action. If that is the case, then the plausibility and credentials of advice do not mean that it must be true, or at least it remains possible that quite contradictory advice might also be true.

Two completely separate father-son instructions from the mid-second millennium BCE also present critiques of advice using a less complicated form of dialogue, in which the son responds negatively to the father's teaching. In the *Instruction of Any*, from New Kingdom Egypt, the son's objection is that it takes more than hearing or remembering to live according to instruction, and that the heart must be receptive; when Any replies that anyone, even any animal can be taught, his son again suggests that teaching must be responsive, and that it is no use just to batter someone with words (cf. Fox 1997). The work seems to explore the idea that real teaching involves more than forcing people to learn long lists of admonitions, and that the conventional format of instruction, therefore, might have serious limitations. An Akkadian work, preserved in copies from Syria and the Hittite capital Hattusa (modern Boğazköy/ Boğazkale), is rather fragmentary, and the reading of the names is disputed. It is now commonly known, however, as *Šūpê-amēli*, which was probably the father's name (see Hurowitz 2007 for the text and a useful discussion). Here the father again offers a conventional instruction, reminiscent of *Šuruppak*, but the son responds with what seems to be a portrayal of an uncertain world, in which his father has thrived but others do not, and in which a birth into sunshine leads ultimately to a death in the shadow of the underworld, where the dead are cut off from the sight of the living. This seems to suggest that success in life must be viewed against the broader background of human transience, and it implies also, perhaps, that the tidy certainties of instruction do not really correspond to the realities of the world.

Any and *Šūpê-amēli* use the basic, father-son convention of instructions to raise questions about the very nature of instruction. There is no reason to suppose that they reflect the thought of different circles or schools of thought, somehow opposed to the more certain, optimistic works. Indeed, we sometimes find mixed feelings in those works themselves: *Ptahhotep*, for example, explores in its epilogue the problem that some people seem fated not to learn, while the generally positive *Ankhsheshonq* indulges briefly in paradoxical sayings about unexpected consequences for actions (since everything is in the hand of fate and God). From an early stage, but still in some of the very latest texts, advice literature shows an awareness of its own limits. This is frequently connected with a religious awareness, which stresses that human behaviour is constrained by the intentions of fate or gods, and sometimes that human accomplishments are limited by human mortality. Near Eastern advice literature is by no means secular, even when it is entirely positive about the virtues of advice, and it does not try to displace the religious ideas current in the various cultures and periods where it was composed. Especially in Mesopotamia, indeed, the readers of this literature are often advised directly to worship and pray to their god: religious practice is itself key to one's survival and prosperity.

With a view to the biblical literature in particular, it is important to note two associated themes, which are a little more specific, and which relate to this tension between giving advice, and accepting the possibility of its failure. The first is that the quest to improve or extend life should not displace acceptance and enjoyment of what one already has: human lives are too short to be consumed by worrying about the future. This idea is found in various contexts, and in response to various concerns. In Egypt, for example, the *Harper's Song from the Tomb of King Intef* (Lichtheim 1973: 194–7) asks whether it is sensible to spend one's time in elaborate preparation for an afterlife about which nothing is really known. In Mesopotamia, the Old Babylonian version of *Gilgamesh* commends enjoyment of life over the pursuit of immortality, and a fragmentary text, known as *Counsels of a Pessimist* (Lambert 1960: 107–9), advises one to be rid of the worries that produce bad dreams, and instead to smile. Lambert (1995: 37–42) notes a further work, originally composed in Sumerian, which observes that 'the whole of life is but a twinkling of an eye', that the famous kings of the past are dead and gone, and that a life without joy is no better than death. This is an idea found in advice literature, then, but by no means confined to that literature.

The second theme is not really a constituent of advice literature at all, but is closely related to the concern sometimes expressed there, that the prosperity or failure of individuals does not always seem to match their behaviour. In Egypt, works like the *Sayings of Neferti* (Lichtheim 1973: 139–45) link this with the intrusion of chaos and failure of order. In Mesopotamia, on the other hand, *Ludlul Bêl Nêmeqi* – 'I shall praise the lord of wisdom' (Lambert 1960: 21–62; 1995: 32–4) – and the so-called *Babylonian Theodicy* (Lambert 1960: 63–89; 1995: 34–6) explore the problem directly in terms of divine action. The former discusses the dispossession and restoration of a man by Marduk, and although it is prefaced by a hymn of thanksgiving (Moran 1983), it is apparently not uncritical of that god. The latter sets up a dialogue between a man in distress, who cannot explain his apparent abandonment by his god, and his friend, who tries to explain and to justify divine action – a scenario which is very reminiscent of the book of Job, although the Babylonian work comes to a rather different conclusion.

Again, we cannot be sure that the writers of Job and Ecclesiastes had any knowledge of, or access to particular such texts from abroad. The very existence of the foreign works, however, makes it difficult to understand the biblical compositions as some new development within Israel, driven by disillusionment, particular historical circumstances, or a theological crisis induced by the Babylonian Exile (as suggested for Job most recently in Perdue 2008: 117–8, and Janzen 2009). That the sceptical works emerged and were transmitted alongside more 'standard' advice literature in Egypt and Mesopotamia, moreover, should make us very wary of seeing their Hebrew equivalents as the products of some group opposed to the optimism of Proverbs. Although specific religious ideas shape the literature in each region, sceptical texts are, again, a longstanding and mainstream feature of ancient Near Eastern literature.

6. The Jewish Context: initial considerations

Having stressed that the foreign texts belong firmly within the broader religious, cultural, and literary traditions of the regions within which they each emerged, it is important to ask whether the same is likely to be true of the biblical works. This is a controversial issue, which we shall look at in more detail in chapter 7, but it is desirable at this stage to offset any false impression that may have been created by discussing the advice literature in isolation. While Egyptologists have borrowed the term 'wisdom literature' from biblical studies, and use it rather loosely to describe a wide range of compositions (some of which bear little resemblance to any biblical wisdom text), they do not generally mean to imply that these works emerged from any historical context or school of thought which was separate from or distinct within the scribal class that produced most other Egyptian litera-ture. For Mesopotamia, the picture may be complicated by an apparent tendency for scribes to specialize in copying and transmitting particular sorts of text, but these specializations do not constitute different schools or philosophical traditions, and the boundaries between different types of literature are often very blurred. There is an interesting example of this in some hymns, described by Lambert (1960: 118–38) as 'preceptive hymns', which include commendations and condemnations of people who behave in particular ways, such as honest or dishonest judges and merchants: these resemble advice literature, but are not advocating ethical behaviour directly. Although we can make useful generic distinctions between different types of literature, then, those distinctions are not absolute – and we should not take them to indicate some broader historical difference, any more than we would presume that novelists and poets somehow represent radically different 'circles' in modern literary culture.

The relationships between wisdom literature and other Hebrew compo-sitions will also be discussed in more detail later on. Without pre-empting that discussion, we should observe at this stage that there is certainly no impermeable barrier between wisdom and other texts, even if the biblical wisdom literature shows little interest in the questions of national his-tory and religion which are addressed by so much writing elsewhere in the Hebrew Bible. Especially in the decades after the Second World War, however, when great emphasis was placed on historical consciousness as a key feature of Israelite theology and thought, the distinctiveness of wisdom literature in this respect led to a suspicion that it did not really belong in the mainstream. Since this dovetailed with the opinion, already current, that the texts were strongly influenced by foreign compositions and ideas, it became a scholarly commonplace that wisdom literature belonged to some particular group, whose concerns were very different from those of the prophetic and historical books, and perhaps shaped by non-Israelite ideas.

Whatever the merits of this as a historical theory, and without also pre-empting our discussion of that aspect, it should be apparent that the foreign materials in themselves offer little support to this way of viewing wisdom texts: if they are rarely interested in historical issues (*Amenemhet* and *Merikare* are notable exceptions), this is not because they have emerged from distinct parties or schools of thought, and they were produced in circles which also composed more nationally or historically orientated literature. There is an unfortunate tendency in biblical studies to suppose that because 'wisdom literature' is scribal in Egypt and Mesopotamia, the scribal class was therefore somehow orientated around wisdom literature. We could as well say that the scribal class in Egypt was the 'narrative' class, the 'lament' class or even the 'hymn' class. The foreign literature, in other words, should warn us against presuming that different concerns must reflect different underlying ideologies.

It may be useful also to observe, more broadly, that our witnesses to literature in Egypt and Mesopotamia may be more representative of the diversity typical within the scribal classes of ancient cultures. The biblical canon is the creation of much later generations, and the weighting of its content toward historiographical texts may say more about the concerns of those generations with the past than about what was actually normative in earlier Israelite literature and thought. In Egypt and Mesopotamia, on the other hand, the preservation of texts, if by no means entirely random, is at least the consequence of very different circumstances, without such an inbuilt bias toward a particular concern. Whilst it is certainly true, then, that the biblical wisdom literature seems very different from much of the other biblical literature, we should not presume either that historical or prophetic texts were more normative in the periods when they were composed, or that the various types of literature could not have emerged side-by-side without representing different groups.

7. Conclusion

Even were we to isolate the biblical texts completely from those of surrounding countries, and suppose there to have been no influence at all, it would be clear that the foreign materials offer potentially important analogies and correctives. In fact, some level of influence is likely, even if it is not easily quantifiable, and that offers us some insights into aspects of the biblical texts, which we shall exploit as we turn to those next. The foreign literature should certainly not be ignored, therefore, but it needs to be treated with some caution. In particular, we need to avoid taking each of the texts too far out of its own context in order to associate it with the others, and to recognize that generic distinctions do not always, or even commonly, reflect historical distinctions of other kinds.

Chapter 2

The Book of Proverbs

Since it bears the closest resemblance to many of the texts found elsewhere, Proverbs offers an appropriate starting point to our description of the biblical books. It is also likely that this work contains some of the earliest materials found in Jewish wisdom literature, but it is difficult to assign a date to the book itself, and it might be misleading, indeed, even to speak of any single date of composition. The problem is that Proverbs is an anthology, which explicitly includes a number of quite different works. Some of those works may themselves have been created out of originally separate compositions, and Proverbs as a whole has apparently undergone some further supplementation, after its initial compilation. The situation is very complicated, and in places controversial.

1. Structure and contents

The book itself offers a series of subheadings:

1.1	Sayings of Solomon
10.1	Sayings of Solomon
22.17	(. . . hear) the Words of the Wise
24.23	These also are of the Wise
25.1	These also are Sayings of Solomon which the men of Hezekiah, King of Judah, ?-ed (the sense of the word is disputed, see below)
30.1	The Words of Agur, Son of Jakeh of Massa
31.1	The Words of Lemuel, King of Massa, which his Mother Taught Him

There are problems involved in understanding some of these titles, but the most interesting point for the moment is that 24.23 and 25.1 both include the word 'also', linking them to 22.17 and 1.1/10.1 respectively, and show-ing that there has been some deliberate attempt to relate the parts; there is a system here, in other words. We would expect that system similarly to include 'also' at 10.1, however, which suggests that a subtitle (and per-haps a corresponding section of the book) has been added: 1.1 is the likely candidate, and this verse now serves as a title for the book as a whole. Because they are not related to other sections, it is difficult to tell whether the Words of Agur and the Words of Lemuel belong to the original series, or are also additions.

The system of subtitles tells only part of the story. There are several places where material appears to have been added, and effectively sub-sumed within sections. It is probable, for example, that the Words of Agur actually finishes in 30.4, and that the miscellaneous sayings which follow are secondary, while the poem about the good wife in 31.10-31 is itself a separate work, and not part of the Words of Lemuel. Earlier in the work, 6.1-19 is usually considered to have been inserted into the first section (chs 1–9), and that section has apparently been disrupted also in 9.7-12, where a short series of sayings fits uncomfortably into a speech. The Greek Septuagint version, furthermore, has certain changes of order and differ-ences of content. These raise the possibility that Proverbs did not achieve its current fixed state until quite late, although it is clear that many of the differences between the Greek and Hebrew are down to translation style, rather than different underlying texts.

At whatever point they were introduced, and despite their limitations, the subtitles do correspond to distinct changes of style, and mark out sections of the book that may reasonably be regarded as separate compositions. All or most of these, indeed, may have enjoyed an independent existence before becoming part of Proverbs, and the majority belong broadly to the two genres of advice literature which we discussed in the introduction and the previous chapter – sentence literature and instruction. The boundaries between these, however, should not be drawn too sharply, and it would be unhelpful simply to run through the book assigning material to one genre or the other.

The issues may be illustrated quite readily from the two main sentence-literature collections, which are in 10.1–22.16 and 25–29 and are both attributed to Solomon. The first consists almost entirely of short, indicative sayings that state a supposed fact or facts; so for instance, 10.12 claims that: 'Hatred sparks dispute, while love overlooks all provocations', and 14.34 that 'Righteousness glorifies a nation, while sin is a disgrace for peoples'. The address is sometimes direct, however, as in 14.7: 'Go up against a foolish man, and you'll not get to know knowing speech' (cf. Judg. 20.34 and Prov. 20.15 for the idioms used here). In 19.27, furthermore, a saying begins 'Cease, my son', which envisages the sort of parental teaching more typical of the instruction genre. Chapters 25–29 include more in the way of direct admonitions, and again address a son in 27.11: 'Be wise, my son' . . . This works both ways: if the sentence literature in Proverbs can pose sometimes as instruction, so too can the instructions sometimes borrow the style of sentence literature. Proverbs 1–9, for example, refers constantly to parental instruction and attaches itself very closely to the instruction genre, but 3.32-35 is a series of indicative sayings very reminiscent of much in 10.1–22.16, framed as the justification for a direct admonition in 3.31. The generic characteristics or markers for each type of composition are found sometimes in the other.

Some commentators have found this a problem. William McKane (1970), for example, correctly observed that instructions and sentence literature are different types of composition in Egypt and Mesopotamia, but wrongly deduced that what is appropriate for one can therefore have no place in the other, and concluded that such apparent mixtures must have arisen from secondary revision of the text. As we have already seen, the fact that instructions and sentence literature are different genres does not make them mutually exclusive elsewhere: the Demotic advice literature, for instance, commonly has the features of both, as does *Ahiqar*. In Proverbs, we do not find such simple presentation of a sayings collection as the advice of a parent, but we do encounter allusions to the instructional setting within series of sayings, and series of sayings within instructions. We also find considerable variation on the basic idea of an instruction. The main instructional section, chs 1–9, consistently portrays itself as parental instruction, but not really as a single testamentary speech, which is the norm elsewhere, whilst 22.17–24.22, despite its dependence on the Egyptian *Amenemope*, apparently presents itself as a written selection of established sayings by 'the wise', and not as a parental speech at all. Only the Words of Lemuel, in 31.1-9, describes itself directly as parental – but even there the attribution to a mother, rather than a father, is itself unique.

So, although we can divide the major sections of Proverbs into different types for the sake of convenience, it is difficult to define clear distinctions between those types, and very probable, indeed, that the original editors perceived most of the materials as closely related to each other – a key factor, presumably, in their anthologization together. With the possible exception of the mysterious Words of Agur in ch. 30, all of the various sections, and the secondary additions as well, can be described broadly as advice literature. Some of the advice offered seems to concern very specific actions: 22.28, for example, prohibits moving a boundary marker, and 25.6 advises against self-promotion. Sometimes those actions are essentially representative, however, as when 25.16 uses eating honey as an instance of overindulgence: 'Should you find some honey, eat just enough – so you don't gorge yourself with it, and throw it up.' Of course, we should beware of assuming that we can always distinguish the two: it is quite possible, for instance, that the prohibition against moving a marker is intended to convey some more general point, like 'Do not change established conventions.'

A great deal of the advice, moreover, relates to much more general patterns of behaviour: righteousness and wisdom are repeatedly commended, often by statements about the benefits which they offer the righteous and the wise. Mixed in with the advice, there are also many general observations, such as 14.20: 'A poor man is unlovely even to his friend, while those who love a rich man are many', or 25.25: 'Cool water on a parched throat – (that is the feeling of) good news from a distant land.' It would be wrong, in fact, to see any part of Proverbs simply as a manual of proper behaviour, and there is much of the variety here that we saw in, for instance, the Mesopotamian collections.

It would also be wrong, however, to generalize too much about the book as a whole before looking at its main components individually. Rather than follow the order of the book, it is easiest to begin with the materials that are simplest in their formal presentation, the major collections of sayings attributed to Solomon and to 'the wise'. We shall move on after that to the intriguing but difficult work in chs 1–9, and to the various materials in chs 30 and 31.

2. The Sayings of Solomon (10.1–22.16 and 25–29)

Both of these collections are attributed to Solomon, and described using the Hebrew term *mashal*. Although there has been much discussion of that word, it seems to refer to quite a wide range of sayings, and it may have been picked instead of other alternatives for no reason more specific than the alliterative effect of the expression pronounced *mishley shlomoh*, 'Sayings of Solomon'. The second collection adds that the sayings were treated in some way by the men of Hezekiah, king of Judah: the verb used is often rendered 'copied', which would make this a unique reference to the transmission of a text. Elsewhere, though, the same verb is used of removing or moving away, not passing on (Weeks 1994: 43–4), and it is possible that we are being offered an explanation for the separate existence of this collection: the Septuagint translation might be taken to mean, 'The unsorted teachings of Solomon which the friends of Hezekiah, king of Judah, expunged.' It is, of course, difficult to confirm or deny the actual attributions to Solomon, but their function is probably not as a simple record of authorship anyway: as with the attributions to other famous individuals from the past, which we saw in connection with foreign instructions, these serve to affirm the validity of the sayings, lending them the authority of a king who had become legendary for his wisdom. Most modern scholars doubt that Solomon was actually involved in the creation of the sayings or collections, and considerable debate continues amongst historians about almost every aspect of his reign. The reference to the time of Hezekiah is more often regarded as historical, but while we have no way of knowing on what information, story, or idea it is based (or even precisely what it means), that too must be treated with caution.

In fact, the dates at which the collections were composed is uncertain, and although it is reasonable to suppose that they were each created independently before becoming parts of Proverbs, it is possible that they reached their present forms as the result of quite lengthy processes. It is certainly not easy to assign a date on the basis of content, not only because that content is rarely dateable itself, but also because the collections may contain material composed at many different dates. A similar problem confronts any attempts to identify a particular ethos and social context in the sayings: they may have been drawn, ultimately, from many different settings. We shall return to that question after looking briefly at the character of the collections.

a. The collections

The sayings which make up the collections do not all adopt the same formal structure, but are much more consistent in the original Hebrew than they appear to be in translation. The great majority consist of two short statements (generally three or four words long), which are set in parallel: in poetic terms, each statement makes a 'stich', and the pair make a 'distich' (the terms 'colon' and 'bicolon' are also sometimes used). So, in 10.1 we have:

(stich 1)   A wise son makes a father happy
(stich 2)   while a foolish son is his mother's sorrow

The two stichs are usually joined by a simple conjunction, w- in Hebrew, but that conjunction has no precise equivalent in English or many other languages. In this example, it expresses a contrast between the two sorts of son, but exactly the same expression can be used to express an equivalence or analogy, as in 16.13: 'A contrary man spreads conflict, while (w-) a mutterer alienates a friend.' Simple joining with a conjunction can even be used to create a simile, as in 25.25, which I translated above. Literally, it reads: 'Cool water on a parched throat and (w-) good news from a distant land.' The conjunction can also express other ideas. So, in 17.11 it seems to denote consequence: 'Surely the rebel looks for trouble – and a cruel messenger will be sent to him.' In the next verse, it seems to indicate preference: '(Better) a bereaved bear meeting a man, and not a fool (meeting) his folly!' With such a variety of connotations, the translation of such sayings obviously requires some degree of interpretation. This does not usually cause any great shift in sense, and it does not matter greatly whether we render 26.14, for instance, as 'Like a door turning on a hinge, so a sluggard (turns) on his bed', as 'A door turns on its hinge, and a sluggard on his bed', or as 'A door turns on its hinge, but a sluggard on his bed'. There are occasions, though, when it is difficult to establish just what is meant.

Other types of saying also tend to adopt the two-part structure, sometimes with the conjunction. In 14.7, for instance, we have a direct admonition: 'Avoid confrontation with a foolish man, and you will not know knowledgeable speech.' Admonitions generally consist of a command or prohibition, followed by an explanatory 'motive clause', as in 25.17: 'Let your step be rare in your neighbour's house, lest he have enough of you, and hate you', or 27.1: 'Boast not about the morrow, for you do not know what a day may give birth to.' Another form encountered several times is the 'better than' saying, like 25.24: 'Better is living in a corner of the rooftop, than a contentious wife and a shared house.' These sayings, again, are naturally in two parts, and so even when there is some variety in the style of the sayings (which is more often the case in the second collection), there remains a general appearance of consistency, with distich following distich, or distichs very occasionally combined to form longer units (e.g. 25.4-7).

In fact, because Hebrew poetry is built from similar units, with stichs set in parallel, the overall effect is to make the collections look like long poems. Especially in 10.1–22.16, the formal consistency is striking, and much greater than in most of the foreign sayings collections. This structural uniformity is reinforced in places by the sense as well. In the first half of 10.1–22.16, most obviously, almost all of the sayings are apparently intended to draw out a contrast (and it is tempting to suppose, indeed, that the collection has absorbed another consisting entirely of such sayings). Throughout, though, we find sayings associated with each other using the sort of devices which we observed in the Sumerian collections, with sayings linked to those around them in various ways, most commonly by their theme, by catchwords, or by a shared first letter. In the many places where they are used, such methods provide a sort of flow from each saying to the next, and show that the arrangement is far from random. We can illustrate the way this works with a fairly typical example from 14.6-8, where there is a broadly consistent theme about the inadequacy of unwise people, but also verbal links between the sayings, indicated by the arrows here:

> 6 The scornful man seeks wisdom and there's none,
>   While knowledge↓ is a trifle for the discerning.
> 7 Avoid confrontation with a foolish↓ man,
>   and you will not know knowledgeable speech (lit. lips of knowledge↑).
> 8 The wisdom of the shrewd is discernment of his way,
>   while the folly↓ of fools↑ is misleading.

It is not always easy to be sure what is a linking device and what is simple coincidence: how much weight can we place, for instance, on the fact that the sayings in 16.20-2 and 17.12-15 have alternating first letters (m-l-m-l and p-m-p-m)? On the other hand, it seems hard to overlook the fact that 15.16 and 17 share a very distinctive form – better something small with something good than something big with something bad – even if they are about different things:

> 16 Better a little with fear of YHWH than much wealth and trouble with it.
> 17 Better a portion of salad and love there, than a fatted calf and hate with it.

We can be fairly certain, at least, that many of the correspondences which we see are intentional, and that they display a strong interest in words and sounds, as well as in the meaning of sayings.

With so much compositional effort on display, however, it is not surprising that many scholars have wondered whether the sayings are being arranged at times to draw out more complicated ideas than they can each individually express. In some places, and on a small scale, this is undeniably the case – as when, for example, contradictory sayings are set beside each other in 26.4-5, or complementary ones a little later, in 26.20-1. We can also observe apparent correlations that extend beyond simple linking to adjacent sayings. Efforts to find larger structures, however, run into serious problems of method: it is very easy to find apparent patterns in this material, but much harder to prove that any particular patterns are deliberate and significant (Weeks 1994: 20–40). Furthermore, it is quite likely that there have been accidental or even deliberate changes to the text in the course of its transmission, and additions, omissions or transpositions can all have a profound effect on our ability to identify the interconnections. Some of the problems may be illustrated by 19.4-9:

> 4 Wealth adds many friends,
>> while the poor man is cut off from friendship.
> 5 A false witness will not get away with it,
>> while a breather of lies will not escape
> 6 Many seek the favour of the generous,
>> while everyone's a friend to a man who gives.
> 7 All the poor man's brothers hate him
>> – how his friends keep their distance from him!
>> Whoever seeks words not them (?)
> 8 Whoever gets a mind loves himself,
>> whoever hangs on to understanding is going to find good
> 9 A false witness will not get away with it,
>> While a breather of lies will perish.

Here verse 5 is almost identical to verse 9, and seems to interrupt a sequence of closely related sayings in verses 4, 6, and the first part of 7. Verse 7, on the other hand, has an extra stich, which is very obscure and may be the remains of another saying, perhaps similar in form to verse 8. It is difficult not to suspect that something has gone wrong, both in verse 7 and with respect to verse 5, but equally difficult to prove that it has. As regards broader interconnections, we have already looked at 14.20, which is very similar to the sayings about rich and poor here, while verse 8 seems very close to 15.32, and there are many other sayings about the false witnesses of verses 5 and 7. Closer to home, there are a number of thematic and verbal correspondences to the sayings in chapter 18 which immediately precede these. However striking we may find such correspondences, though, they are scattered, and it is almost impossible to see what, if anything, they signify beyond a general consistency of interest and expression.

Accordingly, attempts to identify meaningful subsections within each collection have struggled to find criteria that are not simply arbitrary and subjective. If certain correspondences or differences do indeed indicate structure, then we need a way to tell those apart from the many other correspondences and differences. If the subsections are supposed to convey meaning, moreover, then we also need to show somehow that delimiting a sequence of sayings to produce a set in one way yields something more than doing it in another – that the group 19.1-10, for example, is a more meaningful context in which to read each saying than the group 18.24–19.7, say, or the group 19.1-7. Whether we are seeking formal sections or more informal 'clusters' (as Gnut Heim [2001] calls them), it is difficult not to fall back essentially on subjective claims about the superiority of one grouping over another. In short, if we are supposed to read each saying in the context of those around it, then the creators of the collections have rarely made it clear how we should do so, and we have no knowledge of any conventions which may have existed for doing so. Correspondingly, it is difficult for us to know whether any interpretation based on a contextual reading was actually intended by those creators, let alone whether one such interpretation is more authentic than another.

Despite their formal coherence and poetic appearance, in fact, it is far from certain that the collections were designed for continuous performance or reading, or that they intend to provide contexts throughout for their individual sayings. Such collections elsewhere are organized in various different ways, as we have seen, but it would be difficult to make a case in any of them for the sort of contextual reading that is often proposed for Proverbs. The basic nature of ancient sayings collections seems somewhere close to that of almanacs, miscellanies, joke books, or other modern works designed more for dipping into than for reading cover-to-cover, and the skill of arranging the materials seems more oriented in most to finding hooks for sayings, than to any broader composition. The unusual formal coherence of these two Hebrew collections does not necessarily mean that they were different in this respect.

b. The sayings

If they do not obviously provide an interpretative context, the collections are nevertheless important for understanding the character of the sayings within them. Some scholars in recent years (most notably Claus Westermann [1995] and Friedemann Golka [1993]) have argued for a return to old assumptions that the raw materials of the sentence literature in Proverbs are essentially folk proverbs, which would have circulated and been used within the society as a whole. This is not inherently implausible, but it runs into the difficulty, which has long been recognized, that the sort of two-line sayings typical of 10–22.16 and 25–29 are not typical of proverbs attested elsewhere, even elsewhere in the Bible. Compare, for instance, these snappier aphorisms, all described as proverbs:

'Is Saul too among the prophets?' (1 Sam. 10.12)

'It's from the wicked that wickedness comes.' (1 Sam. 24.14 [ET 24.13])

'Like mother, like daughter.' (Ezek. 16.44)

We would generally expect actual proverbs to be much more varied in form than the sayings we find in our collections, and it is striking that we find closer parallels in poetic contexts (such as Hab. 2.4-17, where general sayings are apparently applied to the object of the prophet's attack).

This issue has led to considerable discussion in the past, often guided by the dubious principle that form must reflect setting, and that the two-line sayings of the collections must represent a more evolved, literate form than simple proverbs. Such discussions can draw distinctions which are unhelpful and unrealistic. Proverbial sayings, in the many cultures which use them, are not easily distinguished from certain other types of expression, but they do generally employ elevated modes of speech which are elsewhere associated with poetry or other types of composition: these may include characteristics such as rhythm and rhyme, or the use of figurative and metaphoric language. Correspondingly, in literate and semi-literate societies, there can be considerable interplay between literate and oral usage, with proverbs commonly quoted in literary compositions, while literary aphorisms, or even snatches of verse, come into use as proverbs. We see one side of this in quite a broad range of ancient literature, where proverbs are cited or absorbed into other compositions, whilst on the other side, it is widely assumed that the readers of most ancient sayings collections were looking to use the sayings which they read in their own speech and writing (and, of course, it is quite likely that these sayings would therefore be recirculated into popular usage outside literate circles). Since new proverbs surely continued to come into use, we are not really looking at a context in which sayings passed through some distinct development from 'folk' or 'oral' to 'literate', but one in which there was probably a continuous interaction between the oral and written. If we can speak of different contexts in which sayings might have been used, it is doubtful that we can assign any saying specifically to a single context, or talk about its origin on the basis of its form.

The general consistency of our two collections is probably to be explained not by the development of some special sort of proverb, but by literary intention: the creators have collected sayings which are mostly distichs, or are close enough in length to fit, perhaps in imitation of Hebrew poetic norms. We have no direct knowledge of their sources, and it is possible that they have themselves adapted or composed sayings to fit their adopted style. So, anything we can usefully say about the background of the sayings themselves has to be based on their individual content, and this is, again, quite a difficult area. Between them, for example, the two collections have some twenty-five sayings involving kings and rulers, which have often been understood to reflect an origin in the royal court. The attitudes of these sayings vary greatly, however, and some seem actively critical of kingship, or concerned to subordinate its importance (e.g. 29.26). Courtiers, moreover, are not the only people to be interested in kingship, and the language of monarchy may serve, indeed, to represent government or the powerful more generally. Correspondingly, sayings which express a concern with the poor, another favourite topic, need reflect an origin neither amongst the poor themselves, nor amongst the charitable wealthy: this is a basic ethical concern throughout the ancient world, which goes to the heart of ideas about proper behaviour and the right ordering of society.

We have also to reckon with a sort of metonymy, in which the specific can stand for something more general. Chapter 27 ends with an unusually long piece of advice in verses 23–7, really a short poem in itself and not a proverb, which commends careful attention to one's flocks and herds: wealth may pass, but when the harvest has been taken in, these animals will still provide for the household. On the face of it, this is pragmatic advice for farmers – and it is often read as such – but it also makes a much more general point about the need to take care of basics: we should all attend to those things which keep us secure even when the good times are over. Similarly, 14.4 talks about the need for labour and effort: 'Without cattle, there's just a trough of grain, while with the strength of an ox, there's a massive yield.' Such sayings may conceivably have been composed by or for farmers, and only later perceived by the collectors to have a wider application, but we should note that agricultural themes are quite common in ancient advice literature more generally, and the familiarity of the farming context would have made these themes appropriate vehicles of expression for members of any class. We must be wary, in other words, of being too literal-minded in our assessment of this material: it draws on the everyday and the familiar – a world of farms and small towns, rich men and paupers, law courts and royal courts – to make points which would have been comprehensible to all. A reference to any part of that world, though, does not imply an origin in that part, or a concern solely with that part.

In fact, much of the first collection is characterized by advice so general that it is almost worthless: saying after saying spells out the virtues and rewards of the righteous, the wise, and the upright, along with the corresponding vices and problems of their counterparts – the wicked, the foolish, scoffers, and others. This material exhorts a type of behaviour which it is presumed the audience will themselves understand, but it offers little by way of specific guidance. Indeed, since it is fair to assume that most foolish or wicked people do not see themselves in that light, pretty much anyone could applaud these sayings without in the least being motivated to change their behaviour, let alone being taught how to do so. Such sayings, then, are not really advice, so much as assertions about the nature of the world: those who understand it and behave properly within it will prosper, while those who do not will suffer. These ideas are quite often tied up with declarations about God, which make it clear that he acts to protect those on one side, while condemning those on the other, as 10.3 puts it early on: 'YHWH does not starve the appetite of the righteous, while he pushes away the desire of the wicked.'

Certainly as they stand, in fact, both collections have a strong religious dimension, and in the second collection this is sometimes very explicitly Jewish: 'Those who abandon the Torah praise the wicked, while those who keep the Torah do battle with them' (28.4; compare 28.7, 9 and 29.18, which talks also of prophecy). Compositions from other countries, in particular those closest to Proverbs in date, frequently express a very strong concern with religious ideas, and in particular with divine control of events. If our collections seem focused for much of the time on the mundane, they nevertheless view human actions in a broader context of divine power and justice, and they probably always did so.

3. The Words of the Wise (22.17–24.22; 24.23-34)

The two sections of Proverbs attributed to the wise are rather different from each other, and the first raises some very particular problems, since it is often associated with the Egyptian *Instruction of Amenemope*. It is difficult to know what significance we should attach to the titles of these works, the first of which is almost concealed within the Hebrew text of 22.17: 'Turn your ear, and listen to the words of the wise . . .' (the Septuagint Greek version has a different word order, which makes it stand out more). For reasons discussed earlier, advice literature in the ancient Near East was usually attributed to a named individual, if it carried any attribution at all, and this break with convention – assigning the words to the anonymous 'wise' – is made all the more curious by the fact that both collections include sayings expressed using the first person singular 'I' – indeed, 22.19 goes on to speak of the words that 'I have told you', and the next verse asks, 'Have I not written for you'. The image presented seems to be one of an individual passing on teachings which are explicitly not his own, while the expression 'words of the wise' has perhaps given rise to, or been derived from Prov. 1.6. It need not refer to some particular group, any more than does, say, 'The words of the wicked' in 12.6. There are no secure grounds for dating either section, although there are some resemblances between the first and Prov. 1–9, while the second arguably elaborates, in 24.30-34, a saying found in 6.9-10. It is difficult to assess the direction of influence in such cases, but a date after Proverbs 1–9, and so probably in the post-exilic period, is likely.

a. The first collection: 22.17–24.22

It was mentioned earlier that Adolf Erman drew attention in 1924 to a series of correspondences between *Amenemope* and the sayings in 22.17–23.10. These are too striking to be entirely coincidental, and although a few scholars (notably Norman Whybray [1994a: 132–4; 1994b, and elsewhere]) have expressed doubt about any close link between the works, most accept that there is a connection (recently, e.g., Emerton 2001; Shupak 2005). The nature of that connection is less clear than its existence: Proverbs does not simply reproduce a continuous section of the Egyptian work, and its versions of the sayings vary in some respects. It is unlikely that they share a common source, and highly improbable that *Amenemope* has borrowed from Proverbs (it is somewhat earlier than the Israelite monarchy); most likely, some version of, or selection from the Egyptian was already available, perhaps in Aramaic, and this was used as a source by the Jewish writer. From that point of view, it is interesting that the prologue in Proverbs 1.2-6 also bears a close resemblance to that of *Amenemope*, which is very distinctive, and the influence may spread beyond this one section of Proverbs. One other very distinctive feature of the Egyptian work is its division into numbered stanzas. There are thirty of these, and many commentators reconstruct the awkward Hebrew of 22.20 to read: 'Have I not written for you thirty sayings . . .' If that reading is correct, then it may be that we are supposed to find thirty teachings in this section, as various scholars do in various ways, or perhaps that the number is just a leftover from the source.

This remark about the sayings forms part of a short introduction, in 22.17-21, which exhorts acceptance of what is to follow. Similar exhortations follow in 23.12, 15, 19, 26 and 24.13, 26, in all but the first of which the listener is addressed as 'my son'. This is apparently a reminiscence of the parental context typical of ancient instructions, although the work as a whole seems to present itself as a written composition, rather than as a father's speech. The exhortations, or 'parental appeals' serve not only to mark a connection with the instruction genre, however, but apparently also to divide the section into subsections of various lengths. This is a technique which is used in Prov. 1–9, as we shall see shortly, and it may have been borrowed from there. In any case, such appeals are not a generic feature which can stand only at the head of instructions, as some scholars have claimed (e.g. Whybray 1965), so we do not need to assume that the subsections of this work existed originally as independent, very short compositions in their own right (Weeks 2007: 52–3).

There is, however, a great deal of variety in terms of form and content, certainly as compared with the more formally consistent sayings collections of 10.1–22.16 and 25–29 which we examined above, and the principles of arrangement, if there are any, mostly elude us. Most of this section contains admonitions addressed directly to the reader, a high proportion of them negative, 'Do not . . .' sayings, usually with explanatory motive clauses. The indicative sayings more typical of the preceding collections feature in 24.3-9, but we also find more complicated passages. 23.29-35 is especially striking, with its vivid warnings against alcohol, which begin with questions, and move on to a striking depiction of how the reader will find it to be drunk. In 24.10-12 there is also an unusual, rather disturbing call to rescue those being dragged to slaughter in the 'day of trouble': those who do not must reckon with punishment from he who 'takes the measure of hearts' and watches each individual. Indeed, several of the sayings here are concerned with avoiding opposition to God, and the section finishes with a chilling piece of advice: 'Fear YHWH, my son, and a king: transgress with neither (?), for calamity comes from them suddenly, and who knows what ruin from them both?'

Again, we can say little about context for this material. Even 23.1, one of the sayings with a link to *Amenemope*, does not necessarily reflect some special setting in a court or bureaucracy: 'As you sit down to dine with someone in charge' could apply as easily to lunch with one's boss as to dinner at the palace. Similarly, in the preceding 22.29 it is surely only a figure of speech to say that a skilful man will 'stand before kings'. The sayings here are certainly sometimes addressed specifically to men, but it would be difficult to justify any more precise a setting or target audience.

b. The second collection: 24.23-34

There are just a few miscellaneous sayings in this short section: these address impartiality, the need for preparation before a major project, avoidance of false, vengeful accusations, and the perils of laziness. The last is interesting: it is presented as an anecdote, told in the first person, culminating in a realization that poverty will overtake the slothful; as already noted, virtually the same conclusion is expressed in the briefer 6.9-10. Otherwise there is little which we can say about this collection. The Greek Septuagint tradition places it between 30.14 and 30.15, and if this reflects the order in the translator's copy of Proverbs, it should warn us against the assumption, occasionally made, that it is merely an appendix to the preceding collection (e.g. Whybray 1994a: 145).

4. Proverbs 1–9

The first section of Proverbs, like 22.17–24.22, appears to be divided into subsections by parental appeals. These vary quite a lot, but the first, in 1.8-9 gives a flavour: 'Heed, my son, your father's instruction, and do not forsake your mother's teaching, for they are a lovely wreath for your head, and pendants for your neck.' There are some quibbles over what to count as an appeal, but most commentators recognize some ten to twelve subsections, which vary considerably in length. The first seven verses stand outside this structure as an introduction, although it is not certain whether any or all of them are supposed to introduce Proverbs as a whole, or just chapters 1–9. They comprise, in any case, an attribution to Solomon, followed by a series of purpose clauses in verses 2–6. These may, as noted above, be an imitation of a similar series in *Amenemope*, and they speak of the benefits to be gained from the work by learned and unlearned alike. A concern with those who are still uneducated is characteristic of chapters 1–9, but not really specific to them. In verse 7, however, a motto declares 'Fear of YHWH is the start of knowledge: it is wisdom and instruction that fools despise': this goes, as we shall see, to the heart of some concerns prominent in chapters 1–9, and it is picked up by 9.10, at the end of the section; so this verse, at least, probably belongs with these chapters. There is some confusion in the text of 9.7-12, and 6.1-19 is almost universally regarded as a later addition (we shall look at it separately below), but otherwise the extent and content of the work is fairly clear. Agreement about the content, however, is not matched by any consensus as to how we should read this work.

a. Approaching Proverbs 1–9

The sections of Proverbs that we have looked at already are collections, which may have their own compositional or structural features, but which do not really ever amount to more than the sum of their small parts. It is obvious at a glance that we are dealing with something different in

Proverbs 1–9. Not only are the units of advice typically much longer than elsewhere, but there is also a great deal of continuity in the themes. Furthermore, although there is a strong interest in parental teaching, which associates the work closely with the instruction genre, we hear not just the father's voice addressing his child, but many other voices as well; at points, characters even appear to speak in short vignettes. Throughout, in addition, there is a dense and vivid use of figurative speech, with extended metaphors, personified concepts, and numerous similes. Most famously, wisdom is personified as a woman Wisdom, who stands in contrast, at the end of the work, with a similarly personified figure of Folly. Only in chapter 3 do we find more familiar series of sayings, and even there the thematic consistency is greater than we have seen elsewhere in Proverbs.

Despite this consistency and distinctiveness, some scholars have reacted to the differences in style by breaking the text into small pieces. In particular, Norman Whybray's 1965 attempt to uncover a sequence of original, separate instructions notoriously involved stripping away as secondary large portions of the text, including most of the material that gives the chapters their unusual character. The procedure is indefensible in terms of method (cf. Fox 2000: 322; Weeks 2007: 52–3), but we may have some sympathy with his motives – though more variable in form than Whybray himself supposed, instructions are really not supposed to look like this. Most other commentators have been more moderate in their treatment of the text, but the majority still make an effort to carve something more conventional out of the chapters, usually by isolating some or all of the materials concerning personified Wisdom, and treating these as independent compositions. Even if we succeed in sculpting something that looks more normal, though, significant problems remain.

Chapter 2 is constructed as a single, very long sentence, and seems to offer a preview of the principal concerns that will dominate the following chapters. In this respect, of course, it offers evidence in itself of the work's basic unity, but it also introduces a figure who poses problems for any superficial reading of the text as a collection, or even as a simple instruction. That figure is 'A strange woman . . . a foreign woman who has polished her words, who abandons the companion of her youth, and has forgotten the covenant of her God. For her house reaches down to death, and her paths to the shades. None who goes to her returns, and they never reach the paths of life.' (2.16-19). This woman dominates the text in chapters 5–7, where she is associated with a ruinous relationship and with adultery, appearing finally in chapter 7 as the key character of a story, in which a young man wanders near her house, and is seduced by her as she waits at the corner. In that story she actually speaks, offering a tempting invitation to her perfumed bed, but her power to seduce with speech is always emphasized, along with the deadly danger of listening to her.

Many attempts have been made to read these chapters where the woman appears as a sequence of warnings against adultery, making Proverbs 1–9 seem somewhat obsessive on the subject. Adultery, however, is only mentioned explicitly in chapter 6, while efforts to make 'foreign woman' mean 'another man's wife' (e.g. Fox 2000: 139–40) are unconvincing: 'foreign' in Hebrew means, well, 'foreign' (see Weeks 2007: 198–200). More importantly, time and again the actual advice is not to avoid sleeping with this woman, but to avoid her invitations, and to resist the smooth, seductive speech which is her principal characteristic: the youth of chapter 7 is doomed the moment he follows her, and the story ends at that point, not with some pursuit by a cuckolded husband. The woman, moreover, has much in common with the personification of folly in chapter 9, where a woman Folly also issues a deadly invitation – and that is an invitation to food, not sex. If we take the advice about the foreign woman to be merely about adultery or some other illicit sexual behaviour, we seem to risk ignoring what the text itself says, and squashing it into a predetermined notion of the topics that an instruction should address.

b. Imagery and meaning

If we can only make Proverbs 1–9 seem like other advice literature by removing large sections and imposing new meanings on much of what remains, then it may be better to avoid reading it quite so much in terms of that other literature, and to look more closely at what it actually says. In the case of the foreign woman, the text is in fact no less concerned to spell out how she may be eluded than with the need to elude her. In 7.4, the father advises his son to 'Say to Wisdom, "You are my sister", and call understanding "cousin"', so that he may protect himself from the woman, and this fits the idea in chapter 2 that he will be saved from her by listening to teaching, and so receiving wisdom in his heart. It is teaching that will come to the rescue also in 5.1-6 and 6.20-24, while the youth who is caught in the story of chapter 7 is one of the 'ignorant' or 'untaught'. The role of the foreign woman becomes much clearer if we observe that what she does is to issue persuasive invitations which tempt the ignorant, but against which the educated are protected. Hers, moreover, are not the only invitations on offer, and the untaught are targeted, indeed, by both Wisdom (1.22; 8.5; 9.4) and Folly (9.16) to receive invitations. It is these invitations themselves that are the focus of interest.

More than 30 years ago, Jean-Noël Aletti (1977) observed that Wisdom's speeches are always paired with those of another character. This is clearest in chapter 9, of course, where Wisdom and Folly are presented in parallel, issuing dinner invitations to the uneducated, but in chapter 1 Wisdom speaks after the father describes an invitation by robbers to join them in an easy slaughter of the innocent, while in chapter 8 she speaks after the foreign woman has previously seduced the youth with promises of sex without danger. Aletti concluded, soundly I think, that Proverbs 1–9 is concerned with the problem of recognition: the uneducated youth hears invitations from all sides, many of them attractive, and has no way of knowing which are dangerous and which not. To recognize and accept the invitations of Wisdom, which lead to life and prosperity, one must first receive instruction, which will permit one to know and reject other invitations, typified by those of the foreign woman.

Aletti does not go into the nature of that instruction itself, but other aspects of the work point to its identity. Proverbs 1–9 is filled with references to ways and paths (cf. Habel 1972), which are the key focus of attention in chapter 4. That chapter speaks not only of separate paths for the wicked and the righteous (4.14-19), but of the need to stay away from crooked speech, walking straight forward and never turning aside. For a Jewish audience, such language would surely have been strongly evocative of language used by Deuteronomy of obedience to the Torah, as when Deut. 5.32-3 declares: 'You must take care to act as YHWH your God has commanded you, and must not turn aside to the right or the left. It is wholly in the way which YHWH your God has commanded that you must walk, so that you may survive, prosper and live long in the land which you shall own.' This language of paths and walking straight is picked up widely elsewhere in the biblical literature, and 'turning aside' is a familiar expression for disobedience to God (e.g. Job 23.11; 34.26-7). In Deuteronomy itself, it has a particular association with apostasy – one turns aside to follow other gods (e.g. 11.16).

One may also turn others aside, however, and there is a strong concern in some literature that the Israelites will be led into apostasy by intermarriage with the peoples of the land (Cf. Exod. 34.11-16; Deut. 7.1-4). Although the historical facts are sketchy, it seems that this became a major concern in the community that returned from Babylon after the Exile: recollecting that even Solomon had been caused to sin by his foreign wives (1 Kings 11.1-4 says they 'turned his heart aside'), members of this community seem to have campaigned for Jews to divorce foreign women (Ezra 9–10; Neh. 13.23-7). If 'turning aside' is apostasy, 'foreign women' are the most notorious seducers into apostasy, and it is hard to believe that the 'foreign woman' of Proverbs 1–9 is unconnected to that well-established notion. As a number of scholars have observed, moreover, Proverbs 1–9 uses terms for the father's teaching, including 'torah', which are more normally used of the law or divine commandments (e.g. Baumann 1996: 294–300; Weeks 2007: 104–5). In 3.11-12 the work also associates God with teaching and fatherhood, perhaps alluding to Deut. 8.5. In other words, these chapters are full of terms which would have had a strong religious resonance for the original readership, and which associate the work's 'parental' teaching with Torah. Although we cannot prove that Proverbs 1–9 was intended to be understood as a call to Torah-based piety, it was certainly read that way within a few generations (as we shall see), and if it was supposed to be talking about something else, then its language verges on the misleading.

In sum, this work uses conventional forms and ideas from advice literature, but what it presents is a call to heed and internalize instruction (by implication, the Torah), and so to gain wisdom. That wisdom will keep one on the straight and narrow, able to distinguish what is good and beneficial from what is attractive but dangerous. Those without such an advantage wander through life in constant peril, but those who have secured wisdom enjoy the benefits which she spells out herself in chapter 8: success, prosperity, life, and divine favour. The message is conveyed through a series of poems that draw on instructional motifs, without really constituting an instruction in the traditional sense. They do, however, combine to form a work that has a great consistency of both theme and style: although many commentators have tried to read it as an anthology, it seems probable that it was intended to be read as a unified composition. I am inclined to think that it was written from scratch, in much its present form, apart from the secondary 6.1-19 (Weeks 2007); other recent commentators have concluded that it was created out of existing materials which have been intensively re-edited to create a coherent work (Meinhold 1991), or that a single composition has been supplemented by subsequent editors – Fox (2000: 322–30) believes that a work containing a prologue and cycle of ten poems by a single author was enlarged by a series of secondary 'interludes', added at different times (1.20-33; 3.13-20; 6.1-19; 8.1-36; 9.1-6, 11, 13–18).

c. The personification of wisdom

It has become quite common to assert that Wisdom in Proverbs 1–9 is conceived of as a goddess figure, or more generally, that Proverbs 8 reflects a wider belief in the existence of a goddess Wisdom. The two ideas are conveniently addressed together, although they are distinct: the former may embrace the latter, but it is also possible to argue that Proverbs 1–9 draws on goddess imagery without necessarily believing in the existence of a separate goddess (Fox 2000: 341).

The verses most often thought to indicate a real figure, with some cosmo-logical significance, are 8.22-31. Here Wisdom boasts of her antiquity: she came into existence before the world, and was present to watch it created (perhaps even helping, although it is doubtful that 8.30 is to be read that way; cf. Weeks 2006); she subsequently occupies a position which is still constantly beside God, but somehow engaged with the world. In context, the point of this is to assert her own status: just as in the previous verses she has claimed to furnish the qualities by which rulers rule, and to reward those who love her, now she shows herself to possess incomparable author-ity to advise about the world, because she has known it from the outset, and remains in a close relationship with its creator (cf. Weeks 2006). We should not push too hard to extract a doctrine from what is, after all, a poetic text, but the underlying idea seems to be related to that expressed in 3.19, where God is said to have used (his own) wisdom in creation; we may recall that 'wisdom' in Hebrew also denotes skill in construction or any other area. Correspondingly, the thinking runs, wisdom must have existed before creation, the particular instance of God's wisdom giving rise to wisdom as a concept (just as there was no anger, say, before somebody was first angry). Since the creation, God still has wisdom, but wisdom may also be possessed by others: each instance of wisdom is particular to an individual, but wisdom as an abstract is shared by God and humans. If this is supposed to imply that wisdom can bridge the gap between them, then it clearly involves a deliberate confusion of the particular with the abstract (I am not really linked to someone else by anger when we are both angry). It does not imply, however, any real, physical existence.

Wisdom's femininity, moreover, need not be attributed to any identification with a goddess. The noun *hokma*, 'wisdom' is grammatically feminine in Hebrew, where every noun must be masculine or feminine, and abstract concepts are usually feminine. More importantly, perhaps, there is no evidence for the personification of wisdom in any thought or literature before Proverbs 1–9, and in this work the figure has apparently been conceived in conjunction with that of the foreign woman, and perhaps even secondarily as a counterpart: we are not looking at one female figure, but at a pair, and the identity of each is tied up with the other. If Wisdom is supposed recognizably to be a goddess, what does that make the woman?

Proverbs 8 does not oblige us to view Wisdom as a real, divine person, any more than the next chapter forces us to see Folly as a different goddess. If the text is read as theological exposition rather than poetry, however, it does present a problem. Correspondingly, some scholars have understood wisdom to be portrayed as a 'hypostasis' of God – that is a term used in trinitarian Christian theology to describe the individual persons of the trinity, and it reflects an idea (not always very closely defined) of wisdom being a separate entity while remaining a part of God. That view is of interest: Philo of Alexandria, writing early in the first century CE, associated wisdom with the divine word, or Logos, which he saw as mediating between God and the world, and such speculations may have been influential on the early development of Christianity. Few scholars now, however, would argue that Proverbs 1–9 itself had such a sophisticated idea in mind, and 'hypostasis' is at best a term which we might adopt to provide a secondary theological justification for the writer's presentation of wisdom as both a divine attribute and a separate person.

The modern debate has focused not on aligning the text with later theological sensibilities, but rather on the possibility that polytheistic influences are at work. Some scholars (e.g. Albright 1920: 285–6; Lang 1986) have supposed, quite straightforwardly, that Wisdom was recognized as a goddess in Iron Age Palestine, and is presented as such in Proverbs 1–9 (or, in Lang's view, redefined to suit a monotheistic context). Others, more cautiously, have suggested that the writer is merely drawing upon language and motifs, or even iconography, that was associated with goddesses; such borrowing could be purely literary, and would not necessarily imply that Wisdom was perceived to be a deity. Both ideas have attracted particular interest, of course, because they hold out the possibility that the account of Wisdom preserves a feminine presentation of the divine, which would have important historical and theological implications.

It is not easy, however, to sustain any of the key identifications that have been proposed. There is no evidence of a goddess 'Wisdom' in any other source (a possible reference in *Ahiqar* has been much disputed, and depends on a particular interpretation of a fragmentary passage), while Proverbs 1–9 itself does not describe Wisdom explicitly as a deity, so the various proposals rest entirely on the strength of the correspondences which have been adduced between the attributes of Wisdom and those of goddesses described elsewhere. Most of the interest has focused on supposed resemblances between Wisdom and, on the one hand, representations of *maat* as a goddess in Egyptian iconography (especially Kayatz 1966; Keel 1974), or, on the other hand, aretalogies of Isis, a goddess whose cult achieved international significance in Hellenistic times.

The latter are hymns in the form of a self-presentation, where Isis lists her attributes and accomplishments, rather in the way that wisdom talks about herself in Prov. 8. It is difficult to argue for direct influence, however, since the Isis materials are later than most scholars would date Proverbs 1–9, and although Michael Fox (2000: 336–8) points to certain correspondences (as earlier had Knox 1937), it is also difficult to demonstrate that Prov. 8 is not merely adopting a style imposed by its context, where a speech by Wisdom is required in response to the previous speech by the foreign woman. The influence of earlier self-presentations cannot be excluded, but even if we accept such influence, it is not clear that the original readers would have been familiar enough with such texts to have inferred that Wisdom must therefore be divine.

The problems of identification with *maat* are rather different, although the proposal is obviously attractive to those who believe that this Egyptian concept of order was adopted more generally in wisdom literature or beyond (a view we shall discuss in chapter 6). The main difficulty is that presentations of *maat* as a goddess are largely confined to the sphere of art, and they reflect not so much an active belief in the divine personhood of *maat*, as the need to depict the concept visually. So, for instance, *maat* may be shown embracing kings, or being presented by them as an offering, which are ways of illustrating how those kings are acting in harmony with *maat*, or ruling properly. Famously, the hearts of the dead are weighed on the scales against *maat* (or the feather which is her symbol) when they are judged, and this is again essentially a symbolic representation. As a goddess, *maat* played only a very minor role in the cult (there is a small chapel to her at Karnak), and literary references are almost entirely to the concept, not the deity. If Jewish writers were familiar with this deification at all, they would not have acquired their familiarity from any reading of Egyptian instructional literature.

In all this, we need to bear in mind that Egyptian representations of the divine were extremely fluid and sophisticated (see especially Hornung 1982), and that Egyptian art was highly stylized and symbolic. In certain respects, the deification of *maat* is an embodiment akin to a poetic personification, and the representations of the deity reflect this. *Maat* (like kings and other deities) may sometimes be shown, for instance, holding the stylized sandal-strap used as a hieroglyph for the word 'life' (*ankh*) – because the order represented as *maat* is a prerequisite for life and a source of life. This is entirely analogous to the depiction of Wisdom in Prov. 3.16, where she is said to hold 'length of days in her right hand, riches and honour in her left': it hardly strains credulity, though, to suppose that the same symbolic image might have arisen independently – especially when other Hebrew literature speaks of the right hand holding things which are being offered (Ps. 16.11; 26.10). Equally, *maat* symbols (and many other sigla) could be worn by individuals, but this need hardly be the source of the idea that wisdom might be an 'adornment for your neck' (Prov. 3.22), especially when instruction and faithfulness are similarly described (1.9; 3.3; 6.21). The personification of wisdom in Proverbs 1–9 resembles the deification of *maat* in Egyptian iconography, and what is said about Wisdom sometimes resembles what is said about *maat* (though more often about the concept than about the deified figure). There are many differences too, however, and we need hardly point to direct dependance as the only explanation for those places where two figurative representations of key concepts overlap.

In the end, it is hard either to prove or to disprove that the depiction of Wisdom in Proverbs 1–9 has been influenced, directly or indirectly, by representations of goddesses in the literature, liturgy, or iconography of other countries. About the potential influence of more local goddesses we can say virtually nothing, except that there are no obvious links to known figures such as Asherah (whose influence is perceived by McKinlay 1996) or Anat. It is equally difficult, moreover, to make the case that such influence must be presumed, since there are no good reasons to prevent us from taking that depiction as a purely literary phenomenon: Proverbs 1–9 makes heavy use of figurative speech, with many less sustained personifications of other concepts (e.g. 2.11; 3.2; 5.22; 9.13-18), and it employs other characters with speeches to convey essential parts of its message. In Job 28, where a goddess figure is also sometimes identified, it is far from clear that wisdom is a person at all, and the later accounts of personified wisdom in Ben Sira and elsewhere can largely be traced back to the influence of Proverbs 1–9 – although the influence of Isis aretalogies has also been suggested for Wisdom of Solomon (Reese 1970).

Perhaps the best we can do is to say that the original audiences of Proverbs 1–9 and its successors might have been less inclined to draw such strong distinctions between literary and mythical figurations, and more inclined to understand what they were reading in terms of familiar religious imagery. We certainly cannot say, however, that we must be dealing with a goddess Wisdom, or even that the personification of wisdom must have been shaped by presentations of goddesses. The depictions of wisdom as a woman are potentially important for feminist theology, but we can do no more than speculate about how far, if at all, they offer insights into early Jewish understandings of female divinity. It may well be, in fact, that they reveal more about the void left in Jewish religion by the disappearance of goddess worship (so, e.g., Hadley 1995). Although it was influential, furthermore, this type of depiction is confined to particular works, and does not represent some basic understanding common to the wisdom corpus as a whole.

d. Proverbs 6.1-19

Finally, a few words should be said about this short section in the first half of chapter 6. It has almost certainly been added to Proverbs 1–9, with which it has nothing substantial in common (Weeks 2007: 224–5), but it does constitute a short collection in its own right, containing five fairly long sayings. It may have been inserted here because 6.2 shares a term for entrapment with 5.22, but we can hardly know whether the scribe responsible wished to break up the sayings about the foreign woman in chapters 5–7, failed to observe the continuity of the text, or merely found a convenient margin at this point in his copy. There are some resemblances between the sayings here and those in the second part of chapter 30, while 6.10-11 appears in a longer saying at 24.33-34.

5. Chapters 30–31

The last two chapters of Proverbs each begin with a subtitle attributing the advice which follows, but in neither case is it clear that the work which is named actually extends to the whole length of the chapter. There is a clear division in chapter 31, where the closing verses 10–31 are a poem about the good wife, which most scholars see as an addition to the 'Words of Lemuel' in verses 1–9. The very obscure 'Words of Agur' in chapter 30, however, seems to begin with a series of questions about knowledge of the divine, which stand in contrast to the more ordinary sayings which follow in verses 5–33. The Septuagint's placing of 24.23-34 between verses 14 and 15 has been taken by many scholars as an indication that there was originally a break at this point, but others see the Words of Agur only in verses 1–4, and still others take it to fill the whole chapter. There are various opinions in between, and nothing that could really be considered a consensus. For practical purposes, I shall consider chapter 30 as a whole, but discuss the first four verses separately, because they raise special issues.

a. The Words of Agur

The first verses of this chapter are notoriously obscure, and its beginning seems to have mystified even ancient readers. The attribution is straightforward enough: we are told that what follows is 'The Words of Agur, Son of Yaqeh'; this is followed by a description also applied to King Lemuel in 31.1, which probably means that he is from Massa, perhaps understood to be a tribe in Arabia, but might mean 'the oracle'. The next few words are virtual gibberish, which the traditional Hebrew text vocalizes to include a series of personal names: 'The utterance of the man to Ithiel, to Ithiel and to Ucal.' Whilst this is recognized as very unsatisfactory, none of the many attempts to read it differently has won broad acceptance; since the words usually rendered 'to Ithiel to Ithiel' form a palindrome in the Hebrew, it may be that some compositional conceit has been misunderstood and corrupted.

In verses 2–3, the speaker goes on to declare that he is more brutish than a man, and lacks human understanding; he has not learned wisdom, and has no knowledge of 'the holy ones', or perhaps 'holy things'. If he is expressing ignorance of God, though, he seems also to be implying that knowledge of God and wisdom should be accessible to humans: it is he that is too bestial to grasp them. A series of questions follows: 'Who has gone up to the heavens and gone down? Who has gathered wind in the palms of his hands? Who has wrapped water in a cloak? Who has raised all the ends of the earth? What is his name and what is the name of his son? – For you know!' Despite a certain resemblance to the questions which God asks Job at the end of the book of Job (especially since only Job 38.5 has a similar 'for you know!'), it is not easy just to answer these questions with 'God', especially in the light of the last, and they have a riddling quality which has evoked ingenious responses from some commentators.

From that point of view, the first few verses actually sit quite well with much of the other material in the chapter, throughout which there is a certain colourful quirkiness. Verses 5–6 are sober enough, with a declaration that God's words are true, and must not be supplemented (although it is not clear whether that is a reference to the Torah or to prophecy). They are followed by a short prayer in 7–9, however, which asks God to withhold falsehood, and to grant the speaker neither poverty nor wealth. With its request for these 'two things', the prayer is the first of many sayings here which feature numbers, including several so-called 'graded numerical sayings', in which, for example, 'Three things are too hard for me; four I do not understand' (verse 18). In that particular case, the saying continues humorously: 'The way an eagle's going in the sky, the way a snake's going on a rock, the way a ship's going out at sea, and the way a man's going with a girl.' A certain humour is often perceived in other sayings here. In verse 23, for instance, the last of the things at which 'the world shakes' is a maid succeeding her mistress, while verses 30–31 place the stateliness of a king last in the (descending) list of a lion, a rooster, and a billy-goat.

Where there is no humour, there is still vividness: the oppressors with teeth like blades in verse 14, and in verse 17 the eye which is rude to its parents, plucked out by ravens and eaten by vultures (as it might be in an especially nasty cautionary tale). Verse 20 is a masterpiece of rapid evocation: 'This is how the adulteress does it: she eats, wipes her mouth, and says "I've done nothing wrong!"' There are certain links to the material which had been added to Prov. 1–9 in 6.1-19, but this collection stands out in general against the much less engaging sayings which dominate the others. It also draws more heavily on the natural world, which featured so heavily in Sumerian and other ancient collections, but is rare in Proverbs outside this section. Although it has its own interest in sayings with numbers, therefore, this collection is more reminiscent of the foreign works than are the major collections. As noted above, it is difficult to say which of the sayings we should identify with the attribution to Agur. As a block, they do not sit unhappily with the mysterious first verses, but it is noteworthy that the colourful numerical sayings and natural references fall mostly in verses 15–33, and it is quite possible that the Septuagint break at verse 14 does reflect an original break at that point.

b. The Words of Lemuel (31.1-9)

This is the only section of Proverbs to be introduced formally as the instruction given to a child by their parent, the conventional ancient setting for such works, although, as we have seen, chapters 1–9 also draw on that convention, and 22.17–24.22 makes at least a gesture toward it. Here the introduction tells us that the words were taught to an otherwise unknown King Lemuel by his mother, rather than his father, and the attribution is backed in verse 2 by an apparent address to 'son of my womb': this is unusual, because although other works do mention the role of mothers in teaching and the need to obey them, they are not elsewhere named as the source of literary instructions. Lemuel, like Agur in the previous chapter, is linked with Massa, suggesting that the composition is of foreign origin, or at least that it is supposed to be taken as such. That may explain why we find Aramaic words and forms in verses 2 and 3, although the work as a whole is in Hebrew. Because it is in Proverbs, earlier commentators associated Lemuel with Solomon, but that view is rarely held now, and it is possible that Lemuel is altogether fictional.

The second verse, apparently an appeal to the son, is a little obscure, but the remainder is made up of advice deemed specifically appropriate for kings: they should be wary of women, and avoid alcohol themselves – its power to help people forget is valuable for the wretched and poor, but not for their ruler. Lemuel is also cautioned to stand up for the rights of those who cannot speak for themselves, to judge righteously, and to look out for the poor. This is, in other words, a short recital of a king's duties, and it is reminiscent of the longer and more specific Egyptian instruction to Merikare. Such texts are neither so common nor so consistent that we can very usefully speak of 'royal instructions' as a genre in themselves, but they illustrate the way in which the conventions of instruction can be used to address specific concerns. The responsibilities of kingship are an occasional subject of interest in other types of literature, such as a Babylonian work known as *Advice to a Prince* (which is not itself phrased as direct teaching; cf. Lambert 1960: 110–5), and these are effectively a vehicle for the expression of political ideas. What we have here, then, is not a fragment of royal training but a brief, perhaps mildly cynical, reflection on the need for rulers to avoid devoting themselves to women and wine instead of good governance – and this is safely put in the mouth of Lemuel's mother, perhaps, lest any actual contemporary ruler might think it was addressed to them.

c. The Valiant Wife (31.10-31)

The second part of the chapter is separated from the Words of Lemuel in the Septuagint, and is generally agreed by modern scholars to be an independent composition. Superficially, at least, it spells out an idealized view of what would constitute the writer's perfect wife, and is not really advice literature as such at all – except insofar as it implies that women should behave like this, and that men should seek women who do. Formally, it is also distinctive, since it is composed as an alphabetic acrostic poem: that is to say, the first letters of each line spell out the alphabet, in order. It shows other signs of very careful composition, and appears to be an extremely polished piece of work, probably styled as a hymn or song of praise (see especially Wolters 2001). The contents offer an intriguing glimpse of domestic responsibilities and expectations, although the woman does not merely run her household, but also apparently grows food herself and runs a profitable business selling clothes. She earns respect, moreover, for her wisdom, industry and piety, and not for any beauty, so there is, perhaps, a rather unromantic view of marriage involved, and this is far from being love poetry.

Inevitably, the attitudes and activities portrayed have been of considerable interest to feminist scholars, although there has been some tension between an emphasis on the woman's relative power and independence, on the one hand, and a recognition, on the other, that her sphere of activity is largely limited to the household and its concerns. There has also been much interest, however, in the relationship between this poem and Proverbs 1–9, with which it shares in common not only a striking amount of vocabulary, but also, of course, the portrayal of a female figure associated with wisdom (e.g. Camp 1985: 186–91; Yoder 2001). Some recent scholars, indeed, have gone so far as to associate the woman here very closely with the personification of Wisdom, giving new life to what is a very old interpretation of the poem (e.g. Schroer 2000: 24–5; cf. Wolters 2001: 138–41). That view is not easy to sustain without slipping into much allegorical speculation about the details of what the woman does, but it is attractive to suppose that the poem has been placed here with the deliberate intention of letting Proverbs close with an echo of the women with whom it began. It is also possible that the portrayal of the woman has been influenced by a knowledge of chapters 1–9, and that there is an allusion here, without an actual resumption. It is interesting, in any case, to note that verse 27 contains what many scholars take to be a pun: 'she is watching over (*tsophiya*) the comings and goings of her household' might be read as 'the comings and goings of her household are *sophia*' – *sophia* is the Greek word for 'wisdom'. If that is not too ingenious, then the reference would suggest that the poem probably dates from the Hellenistic Period, after Alexander's conquests spread Greek cultural influence, and so no earlier than the late 4th century BCE.

6. Conclusion

With its many styles and sections, Proverbs is not an easy book to get a handle on, so it is worth saying a few final words about the book as a whole. Obviously, there are many different types of material here, and they defy simple classification. The Words of Lemuel, for example, are quite straightforwardly an instruction, in the sense that they adopt a conventional setting linked with that genre, but elsewhere we find many allusions to that setting without the setting itself, and if we choose to call chapters 1–9 or 22.17–24.22 'instructions', then we need to be aware that the designation is really telling us little about them in itself. Equally, if we bundle 10.1–22.16 together with most of chapter 30 and talk of 'sayings collections' or 'sentence literature', then we risk obscuring the very considerable differences of tone and form between the two. It is useful for some purposes to recognize the different types of composition that existed in the ancient world, but we should not make a fetish of assigning labels. Proverbs is a diverse collection of advice literature, and it may reflect great diversity in the underlying literary culture.

Two sections, of course, sit rather uncomfortably even under the heading 'advice literature'. For all that they do contain some direct advice, chapters 1–9 are more a lengthy commendation of the need for advice, probably to be understood as an exhortation to learn and internalize the Torah. The poem about the good wife in 31.10-31, on the other hand, is a clever hymn to female industry. If the two were indeed placed at either end of the collection to create a certain resonance – also enhanced earlier in chapter 31, perhaps, by the attribution to Lemuel's mother – it is difficult to know whether this is a reflection of some idea, perhaps the influential personification of wisdom as a woman, or no more than a literary, editorial flourish. It is also difficult to know, furthermore, whether any of this material was composed specifically to become a part of Proverbs. It is often suggested, for example, that chapters 1–9 are supposed to serve as a sort of prologue, though that does little justice, perhaps, to the coherence and self-containment of the section. Ultimately, with the book as a whole, as with many of the sections within it, we are left wondering just how much weight we should place on apparent connections, and just how much deliberation has gone into the creation of Proverbs from its constituent parts.

What the anthologization of these various materials does reveal, however, is a perception of some affinity between them, on the part of at least one editor. Whilst we may make generic distinctions between instructions and sentence literature, for example, or different types of saying, the very existence of Proverbs shows that some broader classification may have been operative. If this does not correspond to our own concept of 'wisdom literature', it at least suggests that the association of different styles and contents goes back to much earlier readers, and that our category may not be wholly a later imposition on the texts.

Chapter 3

The Book of Job

The book of Job tells the story of a man whose righteousness and piety was, ironically, the reason for him to lose almost everything which he possessed. Tested to see whether he will retain his loyalty to God even if deprived of everything except his life, he is eventually restored, receiving more than he had before. This story itself, however, takes up little of the book, and serves really as the framework for a series of speeches that are concerned principally with divine justice. Job's troubles are the starting point for these speeches, in which he argues with the friends who have come to comfort him, and ultimately evokes a response from God himself, before the story resumes and narrates the restoration of his fortunes. This format permits the expression of different viewpoints through different characters, with the added twist that most of those characters know less than the audience, who are therefore in a position to test their ideas from the outset against the reality of the situation described in the framing narrative. As we shall see, moreover, the combination of story and speeches creates a number of interesting tensions and problems, which make Job one of the most difficult and intriguing books of the Bible.

1. The book

Obviously, Job's presentation has points of contact both with the other ancient dialogues mentioned earlier, and with the use of different voices in Proverbs 1–9. This is an altogether longer and more ambitious work, however, spanning some forty-two chapters in its present form. Since much ancient literature was probably written for performance, it is tempting to speculate that different readers were used for the different voices, giving Job something of the flavour of a play, even if all the key action happens offstage. We can say little or nothing, however, about the context within which it was composed, and even the date is largely a matter for speculation. The main character, Job himself, is named in Ezekiel 14.14, 20 as a famously righteous man, but that does not mean that the book already existed by the time of the Babylonian exile (the setting of Ezekiel). Daniel is also named there (as is Noah), and the book of Daniel is certainly much later: it is probable that the existing fame of the characters led to their subsequent use by the writers of the books, rather than that the books themselves made them famous. In fact, the context of the passage in Ezekiel seems to suggest that a different story or version of the story existed at some earlier point, in which Job, like Noah, was able to save his children. As with all wisdom literature, however, dating is difficult. Most modern scholars would put the composition of Job somewhere in the Persian period, and probably in the fourth or fifth century BCE, although some would argue for slightly earlier or later dates.

We are almost certainly dealing with a book that was Jewish from the outset, but the story takes place outside Israel, in the land of Uz, which is associated in Lam. 4.21 with Edom (later Idumea), Judah's southern neighbour. That connection is affirmed in an afterword to the Greek Septuagint translation of the book, which identifies Uz with 'Ausitis, on the border regions of Idumea and Arabia' (42.17), and it suits also the description of Job's friend Eliphaz as a 'Temanite' (see Jer. 49.7, 20; Ezek. 25.13). The Greek also suggests (improbably) that Job is identical with Jobab, who was king of Edom according to Gen. 36.33, whilst in Gen. 36.4, 10, the name Eliphaz appears as a son of Esau, Jacob's brother and the ancestral patriarch of Edom. Although the origins of the other friends, Bildad and Zophar, are more obscure, it seems likely that the book is supposed to be set in Edom, and possible that it is set in the patriarchal period, a generation after Esau. This setting may have been dictated by existing legends about Job, but it offers the author an opportunity to explore his themes without the complication of the special relationship with God claimed by Israel. It should not be regarded as historical.

With regard to the structure and composition of the book, we are faced immediately by one very obvious characteristic: the speeches in Job are poetic, while the framing narrative is in prose. This is by no means unprecedented in other ancient literature where a speech is set in the context of a story, but scholars have long suspected that the narrative is a separate composition, and it has commonly been argued that the speeches have been composed to fit an existing story. It is impossible to prove the case either way or, indeed, the alternative possibility that the narrative story was composed to fit the speeches. As they stand, though, the prose and poetic sections seem closely integrated, and any hypothetical reconstruction of what one might have been like without the other would necessarily be very speculative. Most recent interpreters have tended at least to the sensible and economic view that what we have is a single composition, which should be treated as such, even if it has possibly been created using earlier material. As Freedman puts it (1990: 44): 'Whatever the different parts of Job . . . we must deal with the final product that was deliberately assembled.' Newsom (2002, 2003) has argued, indeed, that the generic difference between the narrative and poetry is part and parcel of the way in which the book presents different views and voices without a controlling authorial perspective.

Problems of structure within the poetic section are less easily side-stepped. There are three key difficulties here, which are to some extent interconnected. The first is that, after Job has made his first speech in 3.1-26, he and his friends initially speak in turn, so that we have cycles of speeches:

1st cycle		2nd cycle		3rd cycle	
4.1–5.27	Eliphaz	15.1-35	Eliphaz	22.1-30	Eliphaz
6.1–7.21	Job	16.1–17.16	Job	23.1-25	Job
8.1-22	Bildad	18.1-21	Bildad	25.1-6	Bildad
9.1–10.22	Job	19.1-29	Job		
11.1-20	Zophar	20.1-29	Zophar		
12.1–14.22	Job	21.1-34	Job		

A case can be made for seeing Job's opening lament and responses to Zophar as actually the first speeches in each cycle, and they certainly have a transitional quality. It would be as well, then, not to place too much emphasis on the cycles as disconnected units: they are more a pattern within the continuous discourse. Part of the way through the third cycle, however, the pattern comes to an abrupt end. After a short speech by Bildad, we get a series of speeches (26.1-14; 27.1–28.28; 29.1–31.40) each separately attributed to Job, with no third speech by Zophar. Some of the material attributed to Job, however, seems to reflect the position of his friends, rather than of Job himself. Although it is sometimes suggested that the breakdown of the cycle serves a literary purpose, reflecting the more fundamental breakdown of communication between Job and the friends or a subversive appropriation of the friends' words by Job (e.g. Newsom 2003: 130–68), it seems likely that text has been lost or misplaced here, and most commentators attempt a reconstruction.

The second problem is the poem of Job 28, which is presented as part of Job's discourse, but follows a description of the wicked which is more likely to have belonged originally in the mouth of one of the friends. The poem itself deals with the subject of wisdom, which has not previously been a major theme, and it is not clear to which speaker it should belong. Some scholars assign it to Job or one of his friends, some see it as a sort of interlude, separate from the speeches, and many see it as a secondary addition to the book. As we shall see, this is an important text in its own right, but the problems surrounding its position and authenticity have a significant effect on the ways in which it is interpreted.

Finally, the third problem lies in the sudden appearance of a new character at the beginning of chapter 32. The story had previously announced the arrival of three friends, Eliphaz, Bildad and Zophar (2.11). At the end of the book, God addresses Eliphaz, and is critical of what he and his 'two friends' have been saying (42.7); the same three are listed again in 42.9. In 32.1-5, however, we are introduced, at some length, to a young man,

Elihu, who has become angry with both Job and the friends, and wishes to make his own speech. Broken into sections, this continues until the end of chapter 37, giving Elihu a significant speaking part – but he appears nowhere in the closing narrative, and there is no direct response to his words from Job (whose 'words are ended' already, according to 31.40) or from God, whose own speeches follow immediately afterwards. Everything by and about Elihu, in other words, is contained entirely within chapters 32–37, and if those chapters had dropped out of our text, we would never know that they were missing. This has led the great majority of scholars to conclude that they are, in fact, an addition to the text, and only in recent years has there been a significant body of opinion defending the originality of the chapters.

Up until chapter 26, then, the structure of Job is clear: after that it becomes very problematic, with a probable disruption of the text, and the appearance of two large blocks of material which many scholars treat as secondary. Only with the appearance of God in chapter 38 do we seem to return to more solid ground. Even where the structure is straightforward, however, text-critical and linguistic difficulties combine with a dense, poetic style to make Job a very difficult book to read. Although it has been suggested more than once that it is a translation, there is no real evidence for that idea. Indeed, Job seems immersed at times in other Hebrew literature, and Katharine Dell (1991) has plausibly argued that many parts of the text should be considered parodies of known works or genres. At most, we might go so far as to say that some of the linguistic features could reflect a desire to lend a certain foreignness to the work or its characters, but even that is questionable. This is essentially Jewish literature of a very literary, ambitious sort.

2. The story and speeches

It is possible to summarize the themes and ideas of Job, but to do so is to miss much of the point: ideas are developed in the book through dialogue and confrontation, with the reader forced to hear and consider a range of opinions, expressed in various different ways. Before looking at what the book might be trying to say, therefore, we must first run briefly through its different parts.

a. The initial narrative

The story begins with a description of Job, who is 'guiltless and upright, and he fears God and turns away from evil' (1.1). He is prosperous, with numerous animals and servants, and with ten children – seven sons and three daughters. His sons take it in turns to hold feasts at their own houses, to which their sisters are invited, and after each such feast Job cautiously sanctifies them and offers burnt offerings for each, in case his 'children have sinned and cursed God in their hearts' (1.5). This behaviour impresses God.

On a day when, perhaps echoing Job's family situation, the 'children of God' have come to present themselves before him, the Satan comes amongst them, and reports that he has been 'ranging the earth, and walking through it' (1.7), to which God responds, 'Did you take note of my servant Job, that there is no one like him on the earth? A guiltless and upright man, he fears God and turns away from evil' (1.8).

In order to understand properly what happens next, it is important to be aware that the Satan is not the 'devil' of later beliefs, and that this is not a conflict between the powers of good and evil. In other late biblical literature, his role seems to involve provoking or exposing bad behaviour, so in 1 Chron. 21.1 he encourages David to conduct a census, with disastrous results, and Zech. 3.1-2 shows him in a vision, standing ready to accuse Joshua the high priest, in what appears to be a scene of judgement. The word *satan* means 'opponent' or 'adversary', sometimes in a legal context (Ps. 109.6), and '*the* Satan', seems tasked with prosecuting or uncovering the flaws of those judged by God. We might compare the scene in 2 Sam. 19.22-23 (ET 19.21-22), where Abishai calls for Shimei to be put to death, and David refuses, asking why he is presuming to act as a *satan* for him.

When the Satan responds to God in Job 1.9-11, therefore, he is only doing his job:

> Does Job fear God for free? Have you not put a barrier of thorns all around him, and his household, and all that is his? You have blessed the work of his hands, and his cattle spill out across the earth. Put out your hand now, though, and strike all that is his, (then see) if he doesn't curse you to your face!

Without demur, God gives the Satan permission to do as he will with all that is Job's, ordering him only to refrain from harming Job himself. The Satan, ominously, then leaves God's presence. The challenge he has made, though, is an interesting one. Implicit within it is an expectation, apparently shared by God, that proper piety, or 'fear of God', should involve a motive other than the expectation of reward: the Satan is suggesting, in effect, that Job only loves God for his money. The story, we should observe, does not state or even really imply that 'a question is raised that has apparently never before been asked, in general or in particular' (Clines 1990: 117), and we risk reading into it some great heavenly enquiry about the motivations of piety: the focus is very much on Job, and for all we know God and the Satan have had similar conversations about others many times before. Even at this early stage of the book, though, the reader is exposed to a much broader issue, with the double questioning of assumptions about the connection between righteousness and reward: not only is God prepared to destroy all that Job has, when Job has done nothing wrong, but God seemingly expects something more than righteousness from humans – a proper attitude towards him that is indifferent to his response. It is also important to note God's role in initiating what follows: when he asks if the Satan has seen Job, this is hardly just a conversational enquiry as to whether he bumped into an old friend of his while travelling on the earth. Given the Satan's role, his response can hardly have been unexpected, and of all the beings in heaven and earth, he is surely the one least likely to reply, 'Yes, he is jolly good, isn't he?'

The scene now shifts back to earth. Just as there had been a day when God's children presented themselves before him, now there comes a day when Job's children are dining together at their eldest brother's house. Job receives a series of messages in rapid succession, each reporting an event of which the messenger is the sole survivor: his oxen and donkeys are captured by Sabaean raiders, and the servants killed; fire falls from heaven to consume his sheep, and the servants with them; Chaldaean raiders take his camels and kill the servants; finally, and most terribly, a great wind sweeps across the desert, demolishing the house where his children are feasting, and killing them. The Satan's involvement is not mentioned – indeed, we see the whole terrible day from Job's perspective, as a continuous sequence of disasters in which he loses almost everything within minutes. His response, however, is not despair but resignation: tearing his clothes and shaving his head, traditional forms of mourning, he falls to the ground and prostrates himself, famously declaring 'Naked I came from my mother's womb, and naked shall I return there: it is YHWH who gave and YHWH who took: may the name of YHWH be blessed' (1.21). The narrator points out that Job neither sinned nor saw fault in God throughout all this.

When another day comes for the children of God to present themselves, the Satan and God repeat their previous conversation, but to his description of Job as blameless, God now adds the observation that, 'He still maintains his guiltlessness, although you encouraged me against him, to ruin him without cause' (2.3). The Hebrew word for 'without cause' here is the same as that used in 1.9, where the Satan asked if Job was righteous 'for free': the destruction of Job was not motivated by anything he had done, any more than Job's piety, it seems, was motivated by the material rewards he gained from it. Having failed to make his previous point, the Satan now shifts his ground, claiming that Job has not cursed God because it would be fatal to do so, and a man will give up all that is his to save himself; if his own body is harmed, Job will now curse God to his face. God once again assents, demanding only that Job should be kept alive, but the issue being tested is now different. Where previously Job had to maintain his piety when deprived of the rewards for that piety (given to him by God anyway, on his own admission), he now has to maintain it when suffering positive harm to himself. God is not just ceasing to be his patron, but actively becoming his persecutor.

The Satan's actions are less elaborately contrived this time: he simply leaves God, and afflicts Job with sores across his whole body. Job retreats to the place where ashes are thrown out, and scrapes at himself with a shard of pottery. There his wife, unconsciously echoing God's words, asks if he will 'still maintain his guiltlessness' (2.9), and urges him simply to curse God and die. (The Greek version gives her a longer speech, in which she summarizes their situation, and her own misery – she is herself, it is easy to forget, also a victim of what has happened). Job's response shows his recognition that God is now actively hurting him. Rejecting his wife's advice as foolish – perhaps rather brutally – he asks: 'Should we accept the benefit that comes from God, and not the harm?' (2.10). The narrator tells us, however, that Job did not sin with his lips throughout all this. It is important to observe that Job now, as previously, makes no protestation of faith or religious commitment, and that his acceptance of what God has done is not explicitly rooted in any expectation that things will be put right, or in any understanding that he is being tested. God gives and takes, helps and harms; humans simply have to accept. It is also important to remark, moreover, that the question raised by the Satan has essentially been answered by this stage: Job has refused to curse God, and has given an appropriate response to his suffering. No time limit had been set, and God is perhaps waiting for the next time the Satan is due to visit before he makes his point, as before. In the meantime, however, Job is effectively abandoned on his ash-heap in the aftermath of the test, not as a part of it, and we will be told no more about the conversation in heaven.

Finally, his three friends hear about what has happened to Job, and arrange to meet up and comfort him. He is so disfigured that they do not recognize him until they are close, and then they too tear their clothes and go into mourning, sitting with him on the ground in silence for seven days and seven nights, conscious of Job's suffering.

b. Job's opening speech

With the scene set, and the reader more conscious of the background events than any of the human characters are, the speeches begin in chapter 3 with an explosion of grief by Job. In this first speech, he shows no concern with the reasons for his predicament, but curses the day of his birth, wishing he had never lived to endure this suffering, and wondering why life is prolonged for those who desire only death. In a neat twist, 3.23 evokes the words of the Satan's original charge: where the Satan spoke of God protecting Job with a hedge of thorns (1.10), now Job sees the thorns set around him by God as a barrier against him.

The first cycle of speeches

Eliphaz replies tentatively, anxious to avoid giving offence and apparently making a genuine effort to console Job (Clines 1989: 121; on the positions of the friends more generally, see Clines 1998). Pointing out that Job has himself helped many to overcome their weaknesses, he urges patience now that Job finds himself in a similar situation: Job must place confidence in his fear of God, and look to his own guiltlessness for hope, since it is the wicked who perish, not the innocent and upright. Eliphaz claims to have had it revealed to him, by a spirit at night, that no human can ever be truly righteous before God, who finds fault even with his heavenly servants. Humans consequently die all the time, with no one to care, and without wisdom. It is pointless to call to heavenly beings for help, and anger is the mark of the fool who will perish. Humans are born to inevitable trouble, and Job should place his trust in God, who is marvellously powerful, and who frustrates clever schemes, but acts to save the needy. God's punishments are to be welcomed, because he hurts but also heals, and offers protection from all harm. If Job trusts in God, he will be safe, have many descendants, and live to a ripe old age. 'Behold this!' Eliphaz concludes in 5.27, 'We have discovered it; it is so. Listen to it, and know it for your own sake!' In short, Job is being punished by God, who is just, but must look to a time in the future when God will help him again. All humans are liable to such punishment, and it is pointless to rail against it.

Job's reply is difficult to follow at times, but he seems to begin with a direct response to Eliphaz, claiming that he cannot swallow his suffering, and that he has no strength left for patience. He grumbles that his friends have proved fair-weather: his predicament provokes nervousness in them, although he has asked for no money or help. If they can tell him what he has done wrong, he will be silent – but what are their arguments aimed at? Asking them to watch him, he then apparently addresses God. First complaining of the misery of his existence (and perhaps that of all humans), he notes that it will be brief, all the same, and that he will eventually disappear into Sheol. So why must he be watched all the time, scared by dreams, tested constantly? What does it matter to God if he sins, and why doesn't he just forgive him, since he is going to cease to exist anyway?

When his turn comes, Bildad is shocked, denying that God can act other than justly. If Job's children sinned, they have been punished; if Job himself is really innocent, then God will reward him. Our lives might be brief, but previous generations have passed on the teaching that those who forsake God will perish like rootless plants. God will neither reject the innocent nor support the guilty, and Job will yet be returned to happiness. This is a view which Job then seemingly declares himself willing to accept: his problem is not with the principle, but with the fact that humans are not in a position to justify themselves against this powerful, invisible being. Although innocent, he cannot plead his innocence before one who would crush him, and his inadequacy would make his own mouth condemn him. Since he hates his life, he's prepared to say that it is God who puts an end to the guiltless and the wicked likewise; if it is not him who is giving the world over to the wicked and blindfolding its judges, then who is doing it? He will ask of God why he is struggling with him, destroying what he has made and unleashing all this after years of care. If Job has sinned, then he is done for, but if he is innocent he is still disgraced, and threatened with further trouble if he tries to raise himself up. Again, he just wants to die, and to be left alone by God before he does so.

The third friend, Zophar, will not let Job's claims go unanswered. Hinting that Job himself may be less than wise, he wishes that God would speak, and tell Job the hidden secrets of wisdom. God's depths are unfathomable and his judgements unstoppable, but if Job will put aside his own wrongs and reach out to God, then he will find security and confidence, whilst the wicked are punished. This last speech, then, summarizes what has been the basic position of all the friends, although they have each expressed themselves differently. Job, in their view, needs to turn to God: it is the wicked who will be punished, and if he is basically righteous, then he can be confident that things will be better in the future. Job himself, however, wants nothing to do with God. He craves a release from his suffering through death, and feels emboldened to say the unsayable: life is difficult enough without God breathing over one's shoulder, and innocence is no defence or source of confidence when there is no way to assert that innocence; if there is injustice in the world, it must be because God permits it, and so when the innocent are destroyed along with the guilty, that is God's responsibility. If he tries to pick himself up and dust himself off, then Job fears that he will merely incur further suffering, and he wants God, who has so pointlessly created and nourished him before ruining him, to leave him alone in the remaining days of his life.

At this stage, we may observe, there is little direct emphasis on Job's guilt or innocence. He regards himself as guiltless, while the friends take a range of different positions. Eliphaz allows that Job's behaviour has been excellent, but doubts that any human will be regarded as perfect by God, so even the good must endure suffering sometimes. Bildad speaks to the absolute character of divine justice: Job's children have been sentenced, but Job himself is in a position where appeal to God may actually lead to him being rewarded. Only Zophar is absolutely clear that Job is guilty, and is being punished, but even he does not dwell on this at length. The emphasis of the cycle, rather, is very much on what Job should do now, rather than on an analysis of what has brought him to the current situation, and divine justice is invoked not so much to prove Job's guilt, as to offer reassurance that he will not or need not ultimately suffer. Job is justifiably sceptical about this, but the key characteristic of these first speeches is not Job's defensiveness.

The cautious Job of the preceding narrative, who sanctified his children just in case they had sinned, who accepted gracefully the loss of those children, along with everything else, and who then refused to curse the God who had turned on him, has finally lost his self-possession. His initial lament was grief-stricken but hardly controversial; the response of the friends, though, however well intentioned, has pushed him to express opinions which they find shocking. In the transition from the first cycle to the second, Job's relationship with the friends further deteriorates rapidly. Zophar's rather patronizing speech provokes Job to sarcasm at the start of chapter 12: no doubt the friends are the ultimate embodiment of wisdom, and it will die with them – but he knows a thing or two as well, and what they are saying is obvious. He is angry at being treated with contempt by those who have so far avoided misfortune, and even a plant or fish knows that God is responsible, since every living thing is in his power. Real wisdom, in fact, is with God, along with real power. Where personified Wisdom in Proverbs 8 boasted of her place in supporting the powerful and enabling creation, Job now presents a negative equivalent: God tears down, blocks in, and uncreates. He withholds wisdom from advisors, kings, and elders, bringing them to ruin, releases the waters of chaos, and turns light to darkness. He makes nations great and destroys them, while by depriving human leaders of understanding, he leaves them wandering aimlessly in the darkness. If God has the power to give or take wisdom, that may be a disastrous thing for the world.

In chapter 13, Job moves on to a different matter, although his attack is still firmly focused on the friends. He wishes to speak to God and plead his case, with no expectation of anything except his own destruction; he anticipates, however, that the friends will act as false witnesses against him, biased toward God, but ironically liable to God's punishment when he discovers their bias. Speaking again to God, he asks only that he be permitted to put his case without being overcome by fear; then he will answer whatever charges are brought against him, or else ask God to list his sins. Why, he asks, is God hiding and treating him as an enemy, libelling and constraining him? Finally, he asks why God should be so concerned to confront humans, with their limited lives and their deaths without hope of resurrection. He wishes, though, that he could be hidden in Sheol (the underworld) until God's anger has passed, that there was some prospect of living again, once more actually wanted by God, and with his supposed wrongdoing sealed away. As things are, God destroys human hopes by simple erosion: he always wins because humans always die, ignorant of what will happen to their descendants and conscious only of their own suffering.

c. The second cycle of speeches

Eliphaz, now much less conciliatory, accuses Job of condemning himself, and directs his own sarcasm toward Job's claims of wisdom. He repeats his earlier point, that God puts no trust even in heavenly beings, but applies it specifically now to Job: how will God trust someone so iniquitous, who speaks in this way? He appeals again to the wisdom of ancestors, which matches his own experience: the wicked will suffer, and live in fear. Although it is sometimes suggested that Eliphaz is still holding to Job's essential innocence, and that his description of the wicked man suffering is meant to show that Job cannot be such a man, there is much in this description which might fit Job, leaving open the possibility that Job is, in fact, wicked.

Job's response is also now more personal: the friends are useless comforters. Bildad had earlier called Job's words 'wind' (8.2), and Eliphaz has used the same term to describe his knowledge (15.2); Job now throws it back at them – why do they keep going on with windy words, when he has heard all this before? (16.3). He too could play the comforter if they were in his shoes, but as it is, he can do nothing to reduce his own suffering, either by speaking or by staying silent. God has worn him down, physically attacked him, and left him at the mercy of the unsympathetic and the ungodly. He has set himself exhausted in the dust, but there has been no violence on his part, and his prayer is pure. It is vital that his suffering should not become hidden, because his witness is there, in heaven. Even if his friends scorn him, he hopes that God will uphold the rights of humans in respect of God that they are supposed to enjoy with respect to each other – that God, in other words, will oblige himself to do what is proper. Job cannot rely on his friends to do this, because God has closed their minds: he is an object of derision and condemnation, and he doubts there is a wise man amongst those he is addressing. With the end of life in sight, and welcome, where is his hope? Will it die with him?

Bildad, less harshly than Eliphaz, asks Job to stop and consider. He should not treat his friends as idiots, when his own futile anger is tearing him apart. He goes on, however, simply to reiterate what has already been said, in several different ways, about the inevitable destruction of the wicked. This provokes Job to protest at the friends' repeated torment of him. If he really had done something wrong, that would be a matter for him alone, and it is not up to his friends to make themselves look good by turning his own wretchedness into an argument against him. It is God who has attacked and trapped him, and who has cut him off even from those close to him: he wants sympathy from his friends, not further persecution. In a famous but very difficult passage (19.23-7), he wishes that his words were written down to be preserved for ever, because he knows that there is someone who can vindicate him, who will stand there in the dust one day, after his own flesh is gone: then he will see God finally take his side. If the friends are determined to pursue him and to blame him, they should fear a coming judgement by the sword.

Zophar's speech is predictable. Objecting to Job's criticism, he returns to a now familiar refrain: it has long been known that the wicked will be punished. He presents yet another account of such punishment, which is as vivid as Job's account of his persecution, but does not obviously add anything to what he has said before. The second cycle of speeches, therefore, sees increasing irritation on both sides, and a direct clash between Job and his friends. Although the friends are more concerned, perhaps, to discount Job's ideas and to identify him with the wicked who will be punished, it is Job who shows a greater movement. Increasingly, he emphasizes his hope of ultimate vindication – even if that is to come after his death – and his resentment at the attitude which others display towards him. If God is his persecutor, it is also God who will ultimately vindicate him, and his resentment of the human reactions to his plight consequently drives him to a complicated attitude toward God.

When Job resumes in chapter 21, he is more conciliatory, but directly addresses the point that his friends have been making. Begging their indulgence, and confessing his own dismay at the state he is in, he asks why it is that the wicked seem to live long and prosper, and to enjoy security even though they reject God. Their punishment seems rare, and if it is being postponed to their descendants, why is it not being visited on them themselves? After all, they have little concern with what happens to their families after their own deaths. Is anyone going to tell God what he should be doing, since he is supposed to be judging the powerful? Some die happy and rich, others bitter and poor – but they all die alike. If the friends had troubled to enquire of those with more experience of the world, they would have heard that the wicked man is actually spared, so what right have they to try to comfort Job with meaningless falsehoods?

d. The third cycle of speeches

Job has already questioned whether any sin of his could really have been important to God (7.20) and has asked what profit is to be gained from prayer to him (21.15). Eliphaz now first takes the discussion in a different direction, by picking up the issues of divine and human profit, and asking whether God actually gains anything from righteousness. His questions are rhetorical, and his point apparently that human wisdom, and the corresponding righteous behaviour, are of benefit to humans, not to God. Implicitly, therefore, since God has nothing to gain, his judgement must be impartial – so he can hardly be punishing Job for his piety, and Job must have been very wicked. This is a difficult position for Eliphaz to adopt, since he began by acknowledging Job's essential innocence, and it has given commentators a lot of trouble. The problem is compounded by the fact that Eliphaz then supplies a list of sins which are apparently imputed to Job (not all of which are easy to understand, as the meaning is obscure in places). These are largely social sins, which represent in some way a dereliction of responsibilities to those in society who are supposed to be protected by the wealthy, and some are perhaps the unforeseen consequences of actions that were not harmful in themselves. A number of commentators suggest, therefore, that Eliphaz is not speaking from a knowledge that Job has done these things, but speculating that he must have done them to be suffering as he is, and Clines (2006: 570) takes them to be entirely figments of Eliphaz's imagination. In any case, he goes on to affirm the reality of divine judgement, noting that the wicked may be allowed to prosper before their ultimate destruction, and finally returns to his belief that Job must come to terms with God, putting aside his crimes, humbling himself, and making God his sole delight.

Job does not respond to this directly in chapter 23, but instead repeats his desire to meet God in judgement, to put his own case and to hear that against him. Having earlier expressed his fear of being crushed by him (9.13-21), he now apparently reasons that he might get a fair hearing if he were to address God in God's own place – though he cannot find him. His confidence that he has always acted according to God's will and obeyed his commandments soon gives way, however, to a further expression of fear. God knows all this, but his will is absolute and unchangeable, so he is not suddenly going to stop doing what he is doing to Job. The apparent hiddenness of God leads Job to muse on the invisibility of judgement more generally. God doesn't seem to keep fixed or visible times for judgement, with the result that men oppress the poor and powerless, whose plight he describes at length. They groan and cry for help, but God pays no attention (24.12). Eliphaz had observed that Job, as a wicked man, was plunged into darkness (22.11), and Job has acknowledged that he feels himself to be wrapped up in the dark (23.17). He observes now, though, that such darkness, supposedly inflicted on the wicked, is actually welcome to some of them – murderers and adulterers especially.

At this stage, we begin to run into the textual difficulties that beset the second half of the third cycle. If 24.18-25 belongs to Job's speech, then it begins very abruptly, and must be understood as a quotation of the friends' views about the wicked, followed by a challenge to those views: God appears to give them life and security before they disappear. That much has already been conceded by Eliphaz, however (22.18), and this material seems more appropriate for one of the friends themselves. Some commentators therefore take it to be a misplaced section from the missing speech of Zophar, although it is possible that verse 25 is the end of Job's speech.

In chapter 25, Bildad makes the now familiar point that humans cannot be righteous before God – even the moon and stars seem unclean to him. What follows is then attributed in the text to Job, and the first four verses of chapter 26 may indeed be his sarcastic response, questioning both the helpfulness and the wisdom of what he has been told. Again, however, they could belong in the mouth of almost any of the characters, and although most commentators retain the assignment to Job, Clines (2006: 626) moves them to the end of 25.1, so that they become the beginning of Bildad's speech. After that, verses 5–14 are a statement of God's power as creator and controller of the earth (including in verse 12 a reference to his legendary defeat of the monster Rahab, associated with the sea). This concludes with the observation that, despite all his power, we hear only a whisper of him. Most scholars take these verses to belong to Bildad rather than Job.

Chapter 27 begins with material that is almost certainly Job's: in verses 2–6 he takes a very serious oath by God, despite the fact that it is God who has deprived him of his rights, to tell the truth, to hold fast to his integrity, and to continue to deny that his friends are right. Conversely, the chapter finishes with words that surely belong to one of the friends: verses 13–23 are yet another account of the downfall of the wicked. These have the flavour of Zophar about them, and are usually assigned to him. The central verses, 7–12, are more difficult to assign, and it is not clear that they even constitute a single unit. Verses 7–10 seem to be about the wicked, expressing a wish that 'my enemy' could suffer a fate as bad; this looks like further words of Zophar. Verses 11–2, on the other hand, promise to teach about the hand of God, and address 'all of you', which indicates that Job is speaking.

Scholars are very divided over the assignment of material, especially in chapter 27, but it does seem likely that some reassignment is necessary: the sudden changes of subject and address are too abrupt for us to take them simply as a literary effect. In the end, it probably does not matter precisely how we assign each verse, because the material gives no reason to suppose that any of the characters involved are introducing anything new and unexpected. Job's oath in 27.1-6 is the most striking thing here, and that, at least, is correctly assigned already in the text. The greater puzzle here is just how the text, and Zophar's speech in particular, came to be divided and fragmented to such an extent. If proposed reconstructions are plentiful, satisfactory text-critical explanations are in shorter supply.

e. Job 28

If 27.13-23 were originally part of Zophar's speech, as commonly assumed, they may have been followed by some of the other Zophar material: they do not, in their current form, seem to contain a satisfactory conclusion to the speech, or even to the point that they are making. Chapter 28, however, does not offer an obvious continuation, and if it is Zophar's, then his speech must not only have ranged beyond his usual concerns, but must also have been abnormally long. If it is not Zophar's, then we would expect it to be Job's, since it is now his turn to speak, but Job speaks again in chapter 29, and this chapter does not really fit with what he says there. Given its position, then, we expect chapter 28 to be part of the third cycle, but it is difficult to find a place for it. If, in fact, it is not a part of the cycle, but an interlude or a secondary addition, then it is no less difficult to understand why it has been inserted at this point, unless the speech of Zophar actually marked the end of the speech cycles. A few scholars attribute the chapter to Job (e.g. Good 1990: 292-3, although he considers it ironic; cf. Lo 2003), many more see it as a free-standing poem, whether original or secondary, and Clines (2006: 908-9) has proposed that it actually belongs to the speeches of Elihu, which must originally have stood, in his view, after Zophar's speech.

The poem is about wisdom, and depicts it as something of immense value, which is hidden from all living things, even ingenious humanity. God, however, knows where it is, and the climax of the poem declares that he found it while creating a storm (or perhaps at that stage of the creation when he first made storms): 'Then he saw it and took its measure, set it up and also examined it' (28.27). Finally, he tells humanity about it: 'And he said to the human: "Look! Wisdom is fear of the Lord, and understanding is a turning from evil"' (28.28). If this means that God has shown humans how to be wise, then it sits a little uncomfortably with the rest of the poem, where humans are depicted as hunting high and low for wisdom. Many commentators, in fact, remove the last verse as a pious, secondary addition, which would leave the poem as a declaration that wisdom is inaccessible to all but God.

As the poem stands, however, the point is perhaps a more interesting one. Wisdom is depicted as something with an independent existence, and is not created by God so much as discovered by him. In principle, it is still available for humans to find by themselves, but in practice they cannot do so: only God knows where to find it, and what he offers humans is neither a map to its location nor an offer to take them there. Rather, following his own inspection, he declares that wisdom lies in a proper attitude towards him, and in avoidance of evil. Humans cannot know for themselves how to live their lives, in other words, but must accept a divine assurance that wisdom lies in doing what God wants. Whether this is a good thing or a bad thing, it is presented as an aspect of the inevitable human dependence on, or perhaps subjugation to God, and is not really a statement about the character of wisdom at all. This theme sits quite happily in the broader context of Job, although it corresponds more closely to the ideas treated in the speeches by Elihu and God, rather than amongst the debates about justice which dominate the cycles of speeches, so perhaps the poem has indeed been displaced from later in the book.

f. Job's final speech

Job's last speech, in chapters 29–31, probably belongs within the third cycle, but it also serves as an appropriate conclusion to all that he has been saying. He yearns for his previous life, looking back on the days when he was not just righteous but respected. Back then he helped and consoled others, going out of his way to do so, and was received with awe. He had expected his future to be as good as his present, but he now finds himself an object of mockery and derision, even to the lowest in society. Miserable and in pain, he has become like the dust and ashes into which he has been thrown. When he cries to God he receives no answer, but is persecuted, tossed about by a storm, and doomed to die. In his better days, he had helped the poor and afflicted, but now when he seeks help himself, he gets only hurt. His skin blackens and falls off, and his music has become mourning.

In chapter 31, Job makes a final, comprehensive declaration of his innocence (perhaps partly in response to the charges of Eliphaz). He accepts that the wicked suffer disaster and that God judges his behaviour, and that is why he has not sinned, even with his eyes or mind. If he has committed any crimes, though, he is willing to be punished, even if they are secret crimes, and even if his desire for the respect of others led him to conceal his sins. What he wants is the indictment against him, so that he can answer the charges, and account for what he has done.

g. Elihu

Chapter 32 begins by telling us that the three friends gave up answering Job, because of his conviction that he was in the right, and we are introduced to a new character, Elihu, a young man who has been watching the debate. He is angry with Job, because of Job's concern with his own rightness rather than God's, but also angry with the friends, because they seemed to have no adequate answer. Now that his elders have stopped speaking, he feels able to cut in, and he begins by expressing his dissatisfaction, noting that wisdom is not solely the prerogative of the old. He is bursting to speak, and promises to be impartial.

His first speech, in chapter 33, is addressed to Job. Summarizing Job's position – that he is innocent, but under attack and surveillance from God – Elihu points out that God is greater than humans, and Job should not be seeking an answer from him. In fact, God speaks to humans in two ways: through dreams or visions, and, less obviously, through suffering, which makes the sufferers turn back to him. In his second speech (chapter 34), Elihu addresses the friends and seeks common ground with them. Job's accusations of divine injustice align him with the wicked, and are absurd. God has created the world through his own choice, and does not have to maintain it. All humans are his creations, and he has no bias even towards the powerful: all are judged, and because he knows the ways of all, he has no need for investigations. Often working quietly in the background, he ensures that the rulers who rule beneath him are not ungodly, and do not mislead their people. The next part of the speech is obscure, but is perhaps a call for Job to turn to God and request instruction. He finishes by claiming that wise men will respond to him that Job speaks from ignorance and like the wicked: he should be tried to the very end for his rebellion against God.

The third speech, in chapter 35, is addressed to both Job and the friends, and picks up points made in the earlier discussion. It is humans, not God, who are affected by sin and righteousness. God, moreover, does not answer summonses, even from those who have a right to cry out for help, and someone demanding an audience as a right will just be ignored. God is not even bothering to punish Job for what he is saying, so Job is wasting his time.

The fourth and final speech, in chapters 36–37, continues the address to Job and the friends, and Elihu shamelessly proclaims the truth of what he is saying: 'It is a man complete in knowledge who is with you.' He reiterates that God is powerful, punishing the wicked but caring for the righteous. If they find themselves suffering, he will explain what they have done wrong, and give them a chance to avoid punishment by death. Those who will not ask for his help will, therefore, die young, but it is wrong to dwell on the punishment of the wicked and on issues of justice and judgement, when God is a teacher of incomparable power. We see his work without knowing him, unable to comprehend the lightning storms through which he judges but also feeds, the snow and the rain, the ice and the clouds through which he works. Addressing Job, Elihu asks him how he could possibly presume to address such a being, when he cannot do or understand what God does, when humans cannot even stare at the brightness of the sky. He is beyond our reach, great in power and justice, and therefore to be feared by humans.

Elihu, then, adopts a position that is rather different from that of Job's friends. God judges and ruthlessly eliminates the wicked, but uses suffering as a way of educating and disciplining, not as a weapon. The speeches of Job and his friends have been misguided, because they focus upon the cause of Job's plight, not the reason for it: rather than worry over whether Job is guilty or innocent, all concerned should understand the need for him to learn from the experience. Job, with his presumptuous challenges, is wasting an opportunity, and risks becoming like those others who are destroyed when they fail to respond properly; his attempts to summon God, furthermore, are a complete waste of time. As readers, of course, we know that Elihu is about to be proved spectacularly wrong in at least one respect: God will indeed answer Job. We also know that his understanding of the situation is as misguided as that of the friends, so Elihu is hardly supplying an answer. What, then, is his role in the book?

As we noted earlier, the Elihu section is self-contained, inasmuch as no reference is made to the character or his speeches anywhere else in the book. Elihu's words, however, constantly cite or echo those of other characters, and he does provide a sort of digest or summary of the debate, or at least of the position which Job and the friends have reached by the end of the third cycle. He also provides a separate response to Job's predicament, and although his speeches stand between Job's call for his indictment and God's appearance, they also furnish a backdrop for that appearance, with their vivid portraits of storm and sky foreshadowing God's whirlwind. Whether it is an original part of the work, then, or a later addition, Elihu's appearance seems like a removable, optional section: it adds something new if included, but can be omitted without any great loss. In practical terms, if we think of Job as a work to be performed, then Elihu's is, perhaps, an extra role for an additional speaker.

There are two main reasons for the dismissal of the section as secondary by most commentators, neither of them definitive. The first is its disconnection from the rest of the text, and its apparent intrusion between Job and God – but that is an issue whether the section is original or secondary, unless we think that some later writer went to all the effort of explaining Elihu's presence and writing his speeches, but could not then be bothered to write him into the frame narrative as well and place the section properly. The position is also irrelevant if Clines is right, and the Elihu material initially appeared earlier. The second main objection is stylistic: there are many complaints that Elihu seems ponderous and pompous in contrast with the other characters. That is a subjective judgement in any case, but such differences could also be linked to the characterization of Elihu, who is portrayed as an insufferably smug and conceited character, and who is explicitly holding himself aloof from the heated conversation which has preceded him. In the end, there is no certain answer to this problem, and we should perhaps accept that there are, to all intents and purposes, two versions of Job available to us, with and without Elihu.

h. God

God has been associated with storms and weather a number of times in the book already, and he now appears (as Job had feared he would back in 9.17), from within a tempest. The audience of the book, knowing the circumstances, might expect him, perhaps, to offer Job an explanation, if not an apology. Job himself might expect to hear the charges against him, and the friends anticipate that he might defend divine justice. Elihu would surely expect him to teach, or perhaps to strike Job down with his lightning. God, however, does none of these things. Instead, he demands of Job 'Who is this, that darkens counsel with speech devoid of knowledge? Gird up your loins now, like a man, so I can question you, and you must inform me' (38.2-3). He then showers Job with question after question, asking if he has been where God has been, done what God has done, or has the abilities that God possesses to control creation. The first speech, in chapters 38–39, draws first on God's activities in creation, then on his ability to enter such places as the depths of the sea, the home of light, or the storehouses where snow and hail are kept. It moves on to God's control of the heavens, both the stars and the weather, and then on to his involvement with and creation of animals.

God pauses at the beginning of chapter 40, to demand a response from Job: 'Will Shaddai's challenger yield? (Or) will the man who argues with God answer that?' (40.2). Job refuses: 'I am unimportant – what response could I give? I have pressed my hand over my mouth. I have spoken once, and will not answer, twice and will not do so again' (40.4-5). God challenges him again, therefore, and asks if he really wants to put himself in the right by putting God in the wrong, when he is so much weaker. If Job too could bring down the proud, trample the wicked and kill them all, then he would allow that Job might stand some chance of winning the contest. It is God, however, who created the monstrous Behemoth, just as he created Job, and it seems unlikely that Job could catch or tame another monster, Leviathan. If no human dares stand before such creatures, who could dare stand against God? Or can God owe anything to anyone, when he owns everything? This second speech finishes, curiously, with a further elaboration of Leviathan's terrifying invulnerability.

Although he makes it in different ways, then, God has only one main point: nobody has the power to argue with him, and certainly not Job. To stand a chance of winning against him, or at least of being in contention, the challenger must come close to matching his abilities – but humans cannot cope even with the monstrous animals he has created. That is not to say that he will prevent Job from speaking: on the contrary, he urges him to do so. The futility of such a speech would be clear, however, from the outset.

i. Job's reply

Responding to God in 42.1-6, Job acknowledges his power: God can do everything, and nothing can prevent him from doing what he wishes. He then replies directly to God's initial challenge in 38.2-3, quoting from it, and admits that he had said things beyond his own knowledge and comprehension. With regard to the demand that he answer God's questions, however, the experience of having seen God, about whom he had previously only heard, has led him to a change of heart. What that change of heart consists of is a hotly debated topic amongst commentators, but there is an increasing rejection of the traditional rendering, which has Job despise himself and repent in dust and ashes: the Hebrew more naturally reads 'I reject and repent of dust and ashes' (42.6), although scholars have found many other ways to understand what he is saying, and some have considered there to be a deliberate ambiguity here.

If Job is saying that his experience of God has somehow turned him away from the sense that he had become like dust and ashes (as he put it back in 30.19), then it is interesting to compare Abraham's use of this expression in Gen. 18.27, when he argues with God about the punishment of Sodom: 'Look, I have been prepared to speak to the Lord, when I am dust and ashes.' Perhaps we should understand Job to be saying that his experience has led him not to a new humility, but instead to a greater confidence. After all, he had predicted before, in 9.13-21, that he would be crushed and would condemn himself if God did actually appear in a tempest, and that does not seem to have happened. Job acknowledges, then, that he spoke earlier from ignorance; for him to see God, though, and to have been invited to answer him, however uselessly, has restored his self-esteem. The expression perhaps hints also that he is ready to vacate his current residence on the ash-heap.

j. The closing narrative

Finally, the story comes to an end with Job's restoration. Before that, however, God addresses Eliphaz, as representative of the friends, and tells him: 'My anger burns against you and your two friends, for you have not told me it is settled, as has my servant Job.' This is usually rendered 'you have not said what is true of me', or suchlike, but the Hebrew term involved is not used of truth in the wider sense: it refers to facts which are established (e.g. Deut. 17.4), matters which are settled (e.g. Gen. 41.32), or things which are fixed (as opposed to 'slippery' in Ps. 5.10, ET 5.9) – in short, it means 'confirmed', not 'correct'. Since, moreover, the text is much more easily taken to mean 'said to me' than 'said of me', it does not seem difficult to suppose that God's anger arises from the lack of an appropriate response by the friends. He orders the friends to make a burnt offering; Job will pray for them, and God will express his favour towards him by not doing anything terrible to them (42.8). Job is now again 'my servant', and it seems that he has resumed his role as golden boy.

Of course, if we adopt the usual translation of 42.7, then God is apparently commending what Job has said about him over what the friends have said, leading some modern commentators to suppose that he is acknowledging the accusations of his own apparent injustice, and rejecting the view of the friends, that suffering is inevitably connected to divine punishment or discipline. Perhaps there is some truth in that interpretation even without the support of this verse, and God here certainly favours the rebellious Job over the three friends who have maintained the reality of his integrity and justice throughout. Rather than offering them forgiveness directly, indeed, God makes them dependant upon Job, humiliating them by putting them at his mercy.

God's favour next extends to restoring Job, who receives sympathy and gifts from his friends and family, and who ends up with twice what he had before – at least in terms of animals. His previous children and servants are not somehow brought back to life (and they are, perhaps, the real victims of God's experiment), but Job does get seven new sons and daughters. We are charmingly told the names of the daughters, and informed both that they were exceptionally beautiful, and that they were given rights of inheritance alongside their brothers. It is not clear why we are offered that information, but the last verses show just how fully Job has been restored to divine favour: he lives another hundred and forty years, seeing four generations of his descendants, and finally dies an old man.

3. Does Job have a message?

There is a very beautiful work from Middle Kingdom Egypt that labours under such clunky modern titles as *The Dialogue between a Man Tired of Life and his Ba* – the original beginning and title are lost (see Lichtheim 1973: 163–9 for a translation). In this, a man describes his loathing of life and the attractions of death through a series of exquisitely crafted poems, while his *ba* – the part of him that would pass into the afterlife – protests and threatens not to play its part. Despite the enormous power of its words, however, this poem is not a call for its readers to kill themselves, and its condemnation of life draws not on general principles, but on the state of exhaustion and depression in which the man finds himself. It is an important reminder, in fact, that literature can exploit big issues without trying to solve them, and that not every poem is written to persuade.

It would surely be a mistake to treat Job as a philosophical treatise, and it is certainly clear in some respects that its story is a peg on which it hangs its poems – just how many times, for instance, do we need to hear the fate of the wicked recounted before we take the point? Anyone looking to Job for general answers, moreover, has to confront the fact that its circumstances are far from general: Job is not everyman, but a man of exceptional piety; what happens to him is not usual, but the product of (we may hope) highly unusual circumstances. The friends' ignorance of these circumstances is what leads them to apply general solutions to a problem without precedent, so that they are wrong even in the eyes of those readers who might usually accept what they are saying. The book also avoids offering explicit answers to the questions which are raised: views are expressed through the mouths of characters, with the narrator offering no comment, and God, the character whose opinion would naturally carry most weight, does not seem to engage directly with those questions, except to mention in passing that he does indeed destroy the wicked.

God's avoidance of the issues, however, may be telling in itself. When he responds to Job, it is with an assertion of his power and of his status: he owns the world, so can owe nothing to anyone within it. The questions he asks about Leviathan apply to him too (40.26-30; ET 41.2-6):

> Can you put a reed through his nose and pierce his jaw with a hook?
> Will he ask you many favours? Is he going to flatter you?
> Will he cut a covenant with you, so that you can take him as a servant for ever?
> Will you play with him like a bird, and put him on a leash for your girls?
> Will dealers haggle over him? Divide him between merchants?

This is a God who cannot be tamed, and his actions in the book do not fit some set of rules. If it were possible to guarantee either success through piety or punishment through wrongdoing, then it would also be possible to control God through one's own behaviour: a commitment to humans ('a covenant') would effectively ensure God's servitude to humans. In that light, the bickering between the human characters about who actually possesses wisdom is pointless, since wisdom can never offer a complete understanding. This is what lies also, perhaps, behind Job's ultimate reaction to God's appearance: discourse at the human level, with its focus on divine judgement, had led him to feel misjudged and to doubt God's justice; actual experience of God, however, now makes this way of thinking seem trivial and inadequate, since God has powers, not duties. When Job is subsequently restored, moreover, the writer of the book might seem to be confusing the issues: have we readers not been led to suppose, after all, that there is no true correlation between righteousness and reward? Yet now Job is being rewarded again. It is not the correlation itself that is wrong, however, but the very attempt to devise rules of any sort about God. Divine justice is important, and much of the book has been given over to the topic, but divine justice is a human concept, which has no power to bind God. In a Jewish context, this is also a potentially powerful critique of any attempt to view the Torah as an agreement that places an obligation upon God, and the identification of 'covenant' with servitude is very striking – by setting the book outside Israel, though, the author avoids a head-on confrontation.

Finally, it is important to take on board Job's own disavowal of what he has been saying, not on the grounds that the friends were right and he wrong, but that his position was based on understandings and assumptions which have been exposed as inadequate. Job is, after all, the hero of the book, with whom the audience is clearly supposed to identify. He is, however, a complicated figure, and efforts to make him a role model for the pious or oppressed can idealize him, or overlook his less attractive characteristics. In particular, the original audience might have been more appreciative than a modern reader of the *sang froid* with which he receives the news that his children are dead, but it is striking that Job responds more sharply and fiercely to human criticism than to divine persecution. After being struck down himself, he is patient for a whole week even after the friends have arrived, finally speaking only to express his misery. It is their attempted condolences which seem to provoke his growing sense of grievance, and much of his bitterness is reserved for the way in which he is treated by humans: once a respected pillar of the community, he is now accused, shunned and ridiculed, and he looks for vindication in the eyes of humans as much as with God. Indeed, his attitudes toward God are ambivalent: it is God who is doing this, but also God alone who can ultimately offer that vindication. Job wants a contest with him not because he is under any illusion that he might win, but because he wants to air his side of the case, and put the record straight. Before we sign up to the idea of Job as a tragic hero or spokesman for the oppressed, then, we must remember that he seems more upset by mockery from his social inferiors than by the casual slaughter of his household (see especially 30.1-15, on the scum whose fathers Job would have refused to put with his dogs): the Satan is not entirely wrong to think that Job's greatest concern is with Job.

To sum up, the book of Job was probably not composed to put across some clear and specific message; if that was its intention, indeed, then the many different readings across the years suggest that it failed spectacularly. It serves as a framework within which issues of divine justice provide a focus for poetic debate between the characters, but ultimately suggests that the whole debate is inadequate. God is powerful and frightening, wild and untamed, so that whatever rules we might think he works by, the reality is that no rules constrain him.

Chapter 4

Ecclesiastes

Where Proverbs 1–9 and Job both feature many characters, each with their own voice, Ecclesiastes has just one, and the book is presented as a monologue. The speaker is called Qohelet, or sometimes 'the Qohelet': we have no idea whether this obscure word is a name or title, or even whether we are pronouncing it correctly – the vowels in the Hebrew tradition are based on an idea that it must be connected to a verb meaning 'summon'; this is itself linked to a noun meaning 'assembly', which has in turn given rise to the Greek title Ecclesiastes, or 'assemblyman'. In 1.1 Qohelet is described as 'son of David, king in Jerusalem', and in 1.12 he says that he has been 'king over Israel in Jerusalem'. If we take him literally, then he must be Solomon or Rehoboam – no other descendant of David ruled Israel from Jerusalem in biblical tradition – and it was assumed by early commentators that Qohelet was Solomon, even though he never actually identifies himself directly as such.

This association has been important for the subsequent reception of the book, but there is really nothing else in it which requires that we take Qohelet to have been a king, let alone King Solomon, and various commentators have suspected that the identification was added after the book's initial composition (e.g. Galling 1969). Whether or not it was originally attributed to Solomon, though, Ecclesiastes is most unlikely to have been written by him, and it is usually dated to the last few centuries BCE, principally on the grounds of its Hebrew. This linguistic dating has been challenged (see especially Fredericks 1988), and certainly involves a few questionable assumptions, but it is hard to get round the presence of words borrowed from Persian in the text, which are unlikely to have been used in Hebrew before the fifth century BCE, half a millennium after Solomon was supposed to have reigned. Most scholars place the book later still, in the Hellenistic period.

Qohelet's monologue is followed in 12.9-14 by an epilogue which talks about him in the third person as a teacher and arranger of sayings. Until recently, most commentators have seen this epilogue as an addition, the work of an editor, or several editors who were commenting on an original composition by Qohelet himself. In the last few decades, however, there has been a growing inclination to see Qohelet not as the work's author, but as its protagonist – a character through whom the actual author talks – and this raises the possibility that the epilogue is as much a part of the original work as the monologue (Fox 1977).

The epilogue and the associations with Solomon are not the only parts of Ecclesiastes to have been identified as secondary, and there have been many different attempts to identify layers of revisions in the text. These are usually based on a perception that the book contains actual or virtual self-contradictions, and that no single author would have included such inconsistencies. That is not so logical a basis as it may seem: Qohelet may move through a sequence of ideas which lead him to adopt various positions, and might have had some sympathy with Ralph Waldo Emerson's advice, that 'A foolish consistency is the hobgoblin of small minds . . . Speak what you think now in hard words, and to-morrow speak what to-morrow thinks in hard words again, though it contradict every thing you said to-day.'[1] All the same, many of Qohelet's apparent self-contradictions have as much to do with the interpretation of his words as with the words themselves, and attempts to strip away supposed additions usually rely on no more than unprovable assumptions about what he should or must have meant. Although we cannot exclude the possibility that later hands have tried to improve the text, or to make it more orthodox, we have no objective way to identify such additions, and the text is, in most ways, quite coherent as it stands. Similar problems, incidentally, confront alternative suggestions that the book has not been altered by the addition of different viewpoints, but rather included them from the outset: a number of scholars have argued that we are dealing with a sort of dialogue, either between different voices (Perry 1993), or with Qohelet himself quoting the views of others (Gordis 1968; Whybray 1981). Since there is no specific marking of voices or quotations, however, this again becomes a matter of judging which parts do not seem to fit a given understanding of Qohelet's viewpoint.

The text of Ecclesiastes is not entirely straightforward, then, but it lacks the serious problems of supplementation and dislocation which we find in Proverbs and Job. That advantage, however, does not make the work easier to study, and there is famously little consensus about its purpose and meaning. In the other wisdom books, significant disagreements tend to emerge not over what is being said, so much as over how we are to interpret what is being said. In Ecclesiastes, though, key ideas are expressed in ways that are often difficult to understand or follow, while much is made to hinge on repeated words and phrases that are obscure or ambiguous. This is a very difficult book to read, and was probably challenging even for its original audience. There is much debate over just what is being said in the book, then, even before commentators attempt to assess its significance.

1. The book

The monologue that makes up most of the book is not continuous, since at various points it clearly stops or is interrupted by set-piece compositions, but it is not broken into formal sections. After an initial prologue in 1.2-11, Qohelet speaks in a first-person, memoir style that seems to tell a story in sequence up to the end of chapter 2, and then increasingly to mix recollections and personal observations with other material in a way which seemingly advances discussion of various themes, but is far from constituting a coherent or sequential argument. Any useful description of this material would be as long as the material itself: it defies ready summary. Amongst the set-pieces there are two long series of sayings (in chapters 7 and 10-11) which are reminiscent of the collections in Proverbs, while many shorter series or single aphorisms appear in the course of the speech. We also have in chapter 3 a famous sequence of pairs, which makes the point that there is a time for everything, and in chapter 12 the monologue ends with a beautiful but very difficult description of a scene, which is often taken to be an allegory of old age, but which is more plausibly read, perhaps, as a description of death and mourning (e.g. Fox 1988).

This ending, along with Qohelet's earlier reflections on his experiences and his coming death, suggest that we may be supposed to read his words as those of a man at the end of his life. Indeed, the epilogue's presence, and its brief evaluation of Qohelet's work, add to a sense that this is a sort of posthumous publication, not entirely unlike the tomb autobiographies of Egypt (cf. Uehlinger 1997: 207–10; and Tremper Longman [1991; 1998: 15–20] compares literary autobiographies from Mesopotamia). It is not an instruction, but it shares with the classic instructions a testamentary quality: Qohelet is passing on the fruit of his experience, even if that fruit is, it transpires, more bitter than normal. For all its associations with memoirs, autobiographies, and instructions, however, it is impossible to stick any generic label on Ecclesiastes: we simply have no other work quite like it.

2. The message

a. Humans and the world

The coherence and sequence of the first chapters do show, however, that we are not dealing with a simple collection or miscellany, and we are probably not supposed just to dip into this book. Indeed, what Qohelet is saying, and why he is saying it, seems to be rooted in the experiences that he outlines at the beginning of his speech. Setting aside the prologue, for the moment, we are presented in 1.12–2.26 with a sort of story, or sequence of episodes. Initially, Qohelet describes only generally his failure to find meaning or usefulness in activities, abilities, or pleasure, despite his acquisition of unprecedented wisdom. In 2.3-11, though, after determining to sustain himself until he 'might see where there is any good for humans, which they might do beneath the heavens for the limited duration of their lives',

Qohelet goes on to describe his accumulation of a vast and self-perpetuating business empire, embracing agriculture, forestry and livestock and his enjoyment of a correspondingly luxurious lifestyle (which is comparable to that of a king, but not explicitly royal). He takes pleasure in what he is doing, but when he ultimately looks around at his achievements, he finds no lasting gain in them. As he explains in the following 2.12-16 and 17–23, he finds that the wisdom he had acquired changes nothing – the wise man and the fool will meet the same end, distinguished only by the wise man's ability to see where he is headed, and both will be forgotten. Moreover, all that he has built up will pass to somebody else, who may have done nothing to earn it. This is a crucial point, which leads him to conclude in 2.24-26 that living the good life is possible not because of inherent virtue, but because God assigns ability and pleasure, or else labour on behalf of others, to whomsoever he chooses.

Chapter 3 turns from Qohelet's own experience to a reflection on human activity more generally, set in the context of God's activities and purpose (3.1-15). Human activity is employment, and human actions are tasks that God has given humans to do (although it is not clear that Qohelet thinks in terms of precise, individual assignments). Accordingly, each is the right thing when it happens, and none is permanently or inherently 'right' or 'wrong': we weep when we should weep and laugh when we should laugh, love when we should love and hate when we should hate – the rightness of each action lies not in itself, but in its contribution to the much larger process of which every activity is a part. Here Qohelet is picking up his earlier realization that his own accomplishments will pass to somebody else when he is gone: he has built a business that will outlast him, and his reward for doing so was not the business itself, but merely the pleasure he took in it (2.10-11) – that alone is truly his share (compare 2.21; 3.22; 5.17, 18; 9.6, 9). Similarly, he suggests now that this is true of all human work: as virtual employees of God, we are compensated not with permanent possession of what we accomplish, but by the ability to take pleasure in accomplishing it (3.9, 12–13). Humans conceive of what they do as permanent, but this is because they lack any true knowledge of God's own accomplishments from start to finish (3.11): it is what God does that will actually continue forever, without possibility of change – and one of the things which he does is to inspire human fear of him.

In this discussion, Qohelet deliberately evokes an idea of the world which has already been stated in the prologue (1.2-11), and which can be understood more clearly in the light of these new comments. Pointing to such natural phenomena as the daily rising of the sun, the blowing of the wind, and the flow of rivers, Qohelet demonstrates that actions may accomplish what they are supposed to accomplish without reaching any culmination: the sun, wind and rivers all do their job, as it were, but the job is not then finished. In a world that is permanent, nothing really ends and nothing really starts, but everything is part of a continuing process. Humans are temporary residents in this world: with limited lifespans and limited memories, they can only see, in effect, a snapshot. This can mislead them into thinking that something has just started or finished when it is merely a phase in a process, as though a sunset meant the end of the sun, or the flowing of a river was like the draining of a cup. So now, in chapter 3, humans cannot see beyond their own actions to the broader process in which they each belong, and when 3.9 picks up a question already asked in 1.3 – what profit is there for humans in their work? – Qohelet's answer is that there is no profit as such, and that their reward is limited to their brief time in the world.

b. Judgement and behaviour

After 3.15, as Qohelet turns to the specific ramifications of his insight, a single train of thought is less in evidence, although he seems to pause at times to take stock. In 3.16-22, however, he seems first to add an important qualification to what he has been saying. From the preceding discussion, we might assume that his worldview embraces a sort of fatalism, with humans acting out a script, and that if every human action is right, then humans are not liable to judgement for their actions – that they, indeed, are no more intrinsically good or bad than what they do. In 2.26, however, it was suggested that some humans please God while others displease him, and now Qohelet touches more specifically on the question of judgement. The text is very difficult, but the suggestion seems to be that, although guilt appears everywhere, God will in fact judge who is innocent and guilty on the basis of what they have done. Discernment by humans, on the other hand, is limited by their inability to distinguish themselves from animals; they see only that they die and decay in the same way, taking as little with them when they go. Since they cannot see what will follow them, the best that they can do is take pleasure in their own achievements.

These ideas are picked up again later, in chapter 8, when Qohelet again contrasts divine judgement with the human inability to distinguish the good from the bad, noting now that people are readily confused by the apparent prosperity of the wicked and occasional suffering of the righteous (which is not so very far, of course, from his earlier perception that his own wealth and lifestyle may pass to an undeserving heir). The point is again linked with issues about the obscurity of the future, and is set, indeed, within a discussion about human ignorance of what will come after them, and the need for them, therefore, to enjoy what they can in their lives. In 9.1-10, moreover, the discussion continues first with a further assertion that the apparent culmination of every life in the same end is a serious problem, leading to a human pursuit of evil, and then with a further, lengthier call to enjoy life while one can. In both chapter 3, then, and chapters 8–9, Qohelet seems to link particular ideas together: God will judge; humans see only the same end for all, and nothing of what follows them; humans should enjoy life. This does not look like fatalism, but it is also clear that Qohelet has no concept of a judgement in the afterlife: Sheol, the underworld, is a place of nothingness and darkness for all (9.5-6, 10; 11.8). What, then, is the nature of the divine judgement which he seems so keen to assert?

The ideas about pleasing and displeasing God that appeared in 2.26 are picked up again at the beginning of chapter 6, along with an echo, once more, of Qohelet's resentment at the fate of his own estate. Here he notes the possibility that God may grant a man prosperity and status, which would normally be taken as marks of divine favour, but not grant him the corresponding ability to enjoy them, reserving that for somebody else. Equally, even if a man has a hundred children, another apparent blessing, or lives a thousand years, these are pointless if he has no pleasure in life. The visible marks of divine reward, in other words, may actually be no such thing. The discussion actually continues a train of thought that began in 5.10, where Qohelet noted that wealth does not always provide satisfaction, that it may be lost, and that it is a gift from God to be able to enjoy one's possessions, and so to forget the hardships of life. Later, in the deeply obscure 7.26, we are told again that a man who pleases God is rescued from a dangerous woman, while the sinner is captured. It is clear, in short, that God discriminates between humans while they live, but that he often does so invisibly, as it were, so that the outward trappings of prosperity may be misleading.

This has the unfortunate effect of making it difficult for humans to tell what constitutes divinely approved behaviour: when divine judgement is hard to see, then so is the divine will. Qohelet does not deny, however, that humans should know how to behave. He observes, at the beginning of chapter 5, that it is easy to offend God in some obvious way, by breaking a vow or prattling rashly in the temple, and he calls there for fear of God – later commending that as a quality which preserves and benefits those who possess it (7.18; 8.12-13). Although 7.15-18, furthermore, famously advises against being too wise or too righteous, as this may inflict misery, the matching advice not to be too wicked, or a fool, threatens nothing less than premature death. Qohelet seems to be saying on the one hand, therefore, that the wicked really are punished, and on the other that they often seem to get away with it. The problem is drawn out most fully in 8.10-14:

> And then I saw wicked people who were buried, but they used to enter and depart from a holy place, and cause it to be forgotten of themselves in the city that they had acted thus. This too is *hebel*, that there is no sentence decreed quickly for a wrongful deed – the heart of humans is consequently bursting within them to do wrong – that a sinner does wrong a hundred times, but prolongs things for himself. For I know too that it will work out well for those who fear God, who will be afraid before him, but that it will not work out well for the wicked person, and, like a shadow, he will not prolong life who has no fear before God. There is a *hebel* committed on the earth, that there may be righteous people to whom something happens as if for the deed of the wicked, and there may be wicked people to whom something happens as if for the deed of the righteous. I said that this too is *hebel*.

The term *hebel* is important here: it is a key word in Ecclesiastes, and we shall discuss it in more detail below. It is apparent anyway, however, that the problem for Qohelet lies, at least partly, in the perception rather than the reality of injustice: people forget the behaviour of the wicked, punishment is not swift enough for people to link it to sins, and bad things can happen to good people, or *vice versa*. When these are all characterized as *hebel*, the point seems to be that they are illusory or misleading – they involve failures to remember the past or to look at the longer term, which prevent humans from seeing the actual connections that are present. Rewards and punishments are not instant, and things will go consistently well or badly for no one. It is perfectly possible, in fact, for somebody to kill themselves with righteousness or to preserve themselves with evil (7.15): the deeds do not trigger instant consequences, and righteousness confers neither armour nor immortality. Qohelet draws the pragmatic conclusion that we should neither be too righteous and wise, to our own detriment, nor risk premature death from being too wicked or foolish; it is fine to take one and the other, because anyone who fears God will escape both (7.16-18). Furthermore, he observes, no one is so righteous that they never sin (7.20), and the implication is, perhaps, that God judges people in the round: if one has the proper attitude, or whatever it is that makes 'fear of God' (an expression we shall discuss later), one will not be condemned for occasional sin, and such sin may be necessary for self-preservation. Such divine judgement cannot, by its very nature, be instant.

Divine judgement is emphasized in Ecclesiastes, then, but it is a complicated matter, which is not always obvious and not always punctual. Although its lack of visibility may drive many to simple wickedness, Qohelet's advice is to fear God but also to be practical, neither risking one's life for the sake of virtue, nor throwing it away through wanton wickedness. Above all, however, one must enjoy life and fear God.

c. Wisdom and human knowledge

Qohelet's call to enjoy life is by no means unique in ancient literature, and his most elaborate treatment of the topic in 9.7-10 is quite possibly derived (although probably indirectly), indeed, from a similar appeal in the Old Babylonian version of the famous *Epic of Gilgamesh*, which we mentioned earlier (see Loretz 1964: 116–22; Uehlinger 1997: 180–92 is more sceptical). There Siduri advises Gilgamesh, who is terrified by the prospect of death after the loss of his friend Enkidu, that humans are allotted not only death but the capacity to enjoy life, and that he should pursue that enjoyment instead of his quest for immortality. Parallels are likewise drawn sometimes with an Egyptian work, which I also mentioned earlier, *The Harper's Song from the Tomb of King Intef*. This commends a focus on life, instead of the unknown afterlife – a rather radical message in the context of Egyptian culture (Fischer 1999; Uehlinger 1997: 210–22). It is important to be clear, however, that Qohelet's appeals are not motivated simply by the brevity of life and inevitability of death. To be sure, in 9.10 he calls on us to do what we find to do with all our might, since there will be nothing to do in Sheol, but it is our ignorance of the future which motivates the call to enjoyment in 3.22, and that thought is echoed in 6.12. It is tempting to link this to the famous *carpe diem* cry of Horace (*Odes* 1.11): 'Seize the day, relying on the future as little as you can'; such a message resonates, of course, with Qohelet's belief that no individual future is certain, and that no one knows when their time will come (9.11-12).

The ignorance he is talking about, however, seems to be something much more profound than the uncertainty of death: it is not what happens *to* us, but what happens *after* us that creates a problem: 'Then I saw that there is nothing better than that a person rejoice in his achievements, since that is what is his. For who can take him to see what will be after him?' (3.22). In 6.12, this is specified more closely, 'Who is there who can inform a person what will come after him beneath the sun?', and if we link 8.15 to what follows in 8.16-17, then it appears that the reason for enjoyment being the only benefit available to humans is supposed to be seen in terms of our inability to comprehend the broader picture of activity in the world. For Qohelet, humans are more pawns than players, and we move with no understanding of the game that is being played: correspondingly, all that we can gain is some pleasure from those movements – their repercussions and long-term consequences are beyond us and of no value to us.

This picks up the idea expressed in the first chapter, that human perception of the world can be little more than a snapshot or glimpse of something much bigger, and it obviously poses a significant obstacle to conventional notions of wisdom: how can we know how to live and prosper when we understand so little of the context in which we must do so? Qohelet's response is far from simple. On the one hand, he does not seem to deny the effectiveness of human wisdom within certain bounds: he seems to attribute his own success to his own wisdom, for example, and in 2.19 it is partly the possibility of inheriting success without wisdom of one's own that so upsets him. The difficulty, of course, is not that wisdom can provide no benefits, but that those benefits are of questionable value. Wisdom may provide other things, but it does not provide the only true human good that Qohelet acknowledges, the enjoyment of what one does, and may even be detrimental to the pursuit of that enjoyment.

This is a theme which emerges very early in the book, when 1.18 declares that 'in much wisdom is much exasperation, and whoever gains in knowledge gains in pain.' It is spelt out more clearly in 2.12-16, which begins with what seems like a commendation of wisdom, but rapidly becomes an expression of its limitations:

> Then I looked round to observe wisdom, and confusion, and wrong-headedness . . .
> And I saw that there was an advantage for the wisdom over the wrong-headedness comparable to the advantage of light over darkness: the wise man – his eyes are in his head, while the fool goes along in darkness. But I knew myself that the same turn of events will befall them both, and I said in my heart, 'What befalls the fool will befall me, me too, so why was I wise back then, unnecessarily?' Then I said in my heart that this also had been *hebel*, because there is no memory of the wise man forever, along with the fool, since already in the days which have come, everything has been forgotten, including how the wise man dies along with the fool.

Wisdom, in other words, allows the wise man to see where he is going but not to change course. He will suffer the same fate ultimately as the fool, and both will be forgotten, so that his ability to see that fate gains him nothing – it is like refusing a blindfold before a firing squad. The difficult 8.1 is probably to be read in similar terms: 'Who is like the wise man? And who knows the meaning of a word? A person's wisdom will light up their face, but their confidence will be dimmed.'

Wisdom can be a good thing, then, and is certainly to be preferred to folly, but it offers limited gains, and comes at a cost. It is also restricted in its scope: humans can never find out what is really going on, whatever the claims of the wise (8.17), and it may be better just to hedge one's bets and get on with things than to try to understand and predict them (11.1-6). Qohelet's view of wisdom is consequently rather ambivalent, which makes it difficult sometimes to be clear just what he is saying. In 7.1-13, for example, there is a series of sayings reminiscent of those in the collections of Proverbs, but marked by a recurrent strand of irony. These include some (7.1-6) which seem to commend sorrow and mourning, associating such graveness with wisdom – but they have the net effect of making folly seem more attractive, linking it with partying, singing and laughter. It is hard to tell quite what Qohelet wants us to believe here, and whether or not he has his tongue in his cheek. Elsewhere in the series, furthermore, 7.7 speaks of wisdom's vulnerability to extortion, and the difficult 7.11-12 seem to suggest that wisdom and knowledge do not create wealth so much as benefit from its protection. If, then, Qohelet approves of wisdom and claims to be supremely wise himself, he also portrays it in a way that can be deeply unappealing, and clearly sees no scope for it to transcend the limits imposed on human knowledge and existence.

Although wisdom is often contrasted with folly in the book, Qohelet is sometimes concerned with concepts that seem more complicated: the confusion and wrong-headedness of 2.12, for instance, do not seem to be simple synonyms for folly. The portrayal of folly itself is sometimes interesting, moreover, as when 10.14 links the multiplication of a fool's words to Qohelet's theme that 'No person knows what is going to be, and who can tell him what will be after him?' This picks up a similar link between verbiage and ignorance in 6.11-12, but it also seems to imply that the fool is claiming wisdom of some sort, and certainly places the fool in no worse a light than the wise man of 8.17, who claims more knowledge than he has. Folly is undoubtedly dangerous, then, but it is not a simple matter. As with righteousness and wickedness, perhaps, there is some appropriate balance for the individual to strike between perilous folly and painful wisdom (7.16-18).

d. The term *hebel*

We have already seen several uses of the word *hebel* by Qohelet, and I have deliberately left these untranslated. The literal sense of this word, however, is not really in dispute: it refers to a type of air or vapour, which is linked to breath or wind in Isa. 57.13. Later uses of the word suggest that it is typically exhaled or exuded in some way, and that it is hot. Job 35.16 seems to use it of the hot air breathed out whilst Job 'opens his mouth' and 'without knowledge multiplies words' – the same idea seems to be present in Eccl. 6.11, where Qohelet plays, perhaps, on literal and figurative senses of the term, so that 'a lot of words make a lot of *hebel*'. It is gaseous but detectable, then, something that may be perceived but not grasped, and which is prone to dissipate (see Prov. 13.11). These characteristics, and others, make *hebel* a popular metaphor in a range of contexts, and it is here that the difficulties of interpretation begin. Such figures of speech can have more than one point of reference (we might all rather be 'steady as a rock' or have muscles 'hard as rock', than be 'heavy as a rock' or 'lumpy as a rock'), and they can convey different references simultaneously. Unless a metaphor has become firmly established with a single sense, it may be open to a range of interpretations, and these may be limited by the context, but alternatively kept open (see Miller 2002). When, for example, Prov. 31.30 contrasts beauty in a woman with piety, calling it *hebel*, the image surely evokes not only insignificance but transience: *hebel* is insubstantial, but it also dissipates. On the other hand, in Ps. 62.10 (ET 62.9), the writer seems first to link *hebel* with lying or delusion, but then to focus on its lack of weight: 'Surely humans are *hebel*, the children of man a falsehood: on the scales they'll go up more than *hebel*, the lot of them together.'

Since *hebel* seems not to have had any single connotation or association in biblical usage, we, like the original readers, have to understand what Qohelet meant by the term through the way he uses it, and the contexts in which it appears, rather than identifying its meaning in advance. Correspondingly, when Qohelet's very first words in 1.2 are 'Absolute *hebel*! . . . Absolute *hebel*! It is all *hebel*!', we have to wait to discover not only what 'all' he is referring to, but also what he means by calling it 'breath' or 'vapour'. Since he ends his speech almost the same way in 12.8, after describing many different phenomena as *hebel*, it is clear that he views the metaphor as a fundamental expression of his outlook and message, but we must be wary of presuming that a single connotation is involved even every time that Qohelet declares 'This (also) is *hebel*' (as in 1.14; 2.1; 2.11 [twice], 15, 17, 19, 21, 23, 26; 4.4, 8, 16; 5.9 [ET 5.10]; 6.2, 9; 7.6; 8.10, 14). To some extent, the metaphor serves as a device for linking different points, and it is notoriously difficult to establish one specific meaning that embraces all the uses in the book, let alone to translate *hebel* consistently with a single word.

The traditional English rendering 'vanity' was a good one, in that its own range came close to matching many of the ways in which *hebel* can be used, but for the same reason it never offered any precise insight into the sense, and it has become increasingly misleading as English usage has moved on. Attempts to translate in terms of transience, futility, obscurity, or insubstantiality have won no universal acceptance, and each struggle to explain particular uses. There is, then, no scholarly consensus, but a number of recent commentators have adopted Michael Fox's attractive understanding of *hebel* as 'absurdity' (see especially Fox 1986; 1999: 27–49). For Fox, what Qohelet is expressing by his use of *hebel* is a contradiction between reality and reasonable expectation: things are *hebel* because they are not the way that we think they should be, and they stand as an affront to our reason. Qohelet is protesting, in other words, about what he sees to be a basic irrationality in the world, and in the way that the world works.

Although it does not fit all the uses without a certain amount of shoving and squeezing, Fox's interpretation is valuable and insightful. It faces the substantial objection, however, that *hebel* does not have this meaning elsewhere, and it is difficult to see either how 'breath' could have come to mean 'absurd', or how the original readers were supposed to deduce this meaning. To put it another way, if *hebel* were a completely unknown word, then Fox would have supplied an excellent understanding from its use in the context of Ecclesiastes, but it is not, and his definition jars with the meanings and connotations established from numerous other contexts. If there is a way around this obstacle, it lies, perhaps, in the use of *hebel* sometimes elsewhere to indicate that something is illusory or deceptive – a use which presumably picks up the fact that a breath or vapour is perceptible without being tangible, that it has form, as it were, without substance. Such an understanding may underpin the frequent use of the word with reference to foreign idols, and we find *hebel* aligned on occasions with terms for lying and deception (e.g. Ps. 62.10 [ET 62.9]; Jer. 16.19; Zech. 10.2); a verb derived from *hebel* seems usually, moreover, to be associated with false confidence or assurance, or with preoccupations that have no value.

In this respect, it is important to observe that Qohelet specifies his first declaration that 'all is *hebel*' with a question (1.3), to which the prologue in 1.4-11 is presumably supposed to furnish an initial answer: 'What profit is there for a person in any of his business, at which he works beneath the sun?' As we have seen, Qohelet suggests in the prologue that human life must be set in the context of processes that extend far into the past and future. In 2.11, 18–23, speaking of his own labours, he sees *hebel* in the facts that his accomplishments will pass to another, and that he has seemingly gained nothing from them, and 3.9 once more sets the question about gain from toil in the context of divine plans and eternal processes. To the extent that he is giving the term a single sense, then, Qohelet appears to be suggesting in these first chapters that it is all human works which are *hebel*, and that the reason lies in the lack of any true profit for those doing the work. What they accomplish is not futile or transient – indeed, it may be valuable and outlast them – but it is not ultimately theirs, and so they aspire to what they cannot attain. The sense is similar to that of Isa. 49.4, ' I have toiled for nothing, for emptiness and *hebel* have I spent my strength', or to Isa. 30.7, where vast riches are spent on Egyptian help which is '*hebel* and emptiness' – a bad investment. In Ps. 39.7 (ET 39.6) indeed, a point is made which seems very close to Qohelet's own: 'Surely the human walks in shadow! Surely they roar [?] for *hebel*: he heaps up and knows not who will gather!'

In general, then, Fox's basic perception that *hebel* points to a disappointment of expectation in Ecclesiastes may be sound, but it is easier to align the term itself with the expectation than with the disappointment. Things are *hebel* because they constitute an illusion or delusion, a human aspiration to possess what they cannot own, and to find a profit that will always be annulled by their own deaths. The issue is not that the world is irrational or disorderly, but that human perception of the world is limited and short-sighted. Two similar expressions sometimes used alongside *hebel* (one in 1.14; 2.11, 17, 26; 4.4, 6; 6.9; the other in 1.17 and 4.16) help to clarify this sense, although they present some difficulties of their own. Probably to be translated as 'wishing for the wind' and 'worrying about the wind' (possibly as 'shepherding' or 'pursuing' it), they offer another metaphor based on air, but one that includes the element of wishfulness quite explicitly. What we want, we cannot get, and all that we achieve is ours only in passing: when we leave the world, we go as we came, and all our works slip between our fingers, as though we were grasping at air.

e. Summary

In short, then, Qohelet sees individual humans as temporary residents in a permanent world, who base their desires and understandings on a perception of the world that is limited by the brevity of their lives. Each person may lose before they die whatever they own or have accomplished, but it may just as readily outlive them. In any case, their accomplishments are never really theirs: they cannot, as it were, wind up the business and walk away with a profit, but can at best only take a dividend from it while they live. This seems unjust, especially when prosperity seems to fall in the lap of those who have done nothing to earn it, and the consequent problems of motivation are compounded by the fact that divine judgement of human actions, although real enough, is not always visible or immediate. Since human knowledge is limited by the brevity of lives and memories, human wisdom cannot penetrate to a proper understanding of the world, and if it can help to procure success within the strict constraints of human existence, it also promotes despair by revealing more clearly those constraints. Qohelet's reaction is to commend enjoyment of what we have: our dividend and our reward lies in the pleasure that we can take from our lives, not in anything that lies beyond us. Whilst we must not risk losing the possibility of that enjoyment through false expectations, stupidity or divine disfavour, we must be no less wary of losing it through a dangerous over-righteousness or joyless work ethic. In the end, whether we are good or bad, wise or stupid, we are all going to die, and when that happens we will take nothing with us, and we will find nothing waiting for us.

3. Reading Ecclesiastes

There are other issues tackled by Qohelet that I have not included here, and there are some parts of his speech that are extremely difficult to understand. Even if there is a broad measure of agreement about certain of the key issues, moreover, there are almost as many different interpretations of Ecclesiastes as there are interpreters. In part this is down to wholly different understandings of key terms or passages, but much of the variety comes simply from different emphases. While most commentators would agree, for example, that Qohelet calls on us to enjoy life, there is a significant division between those who see this as a despairing appeal to salvage what we can from the wreckage, and those who see the call as joyful and liberating.

More fundamental problems surround the book's 'orthodoxy', if such a term is remotely appropriate for the late period in which it was probably composed, or, indeed, for any era of Jewish thought before the rabbinic. There is little in Ecclesiastes which is really specific to Judaism, and it has a sort of universal applicability which has undoubtedly contributed to its continuing popularity. This does not mean that it is necessarily a foreign work or a translation, and the book is equally lacking in ideas that we might consider specific to other religions or cultures. Whether it actually contradicts any basic tenets of Judaism is much harder to say. Certainly, Qohelet's rejection of any meaningful existence or judgement after death would be difficult to reconcile with the ideas of the Pharisees, and has contributed to the view of some scholars that the book was written by a Sadducee (e.g. Levy 1912). This is a belief, however, that seems wholly in accord with earlier ideas about Sheol, and, indeed, with widespread Near Eastern and classical notions of death and the underworld. It is more striking, perhaps, that Qohelet seems both to reject human knowledge of the past, when Judaism looked very much to the past for its self-understanding, and to ignore the Torah as a source of guidance for humans – a source which would be much needed in his world of limited human understanding. It is difficult also to see his general pragmatism, his emphasis on personal enjoyment, and especially his advice not to be over-righteous, sitting comfortably with many religious Jews.

It is often said that the book was only controversially accepted into the Jewish canon at a late date. Like most issues surrounding the origins of the canon, however, this is far from clear-cut, and the key rabbinic discussions are more probably to be understood in different terms (see Goodman 1990; Broyde 1995). What we can say is that Ecclesiastes was included amongst the books found at Qumran, and was probably accepted quite widely as scriptural (in some sense) from a relatively early date. Its acceptance, however, came to involve the deployment of an interpretative framework within which the more difficult statements of the text could be read. This means, of course, that we cannot really use its acceptance as a measure of its conformity, but it does raise intriguing questions about the reasons for acceptance of the book in the first place, for which its attribution to Solomon barely furnishes an adequate answer (this attribution, indeed, was itself a problem in some later discussions, since Solomon was viewed with more than a little ambivalence; cf. Hirshman 2001: 88).

One possibility is that we are missing an important point about the way in which the book is supposed to be read, and that the clue to this lies in its unusual epilogue. If Qohelet is a character and creation of the author, rather than just his mouthpiece, then the epilogue may be serving actively to distance the writer from his protagonist. Just as the author of Job presumably did not agree with the contradictory views of all his characters, so it may be that Qohelet's speech is not written to provoke agreement, but to provoke thought, or even disagreement. That might explain why the epilogue starts with a bland description of Qohelet, which seems almost wilfully to miss the point of his words, before moving on to a thoroughly disconcerting portrayal of advice literature in 12.11-12: the wise are like shepherds wielding goads, each with sayings stuck like spikes in their goad – too much reading is to be avoided, therefore, as it tears one's flesh. This is not, perhaps, the warmest commendation ever to appear in the blurb of a book. Martin Shields (2006) has recently pursued this line of thought to paint Qohelet as a sort of parody of a wise man – the problem with this being that Shields is more or less forced to come up with a caricature of his own to provide a model wise man. We need not go so far, though, to suggest that Qohelet's viewpoint is presented for examination more than for acceptance.

In the first place, the questions that he chooses to ask would not, perhaps, be on the lips of everyone. How many people, in fact, then or now, ever perceived the profit that they could make out of life as the most important consideration in living, or were moved to anger by the prospect that someone else would get their possessions after they had gone? Qohelet, it has often been observed, uses a considerable amount of language that we might associate with the world of business, and the questions that he raises are arguably those of the businessman or accountant. He boasts unashamedly, moreover, of his own accomplishments, luxuries, and possessions, draws heavily on his own, avowedly extensive experience, and speaks a variety of Hebrew which may be colloquial, and possibly dialectal. In other words, Qohelet may have been recognizable to contemporary readers not as a professorial or regal figure, so much as a self-made tycoon, trying to make sense of his life and world through a discourse that is both blunt and vivid. That is not to say that we are supposed to mock him, and there is a great deal of beauty and poignancy in his speech. It seems far from impossible, though, that his position is intended to invite a critique of his materialism: having realized too late that he has wasted time on accumulating a wealth which he will lose and a wisdom which pains him, Qohelet faces death, and the loss of those pleasures which, in retrospect, were his only real gain in life.

Other commentators have wondered if the book is a response to Greek philosophy or a polemic between parties within early Judaism; some have painted it as strongly conservative, some as radically innovative. However we are supposed to read Ecclesiastes, though, it seems difficult to resist the suspicion that it is deliberately provocative, and that the difficulties which it has caused interpreters down the centuries are no accident. If Proverbs largely ignores the problems posed by an idea of wisdom, and Job raises them but supplies no answers, Ecclesiastes paints a picture of human knowledge and existence which demands a response, even if it does not command assent.

Chapter 5

Other Jewish Wisdom Literature

As mentioned earlier, there are two apocryphal books usually included within the wisdom literature, and I shall describe those more briefly in this chapter. Few scholars, however, would accept that all the wisdom literature which we have is confined to the biblical and apocryphal wisdom books, and this starts to draw us further into the difficult area of definition. The problems can be illustrated by another apocryphal book, Tobit, which is essentially a narrative set back in the community of exiles from the Northern Kingdom. The work is certainly aware of the Aramaic instruction *Ahiqar*, which we discussed earlier – Ahiqar himself is actually introduced as a character – and it is possibly under the influence of that work that it briefly becomes an instructional text itself. Having prayed to God for death in chapter 3 and therefore expecting to die imminently, Tobit summons his son, partly to pass on some important information, but partly also to offer him parental instruction. Consequently, chapter 4 of Tobit conforms, on almost any definition, to the demands of the instruction genre, but it forms only one section of a book that is clearly not advice literature overall, and which few would classify as wisdom literature. In Tobit, it is a section which is at issue, but in other works it may be themes, vocabulary or other components which seem characteristic of wisdom literature: at what point does such content tip the balance, and make something a wisdom text in itself, and what is the significance of such apparent borrowings from wisdom literature?

One simple answer might be that content never tips the balance, and that genre is a much more complicated matter. The epistolary novels which were fashionable in the 18th century might have told their stories entirely through fictional letters – but that did not make them letters. The problem with this is that biblical scholarship does not operate with a consensus about the definition of wisdom literature as a genre – if, indeed, it is a genre in any meaningful sense. Correspondingly, if someone wishes to declare that wisdom texts are marked by their adoption of certain attitudes or use of particular vocabulary, then it is open to them to define any book with such attitudes or vocabulary as a wisdom text. (In fact, as we shall see later, such criteria are generally presented not as ways of defining, but as clues to identifying wisdom literature, on the assumption that wisdom texts are marked as such by their origin or use; the practical effect, however, is the same.) Even where there are no advocates for the characterization of a text as wisdom literature, furthermore, scholars differ considerably in their attitudes to the presence of 'wisdom' elements in other literature. Proper consideration of such matters must await a later chapter, but the problems leave us in a difficult position if we wish to talk about wisdom texts in bodies of material outside the established wisdom books.

1. Wisdom psalms

This issue is well recognized in the study of so-called 'wisdom psalms': it has been generally agreed for most of the last century that some of the psalms in the book of Psalms should be described in that way (Gunkel and Begrich 1933), but the lists of such psalms are notoriously diverse. An obvious example, on which most might agree, is Psalm 37, which begins (verses 1–4):

> Don't get worked up about the wicked, don't envy those who do wrong:
> For they will swiftly fade like grass, and wither like green foliage.
> Put your trust in YHWH and do good, dwell in the land and protect faithfulness;
> Take delight in YHWH, and he will give to you what your heart requests.

Although they vary a little in length and rather more in form, the psalm consists entirely of sayings, compiled to create a collection on the subject of the righteous and wicked. The composition, in fact, is more sophisticated than it seems in translation: the psalm is also an acrostic, spelling out the Hebrew alphabet in sequence. The first saying here is almost identical, moreover, to Prov. 24.19, and the first stich of the later verse 23 corresponds to that of Prov. 20.24. If this is a psalm, it is also a cleverly composed sayings collection, with links to the book of Proverbs.

Rather differently, the writer of Psalm 49 promises (verses 4–5, ET 3–4) that:

> My mouth will speak wisdom, and the musing of my heart will be under standing.
> I shall turn my ear to a saying, unravel my riddle with a lyre.

He then goes on to discuss the pointlessness of wealth in the face of death: even the wise must die, along with the fool, and both leave their wealth to others, carrying nothing away. The rich are not to be feared therefore, but the psalmist voices his expectation that 'Surely God will ransom my life from the hand of Sheol, for he will take me' (verse 16, ET 15). The tone is more upbeat, but the territory very much that of Ecclesiastes, and the psalm is keen to announce its content as wisdom – musical wisdom, indeed. The theme is apparently the inability of humans to save themselves, and their need, accordingly, to trust in God. There are other conventional motifs from psalmody here, such as the use of a chorus and the appearance of anonymous persecutors, so that although we can recognize common ground with wisdom literature, this work is far from an alien intruder into the book of Psalms.

We do not have to look far in that book, however, to realize that psalms can borrow quite extensively from the themes and vocabulary of wisdom literature without really venturing anywhere close to the ideas and preoccupations of the wisdom books. Psalm 78 offers a striking example, with a beginning (verses 1–4) that could almost be from the parental appeals in Proverbs 1–9, if we substituted 'my son' for 'my people':

> Give heed, my people, to my instruction, turn your ear to the words of my mouth!
> I shall open my mouth with a saying, pour out riddles from the past –
> Which we have heard and known, and our forefathers have recounted for us.
> We shall not keep secrets from their descendants,
>> recounting to the next generation the praise-inspiring deeds of YHWH,
>> both his might and the wonders he has accomplished.

The psalm then goes on to offer an account and analysis of God's relationship with Israel and Judah, embracing the fall of the Northern Kingdom and establishment of the Davidic dynasty in Judah. So, having borrowed from advice literature not only the call to heed instruction, but also the idea of knowledge transmitted down the generations, the writer then presents us with something that is very far from advice literature. Elsewhere, in Psalm 119 (yet another alphabetic acrostic, although each letter here begins eight lines instead of just one), we find various references that might suggest a more general familiarity with Proverbs 1–9, but the topic is devotion to the Torah.

Psalms can also be mixed. Psalm 34, for instance, begins with an account of rescue by God, but then offers a parental appeal in verse 10 (ET 11), offering to teach fear of YHWH, which is followed by advice for anyone who 'likes life, desiring time to enjoy what is good' (34.13 ET 34.12). This psalm is another alphabetic acrostic, and its switch to advice literature occurs precisely at the mid-point of the alphabetic sequence: someone has deliberately created a work that is half psalm of praise, half instructional poem. Although not an acrostic, Psalm 32 does something similar, moving from an account of personal repentance straight to an offer of instruction in verse 8.

On a fairly crude measure, then, looking only at psalms which look a lot like material in the wisdom books, we seem to have psalms which appear also to be wisdom texts, psalms which only look like wisdom texts through some superficial dressing, and psalms which are wisdom texts only for part of their length. At the very least, it is clear that there is no rigid boundary between genres here, and it seems also that some conventions drawn from advice literature are borrowed fairly readily to introduce or characterize other material. Beyond the psalms, incidentally, we see this happening at the end of the book of Hosea, where an epilogue (commonly taken to be a secondary addition to the book) proclaims:

> Who is wise? Then let him understand these things. Understanding? Let him know them. For the ways of YHWH are straight, and the righteous walk in them, while sinners stumble in them. (Hos. 14.10 ET 14.9)

It seems doubtful that any single, simple phenomenon can be adduced to explain all of this. In part, generic or stylistic conventions are being used to shape the way in which material is to be read. So, Psalm 78 calls on the authority of instruction and past tradition to present its historical analysis as something which must be learned and passed on, whilst the addition to Hosea seems to invite the reader to draw some underlying, moral message from the specifics of the prophetic text. In Psalms 32 and 34, however, there is a more specific literary move to unite the experiential aspects of psalmody and instruction: the sufferer who has been saved now offers teaching, with his suffering and salvation furnishing his credentials. This evokes and combines the features which mark different genres in a way that is not unusual in literature – different types of composition are not hermetically sealed from each other – and it is only an issue in itself if we have a reason to believe that some ideological or other barrier would have prevented the writers of psalms from using the conventions of advice literature.

We shall return to that matter later. The more pressing issue which arises from this material is that it exposes the sort of difficulties which face any attempt to define 'wisdom psalms' on purely formal grounds: a search for specific vocabulary or conventions would potentially lead us to include works like Psalm 78, whilst excluding works like Psalm 49. It may well be better to use thematic criteria, and if we adopt the sort of working definition of wisdom literature proposed earlier (and cf. Weeks 2005), then it is possible to create a list of psalms which share the interest of the wisdom books either in affirming the benefits of proper behaviour (so Psalms 1; 19B; 25; 32; 34; 37; 52; 112; 125; 128), or in confronting the problems involved in recognizing such behaviour (10; 14; 49; 73; 90; 94). No such lists, however, offer anything more than an assortment of psalms which match the criteria of our search, and there is no hidden group of poems, ideologically, formally or thematically coherent and self-evidently distinct from other psalms, which suddenly comes to light when we ask the right question. This, of course, is why scholars applying different criteria end up with such different lists, and it means that the whole notion of a 'wisdom psalm' has to be treated with some caution.

The study of the psalms and of the psalter is, of course, a complicated field in itself, and it is beyond the scope of this introduction to assess how or why the collection should contain works that deal with issues similar to those addressed in wisdom literature, or which borrow from the style and conventions of advice literature in particular. One significant point that does arise, however, is the link between wisdom, personal piety, and law. The psalter begins with a contrast between the fates that will befall different types of individual, and this is strongly reminiscent of the contrasts drawn between the righteous and wicked in much wisdom literature. The antithesis of wickedness in Psalm 1, however, is not righteousness or innocence in some general sense, but more specifically adherence to the Torah, in which the man who is blessed finds a source of delight and meditation. Psalm 19B is similarly devoted to praise of the Torah, which will make the uneducated wise, and which offers the prospect of reward, while Psalm 119 has the speaker beseech God to teach him his Torah, which will protect and strengthen him. Many psalms are concerned with personal piety, and these embody a certain type or aspect of such piety, but they also state or imply an association between wisdom and the Jewish law, such as we suspected might underpin Proverbs 1–9. If advice literature had come more generally to be understood in such terms, then the dissemination of its motifs and conventions becomes understandable as a reflection of the increasing focus upon individual piety linked to study of the Torah in post-exilic Judaism: they are markers not merely of a type of literature, but of a conceptual framework in which proper behaviour and piety can be achieved through internalization of the divine instruction. Whether or not it is to be found already in Proverbs, this idea becomes very important in the later wisdom books, and we shall turn to those now.

2. The Wisdom of Ben Sira (Ecclesiasticus)

This work was composed, probably in Jerusalem during the early second century BCE, by one Yeshua ben Eleazar Ben Sira. Originally in Hebrew, it was translated into Greek by his grandson towards the end of that century. The Greek version was ultimately adopted into the Christian canon, but the book was not accepted as scriptural in rabbinic Judaism, despite evidence of its early and continuing popularity. This had two consequences for its later reception. The first was that the book came to be preserved and transmitted almost exclusively through Christian channels and in Greek translation. The second was that its absence from the Jewish bible led to its rejection from the Protestant canon, although it is accepted as canonical, or deutero-canonical, in other Christian traditions. Since the end of the 19th century, however, much of the Hebrew text has been recovered in ancient or medieval fragments – we now possess around two-thirds of it, although the situation is complicated by the existence of separate editions. Recent interest in this period of Judaism has also led to much greater scholarly interest in the book.

The complicated history of the work has left it with an array of different titles. 'Ecclesiasticus' is the name used in the Vulgate, but it is now generally avoided, if only because of the risk of confusion with Ecclesiastes. Since the author's name becomes 'Jesus Ben Sirach' in the Greek, the book is often called 'Sirach', but most scholars prefer the Hebrew 'Ben Sira', which I shall use here.

a. The book

This is a very lengthy work, spanning 51 chapters in the Greek, and although it is difficult to discern an overall structure, the first chapter does seem to serve as an introduction. This begins by declaring that: 'All wisdom is from the Lord and with him for ever'; eternity and wisdom are immeasurable, and wisdom was created by God before anything else. He has poured wisdom out upon his creation, however, and she now lives with all flesh as a gift supplied to those who love him. She in turn offers fear of the Lord, which gives happiness and prosperity. The relationship is described in 1.26-27:

> (If you) desire wisdom, keep (the) commandments, and the Lord will provide
> you with it.
> For wisdom and instruction (are) fear of the Lord, faith and meekness his
> delight.

After that, Ben Sira adopts the stance of a father instructing his children, with addresses to 'my son(s)', and sometimes longer parental appeals. Chapters 2–43 consist of admonitions on a wide variety of themes, which are usually treated in blocks or series of sayings which add up to a discussion of the topic. The material is much more obviously coherent than the sayings collections of Proverbs, and more closely resembles Proverbs 1–9. With that work it shares also a tendency to dwell at length on the importance of wisdom itself, which is sometimes personified, most notably in chapter 24: here wisdom presents herself as having emerged from God's mouth, and covered the earth before being sent to live in the Temple at Jerusalem. We also find other distinctive passages. In 36.1-17, for instance, Ben Sira prays directly to God, calling on him to restore Israel and Jerusalem, while 41.1-4 encourages acceptance of death through a rhetorical address to death. In 38.24–39.11, moreover, he muses on the scribe's need for leisure-time to cultivate wisdom: manual labourers of various sorts are sketched in turn, undertaking the intricate and demanding tasks required by their jobs. They perform an important role, but will never occupy important positions within society: 'they set fast the foundation of the age, and their praying is in the practice of their craft' (38.34). The student of the Torah, however, has the time to seek out wisdom, old and new, and to puzzle out hidden meanings: he will serve among the great, pass on his teaching, and enjoy lasting fame.

With chapter 44, the book suddenly takes a very different turn, as Ben Sira declares 'let us now praise famous men, and our forefathers by generation' (44.1). What follows is an account of powerful, righteous men, from Enoch and Noah through Abraham, Isaac, Moses and various notable Jews, up to Nehemiah and then the high priest Simeon (who served in the closing decades of the third century) – although this last stands as a separate song of praise, after a conclusion in 49.14-16 works briefly back from Enoch and Joseph to Adam. At the end of his panegyrics, Ben Sira brings his work formally to a close, urging his readers to take his instructions to heart, 'For if he should do these things, he will be strong in all respects, for the light of the Lord is his route' (50.29, in the Greek version). Two appendices follow, however. The first (51.1-12) is essentially a psalm of thanksgiving, which praises God for saving the writer from death and danger. Although attributed to Ben Sira by a superscription in the Greek version, its authenticity is questionable, and its pertinence to the rest of the book obscure; it may be the attribution that led to its attachment. A further hymn of praise actually follows this in one Hebrew text. The second appendix (51.13-30) was an alphabetic acrostic in the original Hebrew, and presents itself as the memoir of a love affair with wisdom. Although told in the first person, it is only 'autobiographical' in a loose sense, and although romantic, it is not as erotic as sometimes claimed (cf. Muraoka 1979). Having sought Wisdom from his youth, the writer has become infatuated with her and committed to her; he now invites the uneducated to hear him speak of her, to submit to her, and to profit from her. Again, this is not certainly the work of Ben Sira, and if it is, it is not clearly a part of the book. If it was originally an independent composition (and verses 13–19 are found by themselves on the Qumran text 11Q5), it may have been added because its content, if not its tone, corresponds to one of the book's key interests. It should also be said, though, that its ideas about wisdom conform closely to those of the book as a whole (except, perhaps, that wisdom is more congenial and less ruthless here than in, say, 4.17-19), which would tend to affirm either its authenticity or its dependence on the book.

b. Wisdom in Ben Sira

It would be difficult to do any justice here to the wide range of themes and ideas in this lengthy book, but its preoccupation with wisdom reflects a crucial aspect of the work's self-understanding. This understanding links wisdom, instruction, and fear of God together in a way that echoes the ideas of Proverbs 1–9 – a work which seems to have had a profound influence on Ben Sira. Here, more explicitly than in Proverbs, the Jewish law is also drawn into the relationship, although Ben Sira never equates Torah with wisdom, as is often claimed. Rather, human wisdom is a product of Torah (1.26; 15.1-8; 24.23-6) and of other instruction (6.18, and especially 32–7; 50.28). Personified wisdom, however, is also said to produce instruction (24.27, 32–3), as is the wise man (39.8): one is taught, one becomes wise, and then one teaches, enabling others to become wise, very much as the second appendix suggests. The instruction offered by the book as a whole is presumably to be understood in these terms. Law also defines wisdom in some sense: in 19.20 we are told that 'all wisdom is fear of the Lord, and in all wisdom there is an outworking of law', to make the point that wrongful knowledge is not wisdom. Unlike common cleverness, real wisdom manifests the influence of Torah, and corresponds to fear of God.

This relationship between wisdom and fear of God is less easy to pin down, and the matter is not helped by the fact that we lack the original

Hebrew for some of the key texts. There is a direct allusion to Prov. 1.7 and 9.10 in Sir. 1.14: the verse goes on to say that wisdom is created alongside the faithful in the womb (where they presumably do not yet fear God), while in verses 16 and 18 we are told that fearing the Lord is both the way that wisdom satiates humans and the crown of wisdom. These references suggest that fearing God is a product of wisdom, as in Proverbs 1–9. The reverse seems to be implied by 1.20, however, where wisdom is a tree and fearing the Lord its roots (contrast 1.6), as also by 21.11, where wisdom is the consummation of the fear of the Lord. Matters are complicated by 1.10 and 43.33, where God is said to provide wisdom to the pious (compare 1.26, above), but these verses hint that the acquisition of wisdom is viewed by Ben Sira as a continuing process. We might understand the idea in these terms: those who turn out to be pious possessed a germ of wisdom from the outset, which led them to be filled with fear of God; when that is established, wisdom thrives, and their inclination to receive instruction and obey God's commandments leads them to acquire yet more wisdom. The student of the law in chapter 39 illustrates a stage of this: he is driven by his studies to seek out wisdom beyond Torah, reading ancient books, wrestling with wisdom and other literature, experiencing the world – but he also prays to his creator, who may grant him the ability to focus his ideas and pass on his understanding through teaching, while he continues to glory in the Torah.

Although wisdom is undoubtedly still a quality or skill of discernment in Ben Sira, it is also, therefore, something with which the individual has a continuing relationship. Proverbs 1–9 called on its readers just to recognize and accept wisdom's invitation, but matters are now more complicated – and the lengthy pursuit of wisdom in the second appendix sums that up quite well.

c. Links with other literature

The influence of Proverbs on Ben Sira, and especially of Prov. 1–9, is clear and undeniable (see Corley 2005). It is also apparent that the writer is familiar with much of the material which now forms the Jewish Bible; indeed, the book (along with the prologue of the Greek version) is an important source for our knowledge of Jewish attitudes to those texts in this period. His knowledge of Job and Ecclesiastes, however, is uncertain. In the Hebrew version, Sir. 49.9 refers to Job, who held fast to righteousness, but this is only in the context of the character's mention in Ezekiel. It is perilous to place too much weight on possible allusions, and suggested references to the book of Job are generally very vague. We can certainly say that the description of God's works in 42.15–43.33 is reminiscent of the speeches in Job by Elihu and God, but it is hard to identify specific cross-references. It seems very possible, though, that the reference in 40.3 to a man 'humbled in dust and ashes' is deliberately alluding to Job 30.19; 42.6. Curiously, this lies in a passage which has several possible reminiscences of Ecclesiastes. When Sir. 39.33-34 promotes the idea that everything will be good in its time, it is hard not to be reminded of Eccl. 3, and the subsequent 40.1-11 seems to pick up a number of Qohelet's themes: humans face hard labour from the day they come out of their mother's womb until the day they return; all are perplexed, fearful, and can get no rest at night; humans and animals both face death; all things that come from the ground return there, just as all things that come from water return to the sea. Compare especially Eccl. 2.22-3; 3.19; 12.7; 1.7. Elsewhere, we might compare, for example, Sir. 42.21 with Eccl. 3.14. It might be more surprising if Ben Sira did not know those texts, but whatever the case, they have made little obvious impact on his thought.

Looking beyond Hebrew literature, some scholars have seen links with Greek literature, which would not be at all improbable in this period, and Ben Sira is something of an internationalist in his outlook. The list of professions in Sir. 38 has also been compared by many commentators to the so-called 'Satire of the Trades', which forms part of an Egyptian instruction from the Middle Kingdom, the *Instruction of Khety* (for a translation, see Lichtheim 1973: 184–92). Although both compare the life of a scribe favourably with that of other workers, the tone and point are very different, so a direct connection seems unlikely, even if Ben Sira may have been aware of the work. Another Egyptian link, with the work on Papyrus Insinger, is altogether much less likely. J. T. Sanders (1983) has noted a large number of general correspondences, and that is interesting in itself, but the Egyptian text is probably much later than Ben Sira, who would anyway have had little incentive to learn Demotic Egyptian – the script is extremely difficult, and was only starting to be used much for literary texts at around the time Ben Sira was writing.

It is actually Ben Sira's relationship with Jewish literature other than wisdom literature that seems most interesting. His praise of famous men, in the closing chapters, individualizes Jewish history in a remarkable way, and corresponds to his emphasis on the Torah as something with which individuals must engage for their own benefit, rather than just as the stipulations of God's covenant with the nation. The incorporation of Jewish law into the notion of instruction had probably been achieved earlier by the writer of Proverbs 1–9, and was undoubtedly facilitated by the growing emphasis on study of the Torah as a facet of personal piety, which we have already seen reflected in certain psalms. The book's interest in the Jewish past and expression of hopes for the future, however, seem to have been something new.

2. Baruch 3.9–4.4

Before we turn to the other major apocryphal wisdom book, brief mention should be made of a section in the book of Baruch, which has a reasonable claim to be considered a wisdom text. Baruch naturally falls into two parts: the first (1.1–3.8) contains a confession of sin and prayer for restoration supposedly sent to Jerusalem by the Babylonian exiles; the second (3.9–5.9) presents two poems, one urging the Jews to take hold of wisdom (3.9–4.4), while the other offers encouragement and promises restoration (4.5–5.9). The two main sections of the book are generally regarded as separate compositions, which have been brought together, but the relationship between the poems in the second part is less easy to establish. For our purposes it may suffice to say that, if they are not actually independent compositions, they are at least separate poems. The book as a whole is of uncertain date, and little can be said about the origins of any part. It is widely accepted, however, that the Greek text of 1.1–3.8, passed down through Christian sources, is based on a Hebrew original; it has been argued that the same is true for the two poems, but there is less consensus on that issue (see Burke 1982: 23–6).

The first poem, with which we are concerned, is addressed to an Israel in exile:

> Hear, O Israel, commandments of life;
> pay attention, to know insight.
> Why is it, Israel, why (is it) that you are in an enemy land,
> grown old in a foreign country,
> defiled with the dead, reckoned with those in Hades?
> You have abandoned the spring of wisdom.
> If it had been in the way of God that you had walked,
> you would be dwelling in peace for ever.
> Learn where insight is, where strength is, where understanding is,
> so as to know then where long-living is – and life –
> where light for the eyes is – and peace.
>
> (3.9-14)

After asking 'Who has found its place, and who entered its treasuries?' (3.15), the poem then explains how humans are far from wisdom: rulers of the nations and the beasts have died, and their descendants have lived without knowing wisdom's ways or laying hold of it, so that even the merchants, storytellers and seekers of knowledge among the foreign nations have forgotten its paths (3.16-23). God's estate is immeasurably large, and even the ancient giants died there, because God withheld knowledge and insight from them (3.24-28). No human can get wisdom from the sky or across the sea, and nobody knows the way – except God, who knows all things, and who created the world:

> He searched out the whole way of knowledge,
> and gave it to his servant Jacob, and to Israel, beloved by him.
> After this, it appeared on the earth and lived among humans.
> This (is) the book of the commandments of God,
> and the law that exists for ever.
> All who seize it (are) for life,
> but those who leave it will die.
> Turn, Jacob, and take it:
> travel toward the glow cast by its light.
> Do not give your glory to another,

your advantages to a foreign people.
Happy are we, O Israel, for those things which please God are known to us.
(3.37–4.4)

It does not seem necessary to exclude verse 38 (the third line above) as a Christian interpolation, and whether we keep it or not the sense is much the same. That verse, however, is the only point at which wisdom is clearly personified, and although we can easily substitute 'she' for 'it' throughout, wisdom lacks specifically feminine features here, and is much more like the object uncovered by God in Job 28 than the character in Proverbs 1–9 and Ben Sira. Indeed, 'she'/'it' could refer grammatically, throughout these closing verses, to the 'whole way of knowledge'.

The poem seems to echo Proverbs 1–9 at points, and may well have known Job, but its approach to the nature of wisdom is distinctive: not only does it suggest that wisdom is available through God alone, it also claims that the unique Jewish God has given that wisdom exclusively to Israel. Other peoples simply do not, and cannot, know the ways of wisdom. Further, wisdom is not a quality gained by individuals through the Torah, but is a possession of the nation. Caution is necessary when it comes to understanding the relationship between this wisdom and the Torah: 'This (is) the book' in 4.1 may be identifying the gift of knowledge to Israel, rather than wisdom itself, with the book of the law. In fact, the verse may well be an imitation of Sir. 24.23 'All these things are the book of the covenant of the most high God, the law which Moses commanded us, an inheritance for the congregations of Israel'; that verse similarly relates the law to wisdom's account of her dwelling in Israel, rather than identifying wisdom as law. Since abandonment of the law has earlier been characterized as abandoning the 'spring of wisdom', it is likely that the poem in Baruch retains the older idea of law as a source of wisdom. What it does accomplish, however, is an effective re-expression of a conventional historical analysis through the vehicle of wisdom motifs: Israel has abandoned the law and languishes in exile; rather than waste itself amongst foreigners, it must move back to its source of wisdom to recover its unique insight into the will of God, and so retrieve its situation.

3. Wisdom of Solomon

An interest in history also characterizes the Wisdom of Solomon, the origins of which are more obscure than those of Ben Sira. Almost certainly composed in Greek, it was written no earlier than the Ptolemaic period and probably in the early Roman period, during the late first century BCE or early first century CE (see especially Winston 1979: 20–25). Its writer is usually thought to have belonged to the Jewish community in Alexandria, but its subsequent influence on Judaism was very limited, and the text has been preserved through Christian channels. On the origins and reception of the book, see especially McGlynn 2001: 225–45, and Horbury 1995. Obviously, it is not genuinely the work of King Solomon, and there is no formal attribution to that king in the text; however, 9.7-8 reads: 'You chose me as king of your people, and judge of your sons and daughters. You said to build a temple on your holy mountain . . .' and it seems that Solomon is supposed to be speaking throughout.

The book's Greek is relatively polished, it takes the conventional form of a 'protreptic' or 'exhortatory' discourse, and it probably reflects an educated knowledge of Greek literature and thought (cf. Reese 1970). The extent to which it embodies or reacts directly against specific Greek ideas is uncertain, though, and if it is in part a product of Hellenistic culture, it nevertheless stands also within the traditions of earlier Jewish literature.

a. The book

Wisdom of Solomon begins with an appeal to the rulers of the world in chapters 1–6, calling on them to love righteousness and seek the Lord: wisdom will not enter those who are separated from God by their wrong-thinking, and God knows all that is said because his spirit fills the world. He wants things to live, and did not make death, but the ungodly summoned it. Thinking that life is temporary and death inevitable, they are determined to enjoy living while they can, and have no compunction about oppressing the righteous, or violently testing claims to divine protection. What they do not perceive is that the death of the righteous is an illusion: God accepts the righteous dead like sacrifices, but they will ultimately rule the world under God's supervision. The ungodly, who persecuted them and were foolish enough to reject wisdom and instruction, have no such hope of immortality: their work will prove unprofitable, their children cursed, and their old age – should they live so long – without honour. It is virtue that inspires honour, and even if the children of the ungodly seem to thrive for a while, they will ultimately be uprooted. As for the righteous, they may be snatched early by God from the corrupting power of the wickedness around them, and their short, good lives count for more than any lengthy, bad lives. Ultimately, when the wicked are judged, they will see the right-eous man, who is counted amongst the sons of God, and realize that his was the worthwhile path: their own lives leave no mark, but the righteous enjoy immortality and divine favour. Wearing virtue as armour, God will join creation to fight off his enemies.

In chapter 6, a further direct appeal is made to worldly rulers, threaten-ing judgement but offering instruction and an opportunity to learn wisdom. The nature and activity of wisdom, who appears as a personified figure, will be a major theme from this point until the end of the book, and chapters 6–9 dwell in particular on her virtues (with chapter 10 continuing to speak about her, but forming a transition to the next section). Those who seek her will find her easily, and she seeks out those worthy of her, meeting them in their paths and thoughts:

> For her beginning (is) the truest desire for instruction,
> A concern for instruction is love

Love is the keeping of her laws
Attention to laws is assurance of immortality
Immortality achieves existence close to God,
So the desire for wisdom leads to a kingdom.
If you delight in thrones and sceptres, therefore, you tyrants of the peoples,
Honour wisdom, so that you may reign for ever.

(6.17-21)

The speaker promises to tell what wisdom is, and how she came into being: he wants the rulers to learn because 'Having a mass of wise men is the salvation of the world, and a prudent king is a people's good health' (6.24). In chapter 7 he goes on to describe his own experience. Born like everyone, he prayed and received the spirit of wisdom, loving and valuing her above all else, even without realizing that she was the source of the wealth which he also received: 'For she is an incalculable treasure for humans: those receiving it establish a friendship with God, commended for the gifts of instruction' (7.14). It is God, in fact, who controls even wisdom, and through wisdom's teaching he has granted the speaker his extraordinary knowledge of the world. A whole series of adjectives describe wisdom's qualities in 7.22, and we are told that what she is comes from her relationship with God, and her purity:

For she is a vapour from the power of God,
a pure outflow from the glory of the Almighty:
therefore nothing defiled can enter her.
For she is a reflection of eternal light,
a spotless mirror of God's working,
and an image of his great goodness.
While being one, she is capable of all,
staying constant in herself, she renews all;
and passing on in each generation to holy souls,
she makes friends of God and prophets.

(7.25-7)

In chapter 8, the memoir resumes, as the speaker tells how he came to love her, and sought to marry her. She teaches human qualities and abilities, can pass on knowledge of the past and future, as well as of difficult speech and the solution to puzzles: that is why he wanted her with him, enabling him to become powerful and famous, but also offering rest and companionship. Having the insight to realize that wisdom is a gift of God, he prayed for her to be given, and chapter 9 presents his prayer. Weak himself, but chosen to rule the people and build the Temple, he seeks the assistance of wisdom, who knows the works of God, was present at creation, understands what is pleasing to God, and knows what corresponds to his commandments. She will give him good guidance, so that his own works will be acceptable – this is not something that humans can discern for themselves, and all who have known what pleases God have done so because he has granted them wisdom.

The rest of the book (chapters 10–19) then pursues this theme of divine action and protection by wisdom, although it also integrates a lengthy discussion of the worship of other deities. Chapters 10 and 11 draw on stories from the Pentateuch in which wisdom protects the curiously anonymized characters: there are apparent references to Adam, Cain and Abel, Noah, Abraham, Lot, Jacob, and Joseph in 10.1-14, then in 10.15–11.14 the focus is on Moses, the Israelites and the Egyptians as they take part in the events of the Exodus. This becomes the basis for a discussion of punishment (cf. McGlynn 2001) in 11.15–12.17 – first of its nature, but then of God's ability to punish, which is offset by his reluctance to do so: he punishes and judges even the worst offenders little by little, offering opportunities for repentance. As creator of all, he loves and spares all, but mild discipline can turn to condemnation when it goes unheeded.

Chapter 13 first observes the failure of those who do not know God to see the creator through his creations. They take powerful or beautiful elements of the created world to be divine in themselves, not seeing past them to the power and beauty that lies behind: they cannot be blamed for admiring what they see as they search for the divine, but they also cannot be excused their failure to find God when they have been able to find so much else. Idolaters are worse, because they worship what is merely man-made, but after quite a traditional polemic on the subject, the speaker goes on thoughtfully to examine the basis of such worship. It is not wrong to trust to everything which humans have made, because things made with skill are, by definition, made with wisdom: so a boat may come to shore safely because God wants wisdom to work, even though it is pointless and wrong to pray to an idol for the boat's safety. The speaker speculates, in 14.12-21, that idolatry had its origins in the worship of humans through ever more flattering images of them, talking of a cult founded by a grieving father unable to let go of his son, and of images set up to honour kings too distant for direct veneration. The consequent practices attached to such cults, however, are filled with violence and corruption.

The discussion moves back to its starting point through a further condemnation of idols, which this time focuses upon the cynicism of the craftsman, himself a creation, who sees no meaning in life beyond the pursuit of his trade for money. Referring back to points made in chapter 11, chapter 16 contrasts the punishments of the wicked Egyptians with the kindness and protection offered to God's people: where Egypt was attacked by the sort of animals that they worshipped, God's people was given quails; where storms and fire destroyed the crops of one, the other was given manna. Creation itself adapted, both to accomplish all this, and to make the point that humans survive not by growing crops, but by God's word. In chapters 16–19, the darkness over Egypt is contrasted with the light of the holy ones, the death of the firstborn set against Israel's ability to drive off a plague, and finally the preservation of the Israelites compared with the death of the Egyptians when creation was again reshaped and the Red Sea parted. Things would not have reached this point had Egypt learned its lesson earlier, or had not in the first place enslaved a people who had come as guests and helped them, but the whole process showed both a remarkable adaptation of nature, and God's assistance to his people at every time and place.

b. Key ideas

This is a rich and complicated work, which deserves more discussion than is possible here, but many of its ideas follow on from themes that we have seen addressed in other wisdom literature. The personification and characterization of wisdom, in particular, owes much to Proverbs 1–9, although it receives in Wisdom of Solomon a more theoretical and cosmological basis: wisdom does not merely coexist with God, but emanates from him to permeate creation and to mirror what he does. More generally, indeed, the book places a great deal of weight on createdness and the created world, which so reflects God's work that humans can mistakenly think parts of it divine, when they are actually manifestations of divine activity. A wholly beneficent God loves what he has created, and what he has created is responsive to his will.

Wisdom of Solomon also engages with the ideas of justice and judgement which preoccupied Ecclesiastes, and especially Job. The rules of engagement have now changed, however, since the book believes firmly in a future resurrection of the dead, tied to ideas of eschatological judgement. It is no longer a problem that the wicked may seem to live long and prosper, and the righteous to suffer at their hands, since the righteous will ultimately be vindicated – they may even be taken early to protect their integrity. Death, in fact, is not a part of the divine creation or purpose, but has been brought into being by those whose worldview holds them back from behaving in a way that would assure their own resurrection – 2.24 claims that 'it was through the devil's ill-will that death entered into the world: they experience it who are of that party'. Rather as Elihu had argued in Job, Wisdom of Solomon depicts suffering as a warning or discipline from God, but it can now also be something wholly undeserved, inflicted on the righteous by the wicked.

The depiction of the wicked in chapter 2 is especially interesting. As with much elsewhere in the book, an attempt is made to understand why they do what they do, and the author's explanation is that they are driven by disbelief in a future: life is short and meaningless, so should be enjoyed for itself. Although some have seen here an attack on Epicureanism, there is much that is more strongly reminiscent, in fact, of Qohelet's analysis. That is not to say that Wisdom of Solomon is attacking Ecclesiastes; on the contrary, it may understand very well that these observations about the world are viewed by Qohelet too as the reason why humans behave badly, not as a justification for wickedness. In a sense, this book furnishes an answer to the problem with which Qohelet struggles, because if reward can come after death, then the obscurity of judgement and retribution in life becomes more completely a matter of human perception.

It is not at all clear what form the resurrection of the righteous is expected to take, and the book's allusions to the subject might suggest either a temporary removal from the world and ultimate return in power, or a transformation of the righteous into heavenly, even astral beings. The fact, rather than the mechanism, is apparently more important to the writer. It is also difficult to pin down the work's attitude to human free will, because although it seems to be stated that wisdom and virtue are accessible and repentance possible, some statements seem to contradict the notion that humans are free to choose. In 12.10, for instance, the original peoples of the land are given a chance though inherently wicked, whilst the man snatched away by God before he could be corrupted, in 4.10-14, is hardly given an opportunity to be wicked. The accursedness of children born to the ungodly or through an illegitimate union is especially problematic in this respect (3.12–4.6). The underlying ideas in such areas are not necessarily incoherent, but they are not spelled out.

Finally, and more generally, there is a danger of reading too much or too little into the book from its context. Wisdom of Solomon belongs to an era in which much Jewish literature was shaped directly by recent or contemporary historical events: this was not a quiet or easy period for many Jewish communities. Given the use of the Exodus as a source for interpretation of divine judgement in the second half of the book, and the often precarious position of the Jews in Egypt at this time, there are some reasonable grounds to suspect that nationalistic influences might have shaped the book, or that it might have had polemical intentions. It is difficult, however, to see specifically what those might have been. Although it is keen to emphasize God's protection of Israel, and treats Israel itself uncritically, Wisdom of Solomon addresses itself directly to foreign rulers, urging acceptance of a wisdom that does not explicitly command conversion to Judaism. Moreover, its treatment of those who worship other deities is, if anything, sympathetic and conciliatory, at least by the standards of early Jewish literature: those people have perceived something special in creation, just not perceived enough about the nature of creation. Perhaps there is a swipe at the deification of emperors in the reflections on idolatry, but there is again a certain sympathy visible, whether for the grief-stricken father seeking to perpetuate the memory of his son (14.15), or for those trapped in a system of governance which glamorizes and objectifies its leaders (14.21). Real condemnation is reserved, in chapter 15, for those who market idols, knowing them to be useless but not caring. In some important respects, Wisdom of Solomon perceives the world in a way that is far from black and white, and which suits its idea of a God who loves all that he has made.

4. Wisdom at Qumran

Finally, it is important to mention the significant number of texts discovered amongst the Dead Sea Scrolls at Qumran which have been classed as 'sapiential' or wisdom literature. Of course, this can draw us back into the problems of definition that we encountered at the beginning of this chapter (indeed, Qumran has supplied some new potential 'wisdom psalms'), and those problems are exacerbated by difficulties and controversies surrounding the interpretation of some texts. It would be impractical to engage with those in detail here, and there is a growing body of literature already available on the subject. Rather than attempt to deal individually, therefore, with all of the texts that might be labelled 'wisdom literature', I shall focus on some of the more obvious examples.

a. Wisdom

Although generally difficult to date, most of the relevant texts were probably composed in the first or second century BCE, and most were probably not sectarian works created solely for the Qumran community. It is not surprising, therefore, to find in some of them the expression of themes and ideas found already in Ben Sira or Wisdom of Solomon, and a few contain lengthy references to wisdom.

One of the most difficult is in 4Q185 (4QSapiential Work), which preserves much of fifteen lines each from two columns of a longer text, and rather less of a third column. What we have begins with a reference to judgement, involving angels who wield fire, and then an account of human brevity, reminiscent of several biblical texts, but especially Isa. 40.6-8: humans are like grass; blown upon by the wind of God, they wither and perish, and their days are like a shadow on the ground. After an appeal to pay attention, the people are urged, as uneducated ones, to learn from God's might, and seek for themselves a way to life. A further appeal, addressed to 'my sons' urges them not to rebel; they should conform to the path laid down for Jacob and Isaac, gaining the benefits of that, rather than the risks of disobedience. There follows a macarism, which is a type of saying that begins: 'Happy is (someone who)'. Here the lucky individual is one who has been given something that he should take hold of and get as an inheritance – it promises life, health, happiness and wealth. The item is not specified, but the description strongly suggests wisdom, especially since a feminine noun is required (a direct reference to the Torah is also possible). The wicked should not boast that they have not received it, and God has given it to Israel, whom he redeems. A second macarism blesses the man who does not seek out deceitfully what he has been given; he will inherit it, just as it was given to his fathers, will hold fast to it, and will pass it on to his offspring. The message of the text as we have it, then, seems to be that humans face judgement, and their lives are fragile: the Jewish readers are urged to seek out the safe path of obedience to the Torah. God has given wisdom or the law to Israel, as an inheritance that they should value.

Macarisms are a prominent feature in the best-preserved section of another text, 4Q525 (4QBeatitudes). This lengthy text appears to have begun with a prologue that imitates Prov. 1.2-6, and to have used parental appeals to introduce new sections, so it is clearly influenced by Proverbs 1–9. Much of the rest of the text seems to have involved the offering of advice; the surviving fragments, however, contain many references to disaster or punishment, and the advice may have been backed by vivid threats and promises. The macarisms, presented in a short series, themselves relate the happiness of a man who speaks truth, clings to (wisdom's) statutes, and not the ways of iniquity, rejoices in her, and seeks her with clean hands, not a deceitful heart. The last initiates a longer list, beginning: 'Happy is the man who has obtained wisdom and walks in the Torah of Elyon . . .' (col. ii + frag. 3, lines 3–4); he accepts its disciplines and does not abandon it in troubled times. He meditates on it, is protected from walking in the ways of iniquity, and is raised by it to sit with kings. A subsequent fragment of the text returns to these themes, calling again for a search without deceit, but also admonishing against abandonment of one's inheritance to foreigners, and associating fear of God with walking in the ways of wisdom or the law. Later still, protection is promised against enemies and evil, so that life will be filled with good, peace, and honour, and death will be followed by mourning and remembrance.

Both of these texts, then, seem to presume a relationship between wisdom and Torah, although it is difficult to draw out the nature of that relationship from the surviving material, and both seem also to emphasize the significance of wisdom/ law as protection. There is a strong continuity here, then, between these texts and the apocryphal books, with the influence of Proverbs 1–9 still very marked. In neither does wisdom appear to be personified, but that feature is found in a third work, one of the psalms found in 11Q5 (11QPsalmsᵃ). This work, in column xviii, was known already in a Syriac translation, and called Psalm 154. Here wisdom has a voice and a song, heard from the gates of the righteous and the assembly of the pious; she also has her own gates, as in Prov. 8.34. The psalm is interesting less for the personification, however, than for its statement of wisdom's purposes:

> For it was to make known the glory of YHWH that wisdom was given,
> and to recount the multitude of his achievements was it made known to man
> to make known to the uneducated his strength, to teach the simple his might –
> those distant from her doors, banished from her entrances.
>
> (11Q5 xviii 3–6)

To glorify God is as good as making a sacrifice, and wisdom is supplied as a way to glorify him. When the righteous are together, they talk of wisdom, muse on the Torah, and so glorify God. The same psalm scroll, incidentally, preserves a version of the quest for wisdom which forms part of the appendix in Sir. 51.

If wisdom is personified in at least one text, so too is her female rival from Proverbs 1–9, who appears in 4Q184 (4QWiles of the Wicked Woman). Although there have been other identifications suggested, it seems clear that the woman described in fragment 1 of this text is based on the depictions of the foreign woman and personified folly in Proverbs 1–9. All the elements which made the woman attractive in the original have disappeared, however, and she is now described almost entirely in terms of the danger which she poses: everything about her is sinful and deadly, while to take hold of her is fatal. It may be going too far to say with some scholars, though, that she has become mythologized, or even demonic: the symbolism has merely been pushed to an extreme, and the point of the original largely discarded. Like the woman of Prov. 7, however, she wanders the streets seeking victims, and the path imagery of the original is not only retained but enhanced. Now she seeks not only to lead the uneducated astray, but to corrupt the righteous, tripping them, turning them from the ways of righteousness, and luring them into breaking or twisting the commandments. This is only a portion of a longer text, so we do not know the context of the description, and it may have included a corresponding portrait of wisdom; some of the expressions on the remaining, very small fragments, may suggest that preservation from her is to be achieved through prayer, and there is a probable mention of the Torah. It seems likely that the theme is essentially the need to rely on God and piety to preserve one from a danger that is much greater but less subtle than that posed in Proverbs 1–9 itself.

b. Advice literature

A few texts from Qumran can legitimately be considered advice literature, although this is an area where problems of definition start to intrude. Staying with the clear instances for the moment, perhaps the most straightforward example is 4Q424, a fragmentary text that labours under the inelegant official title '4QInstruction-like composition B'. What we have is a list of admonitions concerning people with particular qualities: one should avoid engaging with them in activities where those qualities would make them incompetent or unhelpful. You should not, for instance, send a deaf man out to investigate a dispute, or get involved in a lawsuit with a liar. Some of these seem forced: it is not clear who in their right mind would send a man with 'smeared eyes' to observe the upright, for example, and they are not, perhaps, intended to be literal, practical advice, so much as to illustrate the point that tasks should be undertaken by the suitably qualified. (The man with smeared eyes, incidentally, is found also on the fragmentary 4Q425, apparently identified with the 'worthless man', so the expression may be idiomatic, with its literal sense employed here to make the point). The list is followed, after all, by another in which the suitably qualified do what they are supposed to do:

> It is a man of insight who will accept instruct[ion],
> A man of knowledge who will obtain wisdom,
> An upright man who will delight in judgment,
> A man of truth who will re[joice in a say]ing
>
> > (4Q424 frag. 3, lines 7–8. The sayings are
> > separated by spaces in the original.)

Much more is preserved of another text, 4QInstruction (also known as 4QSapiential Work A), which has survived in a number of copies (1Q26; 4Q415–18; 4Q423), although we are not in a position to collate all the fragments and establish their order. This work looks, at first glance, like advice literature of a traditional sort, with admonitions about such matters as food, debt, and marriage. Even superficially, however, it reveals some unexpected features. For a start, the recipient of the teaching is addressed throughout as 'understanding one', and then there is a section addressed directly to a woman, which is unprecedented. There is also little interest in worldly success, but an assumption, made explicit frequently, that the addressee is (literally) poor, and expected to remain poor: the text offers advice on coping with poverty, but not on escaping it, while fragmentary references to farming, if to be interpreted literally, suggest an agricultural context, even though poor farmers are unlikely to have been big readers of literature. The preoccupation of the 'understanding one' is supposed to be not with life but with study of something called 'the mystery to be' – a concept related to statements about a divine plan, but the subject of sharp controversy amongst scholars. Without going into the myriad of issues, it looks as though the advice is aimed at someone living a very particular sort of life, against a background of specific religious ideas and revelations. The lifestyle envisaged is not that of the community at Qumran, at least as that is usually understood, but references (in 4Q418 frag. 81, 4Q423 frag. 8) to separation from fleshly spirits and everything which God hates, to God being one's portion and inheritance amongst humans (cf. Num. 18.20), and to honouring him by consecrating oneself, all point to an idea of election, and envisage the adoption of a role which is almost priestly.

There are some fragmentary references to judgement, and it is also made clear that the behaviour which is advocated has some basis in the expectation of ultimate rewards and punishments. To that extent, then, the work shares the preoccupation of wisdom literature with individual benefit. As in Wisdom of Solomon, that benefit may be *post mortem*, and linked to notions of future eschatological judgement. There are some possible references to phrases or ideas found in Job and Ecclesiastes: 4Q418 frag. 95, for instance, warns against 'darkening knowledge' (compare Job 38.2), and frag. 103 seems to speak of material wealth perishing with the individual at death. Proverbs is more certainly an influence, and the fragmentary 4Q418 frag. 221 seems to have another allusion to the prologue of that book. A passage preserved in 4Q417 frag. 1 (formerly known as frag. 2) and 4Q418 frags. 43–45 seems strongly reminiscent of Proverbs 1–9: meditation on the mystery will enable knowledge of truth and evil, wisdom and folly, and every act by its nature, then also discernment of good and evil as expressed in deeds; the 'God of knowledge' is the foundation of truth, and he has set out its foundation in the mystery, expounding everything for humans so that they may walk according to their understanding.

If 4QInstruction is wisdom literature on any reasonable definition, the same is less certainly true of other texts sometimes labelled that way. For example, the Book of Mysteries (1Q27; 4Q299–300; 4Q301?) also refers to understandings of good and evil, but is principally concerned with the eschatological elimination of the wicked, and the overriding importance of understanding the 'mystery', which is the root of wisdom. Some other works, such as 4QWays of Righteousness (4Q420–21), similarly have points of contact with wisdom literature, but are probably not usefully defined that way. Others, like 4Q412 (4QSapiential–Didactic Work A), are really too poorly preserved for a judgement to be made, although they can raise interesting points: 4Q426, for instance, has a speaker declare 'God has put in my heart knowledge and understanding'. We also encounter an issue noted earlier, when we looked at Tobit and wisdom psalms – the employment of content or styles derived from advice literature in very different contexts. For example, we find quite a long, and rather unexpected account of the need to study wisdom in the *Aramaic Levi Document* (4Q213 frag. 1, cols. i–ii), while instructional expressions are used very widely. It is not practical or desirable, then, to establish a corpus of wisdom texts or advice literature at Qumran around which some clear boundary can be drawn.

5. Concluding Remarks

The composition of Jewish wisdom literature does not come to an end with the turn of the eras: there is a great deal more material from subsequent periods, including some which is probably close to the time of Wisdom of Solomon. If space permitted, we could certainly discuss, for instance, the Jewish-Hellenistic *Sentences of Pseudo-Phocylides* (generally dated 100 BCE–100 CE), which incorporates Jewish sources and ideas into Greek gnomic poetry – itself the Hellenistic counterpart of the Near Eastern sayings collections (see especially Wilson 1994: 2005), and there are many later works too (see Küchler 1979). A line has to be drawn somewhere, however, and it has not been possible to examine in depth even the texts which have been described in this chapter. A few points emerge very clearly from these, however, which will be important when we turn to a more general discussion of wisdom in the final chapters. Firstly, although Job and Ecclesiastes leave some mark on the late texts, it is Proverbs – and especially Proverbs 1–9 – that seems to have made the most significant impression. As we saw earlier, this work spoke of instruction in terms that encouraged, or at least permitted, its identification with the Torah. It also presented wisdom as a female figure, who was strongly associated with God, but with whom humans could establish a relationship.

It is probable that much of the later literature picked up these ideas directly from Proverbs 1–9, although it is conceivable that other texts, now lost, had also promulgated them. In any case, however, they supplied an important way of talking about the proper relationship of individuals to God, specifically within a Jewish context of belief in the Torah as a revelation of the divine will. With such instruction available as a gift from God, those who heed it have a significant advantage in the acquisition of wisdom, with its subsequent benefits, and this opens the door also to the association of wisdom with ideas of election. In Wisdom of Solomon and some of the Qumran material, this has further consequences when apocalyptic and eschatological ideas are incorporated into the idea of wisdom's benefits, and the concept of election to potential wisdom also raises questions about exclusivism and determinism.

There is both continuity and change in all this. Arguably the most interesting point, however, is not that the presentation of wisdom and instruction comes to embrace different ideas, but that it does so with considerable ease and little fundamental adaptation. It is a constant that one needs to gain wisdom through instruction in order to gain life and benefits: what changes is the identification of the elements within this framework, especially the nature of the instruction and of the rewards. Just as exhortations to pay attention could readily be borrowed from advice literature to introduce other material, as early as the Psalms, so the basic concept of wisdom and its associated language could be used as a vehicle for a range of ideas. It would be too simple to suppose that wisdom discourse becomes merely a way of talking about things, but there may be some truth in the idea that it does become a way of thinking about things, and of relating concepts to each other.

Chapter 6

Wisdom Thought

The array of literature discussed over the last few chapters seems daunting in its scope and variety, and it is not immediately clear that we can find any core set of beliefs among the mutual resemblances or shared interests that draw all these texts together as 'wisdom literature'. Indeed, we should be wary of presuming that any such common ground exists: shared themes or forms do not always reflect shared ideas. The search for a specific and distinct outlook in wisdom literature, moreover, has often been driven by assumptions which lie outside the texts themselves. If, for example, we could be sure that the sort of covenantal or salvation-historical ideas to be found in much other biblical literature were normative in Jewish theology of the biblical period, then it would be reasonable to seek a particular basis for any dissenting voices. Equally, if we could be sure that wisdom literature emerged from a specific social or religious context, then it would be fair to look for an ideology associated with that context. Such beliefs, to which many scholars subscribe, must await examination in the next chapter, but we can have no real certainty in these matters, and it is clear that much of the discussion about wisdom thought has become caught up in a sort of circular argumentation: theories about the content of the texts are used to bolster theories about their origin, and theories about their origin used to bolster theories about their content.

If we are to avoid such circularity, then it is obviously important to approach the texts, so far as possible, without presupposition. The problems of method, however, do not end there. Difficult though it may be to date them, the various wisdom books clearly emerged over a long period, during which, it is fair to suppose, ideas may have changed and developed considerably in the face of altered circumstances and new influences. Correspondingly, there is nothing inherently wrong, for example, in the common supposition that Ben Sira might have adapted whatever basic outlook he inherited from earlier wisdom literature, and possibly discarded some elements of it while incorporating other ideas. Nobody, furthermore, would find it controversial to suggest that even the biblical wisdom books express considerable differences of opinion about some significant ideas.

Consequently, if there is some body of wisdom thought, it is evidently neither static nor entirely consistent, and we can find ourselves in a position where we start to describe as 'wisdom thinking' not just concepts which are found in every wisdom text, but concepts which are found in any wisdom text. Indeed, a high proportion of the statements made about 'wisdom' in modern scholarship are, strictly speaking, statements about particular ideas expressed only in one or more sections of the book of Proverbs, and we have absolutely no idea how generally some of those ideas were held, or even known.

There is a further wrinkle to this problem. The book of Job certainly, and Ecclesiastes very possibly, make use of characters who are described as 'wise', but whose views are not necessarily shared by the writer or by other 'wise' characters. Disagreement between the wisdom books may be mirrored by disagreement within the wisdom books, and in that case who, if anybody, is expressing 'wisdom thought'? If we set out to find such a thing, then it is as though we are stepping into the middle of a vigorous debate, searching not for some explicit consensus between the participants, but for the common ground which underpins their different views. It is not difficult to understand, therefore, why much of the scholarly discussion of this subject has focused upon such things as wisdom's understanding of cause and effect, or its methods for ascertaining knowledge: wisdom thought is usually described not as a set of specific opinions, but as a worldview, or perhaps a methodology.

Describing even this presents difficulties. When most of the wisdom literature is poetic and some is aphoristic too, then it can be difficult to determine the explicit opinions being stated, let alone the implicit outlook: we are not dealing with a type of discourse in which all the 'i's are dotted and the 't's crossed, but with compositions that rely heavily on figurative speech, and which may value vividness or brevity over clarity and precision. This can lead to sharp divisions within scholarly opinion, as when some scholars read Prov. 8, for example, as a literal or mythological account of wisdom as an independent being, while others see a figurative, literary affirmation of wisdom's relationship to God. In the sayings collections, similarly, most scholars these days would assume that statements about reward and punishment presume some form of divine judgement, but it has been maintained vehemently by a few that God goes unmentioned not for lack of space in these aphorisms, but because some other mechanism of retribution was assumed. Without going into those particular problems just yet, it should be apparent both that it may be difficult to uncover the assumptions of the texts, and that what we find is going to depend very much on the ways in which we approach the texts.

1. Creation and world-order

Some of the problems of method become clear if we turn first to what is often seen as wisdom literature's most important and distinctive feature: an interest in the created order, both as a source for human knowledge and as the context for human behaviour. Before examining that directly, however, we have to step back a little.

a. Wisdom, religion, and nation

Nobody would attempt to claim that the Jewish wisdom literature which we possess is itself 'secular' – not least because it refers frequently to God, and has a marked interest in divine retribution. It has sometimes been suggested, however, that our texts derive from a tradition that was originally rooted in pragmatism and individual experience, rather than in any sort of piety. Indeed, some attempts have been made, most notably by William McKane (1970), to separate out within Proverbs itself an original layer which was essentially devoid of religious ideology before later revision and supplementation of the material gave it a religious tone (cf. also Whybray 1979). Those attempts fail to make their case on literary grounds: claims that the early 'secular' layers can be uncovered using objective internal criteria have failed to survive subsequent scrutiny (see Weeks 1994: 57–73, and the sensible comments in Boström 1990: 36–9). Appeals to the earlier, non-Israelite literature are also unconvincing, not least because that literature is itself often deeply religious. We have no particular reason, then, to suppose that our literature either emerged from or itself manifests a tradition of secular minded pragmatism, and it is likely that Jewish wisdom literature embodied religious ideas from the outset. The nature and distinctiveness of those ideas, however, has been the topic of much discussion.

One of the first characteristics which we noted earlier about the biblical wisdom literature was its apparent lack of interest in the national aspects of Jewish religious thought: it does not present an analysis of history, an explicit covenantal theology, or, indeed, anything which is very exclusively Jewish beyond the use of the divine name. Our subsequent survey of the literature has thrown up nothing which might lead us to discard that description, or even to modify it substantially, but it has raised a number of points which might help us to put the non-nationalism and absence of history in the texts into a clearer perspective.

Firstly, it is clear that some sort of relationship exists between our texts and many pieces of foreign literature, even if it is difficult to characterize that relationship with any precision. It is also obvious that some later Jewish texts draw heavily on Proverbs, at least. Our texts lie, therefore, somewhere between various others – but amongst those others, we find less reluctance to engage with national and historical issues. Most Egyptian texts do not present historical analyses, but some do (e.g. *Merikare, Amenemhet*), and quite a lot of them subscribe explicitly to the ideology of kingship which is a strong feature of Egyptian political and national thought. Equally, Ben Sira and Wisdom of Solomon, to take just the major late works, have an interest in history as a resource for understanding human or divine behaviour, even if they do not present straightforward salvation-historical or covenantal outlines of the past; they are also interested in ideas of election and Torah. Unless the biblical literature, therefore, was radically different from what preceded and what followed it, we should not presume that its silence about history and the nation reflects some necessary and inherent characteristic, let alone suppose that the writers positively rejected historical and national ideas under some ideological or generic compulsion.

In fact, the biblical wisdom books seem to have very varied attitudes in this general area. The ideas presented in Job are probably least compatible with the sort of historical and theological ideas associated with Deuteronomy and the Deuteronomistic history: it is difficult to imagine the God of that book binding himself in a covenant relationship, or adopting any sort of self-limiting relationship. While it seems unlikely, however, that the book was deliberately written to symbolize Israel's destruction and restoration (as is sometimes suggested), its questions and ideas can fruitfully be applied to that situation, and lead us into the sort of territory occupied by Second Isaiah, with a supremely powerful deity and issues around the purpose and degree of suffering. Job is not covenantal, and sets its story outside the scope of Mosaic law, but its ideas resonate all the same with those found in some more historical post-exilic literature.

The various works in Proverbs 10–30 have little to say that is relevant here, although some sayings surely raise questions about their underlying ideology and its relationship with other Hebrew writings, e.g. 'A righteous man is immovable for ever, while wicked men will not dwell in the land' (10.30) would surely have Deuteronomic resonances for a Jewish reader, even if 'in the land' might simultaneously be taken to mean 'on the earth'. Proverbs 1–9, however, leans strongly towards an understanding of instruction as Torah, and probably draws on the exclusivist language of a post-exilic debate on identity for its idea of the 'foreign woman', so it is hardly cut off from covenantal and nationalist discourse. It is not itself non-covenantal for any apparent theological reason, but because it maintains a focus throughout on the individual (sometimes in relation to their community), rather than on the community or nation, and it does have some links with the more individually centred concept of a new covenant in Jeremiah and Ezekiel (see Weeks, 2007: 112–3). There is a clash here in theory – Deuteronomy thinks in terms of collective reward and punishment – but in practice it seems hard to believe that even the most vehement Deuteronomists would have paid no attention to questions of individual reward or punishment in everyday life.

The attitude of Ecclesiastes, finally, is very hard to judge. On the one hand, Qohelet shows no interest at all in the nation, but on the other he draws several times on the past to make points, albeit vaguely (e.g. 9.13-16), and has a very definite interest in time itself. His focus on the hiddenness of divine purposes might seem to preclude the revelation of Torah, but his apparent belief in the existence of such purposes and his emphasis on the reality of judgement both give him some important points of contact with apocalyptic literature. The nation may not be important, but in Qohelet's monologue, human life is very much played out against the backdrop of past, present and future.

All three of the major biblical wisdom texts, then, have points of contact with more historically orientated Hebrew writings, but the points of contact and the writings are different in each case, and there is no consistent ground of disagreement with salvation-historical or covenantal ideas. In other words, the wisdom books share a lack of concern with Jewish history, but they do not share any obvious motive for that lack of interest or possess any single view on related areas. Given the openness to history in earlier and later works, it would seem deeply problematic to derive any sort of defining characteristic of wisdom literature from this phenomenon, and their relationships with ideas of national history and covenant seem as much to divide as to unite the wisdom books. To put it another way, the biblical wisdom literature is not apparently underpinned by any specific antipathy to religious ideas rooted in concepts of nation or history.

b. Wisdom and creation

A significant number of scholars have proposed, in fact, that the distinctiveness of biblical wisdom literature in this respect actually reflects not the rejection of national ideas, so much as the adoption of a different, more basic theological foundation in the notion of the created world. Correspondingly, it has become quite common to speak of a 'creation theology' in wisdom literature, but this tag embraces a number of different observations, and it is important to be aware that the wisdom literature itself does not draw these together into a clear or coherent system of thought.

Among the biblical texts, there are explicit references to God's initial creation of the world in Proverbs 1–9 and Job. The former is particularly concerned with the validation of wisdom, emphasizing that God used it in his creation (3.19-20), and extrapolating from this (in 8.22-31) the antiquity of wisdom's association with the divine. In Job, on the other hand, the principal purpose of the references is to demonstrate God's power and independence (9.4-10; 26.5-14; and especially the divine speeches of chs 38–41); wisdom, according to Job 28.23-28, is not the key to all creation, but almost an incidental discovery, made while God was creating stormy weather. When Ben Sira and Wisdom of Solomon pick up the theme, they are clearly doing so under the influence of Proverbs 1–9 (cf. Sir. 1.1-10; Wis. 9.9), although they introduce ideas of their own. The obscure 'Words of Agur', however, apparently draw on a comparison with divine power over the world at creation (Prov. 30.4), which is more reminiscent of Job.

Elsewhere, Proverbs 10.1–22.16 contains a number of sayings about God's creation of individual humans or their attributes (14.31; 16.4, 11; 17.5; 20.12; 22.2), and Prov. 29.13 may express a similar idea. The reference here, however, is not to primeval creation, but to a continuing divine activity in the creation or shaping of human lives. This idea is also present in Ecclesiastes, which has God create events and assign tasks or times (see, e.g. 3.10-11; 7.14), and, indeed, portrays him as maker of everything (11.5) and everyone (12.1). The book does not, however, ground his creative activities in a specific act of creating the world. Perhaps this is to be linked with Qohelet's notion of perpetual, endless continuity, and it is noteworthy that the depiction of natural processes in his prologue (1.4-7) avoids any mention at all of God's role.

When it comes to the primeval creation itself, then, some of the wisdom literature is interested in using it as a way to affirm the significance of wisdom or the power of God, but it would be difficult to maintain either that this interest reflects some single, defining set of ideas, or that much of it is especially distinctive (see, for example, Ps. 33.6-9; Isa. 45.11-12 or Amos 5.8-9 for affirmations of divine power based on the creation). More importantly, it is an interest confined only to certain of the texts. The discussion of creation theology in wisdom literature, in fact, has less to do with the creation *per se*, than with a perception that the literature is interested in the ordering of the world: the issue is not the fact of creation, in other words, but the result of creation. Especially in German-speaking scholarship of the last fifty years, there have been a number of attempts to find in wisdom literature (and sometimes beyond) a concept of order inherent in the created world, which forms the basis of that literature's outlook.

c. World order

These attempts have focused, in particular, on the way in which consequences flow from actions, and the extent to which they do so as a result of something inherent in the actions or the world, rather than because of a specific divine intervention – some scholars speak of the 'deed-consequence' relationship or nexus (see especially Koch 1955, which extends the idea beyond the wisdom literature, but understands it to be challenged in Job and Ecclesiastes). This is an area, however, in which it is very difficult to assess the evidence. On the one hand, Proverbs in particular commonly speaks about consequences without specifying the means by which they come about, and we can hardly presume that when the writers fail to mention God explicitly this must be because they considered his direct involvement unnecessary. Some scholars have also complicated matters by supposing there to be a mixture of ideas from different periods in the material from Proverbs, which would make it difficult to extrapolate any general view from those statements which actually are explicit. On the other hand, it is not clear that one size fits all when it comes to statements about cause and effect. Hartmut Gese, for example (1958: 34–35), understands the wisdom literature to state that the hard-working man will become wealthy through his actions and the lazy man poor, as the consequence of an order inherent in the world, 'and likewise the righteous will attain success, the unrighteous failure.' It is not at all clear, however, that the cases of work leading to wealth and of righteousness leading to success are comparable, and it is only the claim that they are which necessitates an appeal to some underpinning order; Gese, in other words, is begging the question. The wisdom literature itself gives us no reason to suppose that its writers understood there to be some single principle of causation behind all events.

Appeals to external evidence are also unhelpful here. Hans Heinrich Schmid (1966, developed further in Schmid 1968) has tried to make a case for the existence of a single basic concept of world-order across the ancient Near East, but the variations he is forced to allow across the separate cultures dilute the notion to the point where it is all but meaningless. Many others (including Gese) have looked more specifically to the Egyptian idea of *maat*, which we encountered earlier, but that is by no means just a mechanical principle of cause and effect, as biblical scholars sometimes assume, and it is inseparably bound to a whole range of other Egyptian ideas (see Fox 1995; Assmann 2006). As has sometimes been pointed out, moreover, Egyptian culture had itself shifted substantially to an emphasis on direct divine control and activity some considerable time before Israel came into existence, so is unlikely to have contributed a concept of world order which downplayed the direct role of God (see Boström 1990: 95–6).

The evidence hardly pushes us, then, towards an assumption that wisdom literature is based on or informed by a particular notion of consequences built into the structure of the world, or inherent in every action. Qohelet's views are interesting in this respect, since he combines an interest in quite autonomous natural phenomena (1.5-7) with a strong belief in divine judgement and control. In Eccl. 11.3 he notes that, 'If the clouds are full of rain, it is on the ground that they'll empty themselves, and whether a tree falls in the south or in the north, the place where the tree falls is where it will be', and he follows this with advice not to waste time by watching the clouds and wind – but these observations are set in the context of human uncertainty about the future and about God's activities, which lead him to advise a cautious, belt-and-braces approach to life (11.1-2, 5-6). At one level, therefore, cause and effect is trivial – clouds rain on the ground, trees lie where they fall – but on another level, everything is subject to the powerful but unknowable actions of God. Although Proverbs, in particular, is more confident about how one should behave, there is no reason to assume that any of the wisdom literature is very different in this respect: it recognizes that certain consequences may flow predictably from certain actions or phenomena (that there are, we might say, laws of nature), but also that there are deeper principles or influences at work, potentially linked to divine activity.

If there were no cause and effect, and if the world behaved in an entirely random and unpredictable way, then there would be no possibility of human wisdom – and human survival, indeed, would be a tricky proposition. To the extent that it resists such a notion, wisdom literature correspondingly asserts the existence of order in the world, but this remains subject to the interference of other forces, and it is hard to see how we are dealing with a concept more powerful or integrated than most commonplace human expectations about causation, at least until the very late Wisdom of Solomon declares '. . . reliable knowledge of those things which exist, to know the composition of the world and action of the elements' (Wis. 7.17).

d. Empiricism and natural theology

If it is difficult to isolate a particular theory of order or creation in the texts, Qohelet's remarks point to what may be a more fruitful area for discussion: the interest of wisdom literature in observation of the world, which might loosely be considered the practical aspect of a creation theology. Advice literature, of course, conventionally roots itself in human authority and experience, and this is true even in Proverbs 1–9 and Ben Sira, when the advice itself may include the divinely revealed Jewish Torah. To this extent, wisdom literature presents a counterpart to the emphasis on divine revelation found in much other biblical literature, and it is sometimes described as offering a natural theology, or an understanding of the divine extrapolated from experience of the divinely created world (see e.g. Collins 1977; Barr 1994: 90–94; 1999: 476–8). That is an attractive idea, and it is not difficult to point to places where the writers or their characters draw on personal observation (e.g. Job 15.17-19; Prov. 7.6-27; 24.30-34; Eccl. 9.13-16). In many cases, however, they are just employing illustrative anecdotes rather than formulating general conclusions on the basis of specific experiences, and when we examine its attitudes to experience and observation more closely, it becomes clear that the wisdom literature holds rather complicated views on the subject.

Because he is often noted for his empiricism, Qohelet provides a good starting point here: this is a character, after all, who apparently draws on natural phenomena to present his view of the world (1.4-7), who recounts at length his own experiments and experiences (especially 1.12–2.26), and who frequently punctuates his monologue with statements about what he has seen. The natural phenomena, however, serve as evidence for his conclusion that human perception is necessarily limited (1.11), and the insights which he gains from his experience are not into the hidden processes of the world, but into the ignorance and transience of humanity. He realizes, moreover, that what humans see, and the conclusions that they draw from it, may be deliberately confusing (1.16-22), or even disastrously misleading (8.10-13): his repeated affirmation of divine judgement, one of the few things in which he places continuing confidence, is not drawn from observation, and is presented as contradicting common human experience. So, when he finally advises against watching the wind and clouds rather than working (11.3-6), Qohelet is making an important point about the inadequacy of observation, the impossibility of genuine insight, and the need to get on with life all the same. If there is empiricism in Ecclesiastes, there is also seemingly a strong critique of empiricism.

The treatment is different in the book of Job, but no less critical: as readers we see for ourselves that the knowledge claimed from experience by the friends is unable to comprehend an unprecedented situation, whilst Job's own stance is transformed not by his acquisition of new experience, but by his direct encounter with God (42.5). The fact that the issue is dealt with through debate, however, does raise the possibility that Job's friends are actually presenting a conventional opinion, and that the criticisms of human experience in Job and Ecclesiastes are in fact an indication of the weight placed on such experience by earlier, less 'pessimistic' wisdom writers. That idea, though, runs straight into the problem that other wisdom literature seems no less cautious. It is apparently basic to the ideas of Proverbs 1–9, after all, that human perception of a situation may be false unless it is informed by prior instruction, and that bad things may very easily seem good. This theme is found elsewhere in Proverbs (e.g. 16.25), and the book's interest in human advice or learning from experience lies alongside a parallel interest in obedience to words and commandments which are probably divine (note 13.13; 16.20; 19.16; 30.5-6). It is difficult to make a case, then, that earlier wisdom literature was more straightforwardly rooted in human experience of the world.

In fact, too great an emphasis upon empiricism risks imposing upon the literature a dichotomy between 'natural theology' and 'revelation' which owes more to later Christian modes of discourse than to the biblical literature itself. Human and divine sources of knowledge are not so easily separated even in the earliest Near Eastern advice literature: the Egyptian *Ptahhotep*, for instance, validates its content by means of the protagonist's own success in life – personal experience – but traces that content back through a chain of ancestral transmission to an initial divine revelation. Much later, Wisdom of Solomon presents something that looks rather like a natural theology in 13.1-9, when it discusses human attempts to find the divine through God's creations – but the book condemns these as inadequate, and contrasts them with the superior relationship offered to Israel. Ben Sira also hints at the possibility of a natural theology when he says of wisdom that God 'poured it out upon all his works' (1.9), but he immediately makes it clear that humans can only attain wisdom by divine gift, and later has wisdom dwell specifically in Jerusalem (24.8-12). In between the early and the late, it is difficult to identify any wisdom literature which is solely and explicitly rooted in human experience, and if we overemphasize the experiential, empirical aspects of our texts, then we risk forcing upon them a separation of ideas which would have been alien to the writers themselves.

It is true that the biblical wisdom texts show little interest in the prophetic revelation which is central to much other Hebrew literature, and that they do not all seem keen to embrace the idea of a revealed Torah – although visionary and cultic modes of divine communication are hardly excluded (e.g. Prov. 29.18; Job 33.14-18; Eccl. 4.17–5.6 ET 5.1-7). It hardly seems necessary, however, to attribute this lack of interest to some fundamentally different outlook. In the first place, direct divine revelation is elsewhere portrayed as central to the relationship between God and Israel, but not to the running of most people's day-to-day lives, so that its subject matter may be a key reason for the different focus of our literature. We should not project the national, historical concerns of the historical and prophetic books on to every area of Jewish religion. More importantly, perhaps, we must reckon with the fact that there is a strong strain of thought which does link wisdom to revelation of the divine will, and which runs from Proverbs 1–9 through into the later Jewish texts. Even if such insight is questioned or seriously limited in Job and Ecclesiastes, we can hardly take a rejection of divine revelation to be basic or intrinsic to wisdom literature.

In short, wisdom literature does draw on human experience, but not in some consistent and programmatic way which might lead us to think in terms of a particular wisdom epistemology. It is not wrong to observe that wisdom literature has an interest in the importance of human experience, but when it nowhere explicitly develops any general approach based on this, and instead asserts the limitations of that experience, it would seem perverse to conclude that the interest is underpinned by some conscious and distinctive natural theology or philosophy. Our own categories might lead us to suppose that the writers must have had such an approach even if they were not aware of it, but it is difficult to impose those categories when the texts themselves do not clearly share our own distinction between observation and revelation, and when their focus may be as much a product of their subject matter as of any underlying ideology.

e. Conclusions

Whatever the assumptions behind our texts, to speak of a 'creation theology' or suchlike in wisdom literature is potentially misleading just because it implies a purpose and deliberation where there is surely none. The writers give no indication that they have formulated a particular approach in this area, let alone that they are attempting to promote such an approach. As Roland Murphy once shrewdly observed, '. . . wisdom's alleged search for order is our modern reconstruction. It asks a question never raised by Israel: On what conviction is your wisdom based?' (1978: 41 n. 4; cf. 1996: 116). There is a risk also that we may be imposing distinctions which would not have been recognized by the writers and their audience, not least when we contrast direct divine revelation with attempts to understand the divine will based on personal or accumulated human experience, or try to distinguish between natural causation and divine retribution. It is in the nature of theological hermeneutics that we should attempt to interpret biblical texts in terms of our own questions and categories, but it is also important that we should not read our results back into those texts and suppose them to reflect the conscious views of the original writers. We may find a creation theology in wisdom literature, but that does not mean that the writers must have put one there.

In fact, though, it is doubtful that this is a very helpful way of understanding the literature, even if we set aside questions of intent. Creation itself is not a major concern for all or most of the biblical wisdom books, and it is not treated in a single way; theories about a world order or a principle of causation in the created world are controversial and problematic, except when understood in the vaguest terms; empiricism and a quest for understanding through observation, finally, are condemned at least as much as they are employed in our texts. We may very well wonder whether wisdom literature would ever have been credited with a creation theology were scholars not concerned to identify a theoretical basis for apparent differences between these texts and others. An emphasis on those differences, moreover, can easily lead us to neglect or consign as secondary those places where the biblical wisdom writers (and their successors) did in fact draw on ideas of revelation or Torah, which sit uncomfortably in the 'creation-theology' paradigm.

2. God

Alongside its concerns with humanity and the world, wisdom literature has a profound interest in God and in divine action, especially but not exclusively divine judgement. Correspondingly, much of the literature seeks also to understand the relationship between the human and the divine, in terms of both the influence of God on human lives, and the appropriate response of humans to the power of God over them. Again, there is no unanimity amongst the writers, but there is, perhaps, a greater degree of consistency than is sometimes assumed.

a. The unity and power of God

It hardly needs saying that Job and Ecclesiastes both affirm, very emphatically, the supreme authority of God, and the inability of humans to constrain, or perhaps even to comprehend, divine action. Proverbs 10.1–22.16 also emphasizes, in a number of sayings, the ability of God to overrule human intentions and to control human lives:

> The mind's arrangements are up to man, but the tongue's response is from YHWH. (16.1)

> A human's mind may plan his route, but it is YHWH who places his steps. (16.9; cf. Jer. 10.23)

> Many plans are in the mind of a man, but what will occur is what YHWH has planned. (19.21)

> The steps of a man are from YHWH, and a human – what can he understand of his way? (20.24)

> There is no wisdom, and no understanding, and no plan that stands in the way of YHWH:

> A horse is readied for the day of battle, while the victory is YHWH's. (21.30-31; cf. Ps. 33.17)

Similar concerns are found in advice literature from elsewhere, for instance 'The words which men say are one thing, but that which the god does, another' (*Amenemope* 19.16-17). It is difficult, therefore, to see them as a secondary Jewish religious attempt to impose limits on the ambitions of advice literature, and the most we can say is that our other major biblical work, Proverbs 1–9, is more concerned with the power of God to enhance human life than with his ability to control or thwart human intentions. So far as we can tell, wisdom literature always operated with an assumption that the human quest for success in life was constrained by divine actions and intentions, and that should hardly surprise us: it would be strange if the writers did not share the fundamentally religious worldview characteristic of their culture. We shall turn shortly to one significant implication of this – the need to align one's behaviour, so far as possible, with the divine will. It is important first, however, to observe some of the more strictly theological consequences, and in particular the role assigned by the literature to God.

One of the most distinctive features of the Egyptian instructions, which has provoked much discussion, is their marked tendency to speak not of individual deities within the polytheistic Egyptian religious system, but of 'the god'. Since other deities are sometimes mentioned as well, it is clear that this does not indicate some separate, monotheistic inclination, but it does point to the need for the literature to express divine power and action within the world without some confusing distribution of responsibilities between different gods (especially when different readers might attribute particular qualities to different gods); the convention is sometimes found in other Egyptian literature when the same degree of generality is needed (see especially Hornung 1982, and further references in Weeks 2007: 30–32). It is difficult to assess the underlying theological ideas, and we should be wary of thinking in terms of a 'godhead', if that is taken to imply an actual entity. Elsewhere, *Ahiqar* tends to speak of 'the gods' in general contexts, although Šamaš, as god of justice, is also invoked, while the analogous texts from Babylon often refer to 'your god', or similar.

The religious situation within early Judaism is complicated and controversial, and monotheism, as we would define it now, is not assumed by all scholars to have been the religious norm in Israelite or Judahite society. Be that as it may, and whether or not, say, Job's references to the 'children of God' should be understood in polytheistic terms, the biblical wisdom literature resembles its Egyptian counterparts in treating a single God as the total embodiment of divinity. A variety of divine names is used, to be sure, with Proverbs generally preferring 'YHWH' and Ecclesiastes 'Elohim', while Job mostly uses 'El', 'Eloah', and 'Elohim', but also 'Shaddai', with 'YHWH' appearing outside the narrative sections (chs 1–2; 42) only in 12.9; 28.28, and in the introductions to speeches at 38.1; 40.1, 3, 6. There is no single way in which the texts refer to God, therefore, but it is also clear that they are each referring throughout to a single being. This deity is supreme god, creator god, and judge of humanity, who watches, controls, and intervenes. He is not explicitly linked to a specific place or nation before Ben Sira, but is effectively god of the whole world, and while he may have particular attributes – the God of Job, for example, is frequently portrayed as a storm-god – he is not confined to a single divine role by those attributes. Whether or not the context in which they emerged was effectively monotheistic, then, the texts speak about God in a way which is unconstrained by ideas of him as the god 'of something' or 'of somewhere'.

This frees the writers to talk about humanity and divinity in very general terms, without reference to the role of any other deities or differentiation between human nations, and the biblical wisdom texts are correspondingly free of explicit concerns with apostasy, idolatry, or any of the religious polemic often associated with universalist claims elsewhere in biblical literature. The wisdom books before Wisdom of Solomon, at least, do not promote the uniqueness or supremacy of their deity, but presume it as a basic constituent of their discourse. On the other hand, the convention (if we may describe it as such) also places God in a role very different from that of a national deity, who is bound by a different set of duties and expectations, and when Ben Sira and Wisdom of Solomon later introduce this dimension, it is the role of the nation which is redefined, rather than the universal role of God. If Proverbs 1–9 already has similar ideas about a special role for Israel and its Torah, it is careful to express them without explicit reference to the nation.

While, then, it is problematic to speak of a 'creation theology' in wisdom literature, it is much less difficult to speak of a 'creator theology', which may not be unique to that literature, but which is intrinsic to its character. The texts portray God in a way which is congenial to the modern theological mind, and so may seem to us unremarkable, but that portrayal is distinctive in the ancient context. Furthermore, the obvious artificiality with which the Egyptian texts achieve something similar may tell against it being simply a product of some more general trend toward universalism or monotheism in the post-exilic period, and suggests, indeed, that we may be looking at an expectation associated with such texts for reasons connected with their genre and scope. We have good reason to suppose that the Egyptian writers shared the basic religious presuppositions of their contemporaries, but adopted a particular mode of theological discourse within their instructional writings, and it is not unreasonable to suspect that something similar was true of the Jewish wisdom writers. That is not to say that there are no differences or even contradictions to be found if we set, for instance, Job and Deuteronomy side-by-side: the point is rather that they were not intended to be set side-by-side.

b. Fear of God

Just as there are different divine roles and aspects of divinity, so there are also different ways and levels at which humans may respond to the divine. Wisdom literature is conscious of such day-to-day activities as prayer and sacrifice (e.g. Prov. 15.8, 29), but it has a particularly strong interest in the 'fear of God', or 'fear of YHWH' (see Murphy 1987). This expression is used quite commonly in other biblical literature (Plath 1963; Becker 1965; Derousseaux 1970), has counterparts elsewhere in the ancient Near East, and probably originates in ideas about the actual fear or awe which may be inspired by the divine (Gruber 1990). It sometimes retains some of this flavour even in late texts (e.g. 2 Chron. 20.29; Isa. 59.18-19), but it more typically describes a proper position or attitude adopted by humans in relation to God, rather than an emotional response to God.

In many contexts, we could loosely substitute 'piety' for 'fear of God', but there are a number of other connotations, and the implication can vary even within the same texts: when, for example, the reluctant prophet Jonah says that he fears YHWH, he is expressing his religious affiliation (Jon. 1.9), but when the sailors fear YHWH a few verses later (1.16), we are being told of a reaction to his power, which provokes efforts to appease him. Although it is not generally difficult to understand what the expression means in any given context, therefore, it is not easy to provide a specific definition which covers all the uses, and there may have been neither a single, precise understanding, nor any fixed development of the expression over time. Just as words like 'faith' can be used quite freely in modern religious discourse, even though the underlying concepts may be understood in a variety of ways, so 'fear of God' probably encapsulates a common understanding that there is a proper relationship with God, but does not in itself specify that relationship.

It is particularly striking to observe that, for some writers at least, 'fear of God' is by no means simply a posture of subservience, and involves something more than just deciding to accept or obey God. In Deuteronomy, for example, one learns to fear God through exposure to the Torah, and this fear is something that can be taught (4.10; 17.19; 31.12-13): it is a willingness and ability to obey the commandments that is acquired through education in them. This is subsequently picked up in the idea of a new covenant, when Jeremiah has God declare, 'I shall give to them a single mind and a single way, so as to fear me all the time . . . and I shall put the fear of me in their minds, so as not to turn from me' (Jer. 32.39-40). Similarly, Isa. 11.2 speaks of the 'stump of Jesse' being endowed with '. . . the spirit of YHWH, . . . the spirit of wisdom and of understanding, the spirit of counsel and of power, the spirit of knowledge and of the fear of YHWH.' These texts appear to view the fear of God as something that one must acquire, by gift or effort. For Deuteronomy and Jeremiah, it is a prerequisite for obedience, and in Isaiah it is an intellectual skill or quality. Psalm 119.34, where the psalmist prays for understanding so that he may keep the Torah, drives home the point that for some biblical writers, at least, it is not enough just to want to do the right thing: one must know how to do the right thing, and fear of God is associated with such knowledge.

This general idea appears to underpin the understanding of Proverbs 1–9. In chapter 2, fear of YHWH is promised as a reward for heeding instruction, in the context of that chapter's complicated conditional construction: 'My son, if you accept my words . . . so as to bend your ear to wisdom . . . then you will understand the fear of YHWH and find knowledge of God. For it is YHWH who gives wisdom . . . then you will understand rightness and justice and equity – every good path. For wisdom will enter your heart . . .' (Prov. 2.1-10). Fear of God is something gained through instruction, and facilitated by wisdom, while the structure of the poem sets understanding the fear of God in parallel with understanding rightness. Here too, therefore, fear of God is not simple piety or an initial religious impulse, but something which must be understood through teaching, and which is associated with the prior gift of wisdom. To paraphrase a little: one must accept teaching and receive wisdom in order to know God and understand how to behave as he wishes, because it is God who provides the wisdom which will shape the way one thinks.

Correspondingly, as we noted earlier, the mottoes at the beginning and end of Proverbs 1–9, are not an assertion that one must be pious to be wise, but, as the Hebrew is most naturally read, a claim that understanding of the divine will is achieved through wisdom:

> Fear of YHWH is the start of knowledge: it is wisdom and instruction that fools despise. (1.7)

> Fear of YHWH is the beginning of wisdom, and understanding is knowledge of the holy. (9.10)

A similar idea seems to be expressed elsewhere in Proverbs, when 15.33 claims that 'Wisdom's teaching is the fear of YHWH, and humility goes before honour', which apparently means that one must submit to teaching before achieving the rewards of fearing God; compare 22.4: 'The reward for humility is fear of YHWH – wealth, and honour, and life'. In Psalm 34, the second half of which is instructional, the psalmist promises to teach his 'sons' the fear of YHWH (which the next verse associates with long life and enjoyment of what is good), and Ps. 111.10 echoes Prov. 1.7.

This understanding of the fear of God, however, does not permeate all the wisdom literature. As we observed earlier, Ben Sira's ideas about wisdom as a process lead him to a more complicated presentation (albeit one probably rooted in the claims of Proverbs 1–9), while in the poem of Job 28, fear of 'the Lord' (Hebrew 'Adonai' here, not YHWH) and avoidance of evil are more simply equated with wisdom and understanding. The expression is used elsewhere in Job and in Ecclesiastes, but not directly in association with wisdom and teaching. The fact that such an association is still made in 4Q525 (4QBeatitudes), however, suggests that we are not dealing with the transformation of an idea over time. Some literature, including both Deuteronomy and Proverbs 1–9, picks up the common concept of fearing God, and gives it a particular association with an acquired understanding of how to obey God, which can be expressed in terms of wisdom, teaching, and divine gift. This is not an association confined to wisdom literature, or even present in all wisdom literature, so we should be wary of claiming it to be 'wisdom thought'.

If it is difficult to find some specific connotation for the expression running through our wisdom literature, the fact that it is used at all should not be neglected. Although those scholars who seek a secular basis for wisdom naturally try to exclude the occurrences in Proverbs as secondary, the notion that humans should stand in a particular relationship with God seems fundamental to a literature which is so interested in human life, divine judgement, and the supremacy of God's will. In Job 15.4, Eliphaz accuses Job of 'shattering fear and hacking back what can be contemplated before God', because his wisdom has become empty and his words perverse: it is a key task of wisdom to preserve or instil a relationship with the deity which is properly submissive, but which is not devoid of intellectual content. As we saw earlier, for Qohelet it may be the possession of this relationship which ultimately counts for more than individual deeds, and for Proverbs 1–9, standing in such a relationship offers the crucial benefit of insight into God's will. The biblical wisdom literature emerges within the context of Jewish religion, is concerned with human survival and prosperity in the world, and views God as creator and controller of that world: it is surprising, then, neither that it should seek to establish the proper relationship between humans and God, nor that it should use the common Hebrew expression for such a relationship. Of course, this expression may be associated with ideas of obedience and Torah, but it is part of the terminology of individual relationships, and does not in itself evoke particular ideas about relationships with God mediated through membership of a nation.

c. Conclusions

There is much more that could be said about the presentation of God in the individual texts, but if we are looking at the literature as a whole, what stands out is the strong emphasis on God as god of the world. This enables the writers to speak about very general issues and concepts without reference to specific national and historical relationships, and is a type of discourse found also in analogous literature from elsewhere. Whether or not that literature has exercised a direct influence on the Hebrew writers, it is fair to suppose that they, like their foreign counterparts, are motivated by a desire to engage with the questions at this level, rather than by an ideological rejection, as such, of theological ideas rooted in more local or national concerns. Corresponding to this presentation of God, we find an interest in the proper human relationship with God that is again largely unconstrained by such concepts as covenant or election. Neither the presentation of God, however, nor the expression of that relationship is unique to wisdom literature, while the individual wisdom texts treat each as a starting point for their own discussions, rather than as a fixed and detailed doctrine. We cannot really speak of wisdom thought here then, so much as of common ground occupied by the wisdom writers, or of a mode of discourse that they share, but over which they hold no strict monopoly.

3. Wisdom and instruction

After the broader questions about the world, God, and human relationships with God, it is important not to overlook some of the issues which have more to do with the literature's understanding of its own nature and function. Of course, we have touched on these questions much earlier in this introduction, and there is no need to look again directly at some of the issues covered there. It may be helpful, however, to begin by reaching back to the very start of our discussion.

a. The teaching of wisdom

One key characteristic of wisdom literature that we singled out in the introduction was the shared interest of the wisdom books in wisdom itself. It would mean little to say that this has been affirmed by the subsequent discussion, since we have used it as a rough criterion for admittance to the corpus, so it has naturally been a feature of the books that we have surveyed. We can say, however, that the nature of that interest, and the understandings of wisdom itself, show a degree of consistency which tends to support such use of this as a criterion.

Much earlier, we also described wisdom in terms of the quality or skill which enables individuals to live their lives as successfully as possible; the texts generally confirm this, but it is important to emphasize that they portray it very much as a skill – wisdom is not itself really a body of knowledge. For Job and his friends, the wisdom which they claim or deny seems more specifically to be the ability to understand the way in which the world works, at least in terms of its interaction with the divine. When Proverbs 8 validates wisdom by claiming a place for it in creation, the implication may be something similar: wisdom is aware of the world, or of the way in which it has been constructed. Qohelet probably shares this understanding too, although he tends also to speak of wisdom as a sort of tool (e.g. Eccl. 1.13; 2.21), and his assessment of its value, of course, is more mixed: he sets severe limitations upon the human capacity to know the world, and to achieve anything from that knowledge.

Although humans apparently have to be taught in order to acquire wisdom, what they are taught by fellow humans is not usually wisdom as such – Elihu's claim to teach it is unusual, and perhaps a mark of his arrogance (Job 33.33). More typically, humans demonstrate wisdom and observe each other's wisdom, but do not actually pass wisdom itself on directly: although closely associated with knowledge, wisdom is essentially a faculty developed by teaching and learning (or more rarely, outside the wisdom literature, placed straight in the mind by God, e.g. 1 Kgs 5.9; 10.24; Isa. 11.2); it is not itself the content of teaching. Once acquired, it can be enhanced, and can provide the basis for teaching others, perhaps like any other skill, but it is difficult to translate the concept directly into modern terms: in all probability, the cultures which produced our texts did not clearly recognize the distinction which we would now make between innate intelligence and acquired knowledge or skill. Correspondingly, when proper instruction is received properly, it is considered not just to inform, but somehow to transform the mind and self. Although it is not a precise equivalent, the modern concept of being 'educated' provides an analogy of sorts.

The sort of teaching required to achieve wisdom is described less consistently. Qohelet talks largely about the extent to which he cultivated his own wisdom, and only the epilogue to Ecclesiastes shows any significant interest in education, speaking of it very much in literary terms: the wise collect sayings, and they are passed on in books (Eccl. 12.9-12). The book of Job is interested in wisdom as the consequence of experience: Job himself claims that it is something possessed by the old (12.12), and Eliphaz assents to this (15.7-10). The young Elihu, however, having originally accepted that view (32.6-7), now declares that, 'Surely it is a spirit in a man, and the breath of Shaddai, which give understanding', although it is not clear from the difficult 32.9 whether he denies wisdom to the aged, or merely believes that the young may possess it too. There is an acceptance that God may teach wisdom (e.g. 11.6), and that wise men may pass on their experience (15.17-18), but little or no interest in any type of formal teaching. Despite the polemical tone of their discussion, the characters assert their credentials without ever evoking the quality of their education or their teachers.

The emphasis on listening to parental instruction in parts of Proverbs, then, should not be taken as representative of the tradition as a whole: wisdom literature is far from being an advert for formal education, and there is a certain looseness about the understanding of just what teaching it is which imparts wisdom. This is true even in those works which apparently take the Torah to be central, since it is clear from all the additional advice, in Ben Sira especially, that the Torah is not the only instruction of value, and this perception opens the way for some of the Qumran texts to place 'the mystery to be' at the heart of the process. Although there is a fairly consistent understanding of what it is to be wise, then, the literature as a whole does not impose any close definition of the process required to achieve wisdom.

b. Being wise

Finally, we may touch more briefly on the issues of character and ethics associated with wisdom. Is there a particular and distinctive type of behaviour or character that the wisdom literature advocates?

That question is more difficult to answer than one might expect: given that a significant proportion of the literature claims to offer advice about behaviour, it is sometimes surprisingly difficult to pin down its expectations. Proverbs 1–9, for instance, offers little specific advice outside chapter 3 and the secondary 6.1-19: the warnings against the foreign woman in the second half are apparently geared to the work's figurative presentation, and much of the rest exhorts acceptance of wisdom and instruction, but does not go into specifics. In Proverbs 10.1–22.16, there is more advice implicit in the many observations, but still a high proportion of sayings which merely exhort in a different way, contrasting the fates of the righteous and the wicked, for instance, or of the wise and foolish. It seems to be very widely assumed that the reader will know already what they must do to be placed in one category or the other. In Proverbs as a whole, there are quite a lot of sayings, too, which state a supposed truth, but which have no direct implications for how one should behave (e.g. Prov. 29.2), or at least for how the majority of readers should behave (e.g. 29.12; 31.4). Matters are similar in Ben Sira, and altogether more complicated, of course, in Ecclesiastes: the advice literature seems an erratic source of advice, and its usual reluctance to organize materials thematically makes Proverbs, in particular, very difficult to consult as a guide. The foreign materials, incidentally, vary in this respect, but the late examples, such as *Ahiqar* or the Demotic instructions, are generally similar.

If we set out to extrapolate general behavioural or ethical principles from our texts, then we are doing something which seems to be important to them, in that they are concerned with being wise or righteous in a general way, but which they seem more than reluctant to do themselves. Correspondingly, there is a danger that any epitome of 'wise behaviour' which is compiled by combining or rearranging the sayings will go beyond what the literature itself intends, and create something which would have been alien to the original writers. At the very least, such abstractions can present a misleading picture of the relative emphasis placed on different ideas, and by their very nature they tend to make recommendations of specific behaviour seem more central to some of the texts than they really are. All the same, if we go down that route, then the results can be disappointing: there is little in the literature with which most readers could reasonably disagree, and it is difficult to discern a pattern of behaviour that is truly distinctive.

Its advocacy of wisdom and righteousness aside, the advice literature in Proverbs generally focuses on self-restraint and discipline in one's private life, and on honesty and equity in one's dealings with others. Not everyone might wish always to be sober, careful with their words, and industrious (a reluctance with which I am wholly in sympathy), but it is difficult to believe that Israel or Judah was filled with people who positively opposed such things, and actively advocated drunken chatter or laziness as the secret of prosperity. It is no easier to accept that many people deliberately opted to be wicked or foolish, or that even the most evil amongst the population considered themselves to be evil. The aspirations of our advice literature are so broadly expressed or so universal that they can hardly be considered to constitute a distinctive system of behaviour. Any significant distinctiveness lies not in the content but in the fact that the texts explicitly address such matters.

Turning to the biblical wisdom literature more generally, we find in Ecclesiastes, despite its many offers of advice, a certain resistance to the idea that there is any place at all for human ideas about proper behaviour. In Job, we might look to the behaviour of the protagonist for a model of behaviour, but specific behaviour is itself a matter of virtually no concern to the book's characters, except insofar as the friends condemn the way Job is speaking. There is, then, no discernibly distinctive pattern of behaviour advocated in the advice literature, and no specific interest in behaviour sustained across the corpus of wisdom literature more generally. Again, therefore, it is difficult to ground any idea of wisdom thought in this area.

3. Concluding remarks

In view of the difficulties outlined at the beginning of this chapter, we have concentrated not on finding specific points of agreement within the literature, but on identifying assumptions shared by the different writers. It would be difficult to claim, however, that we have come away with much to show for our efforts, at least in terms of particular ideas. Wisdom literature is not clearly united or distinguished from other literature by some underlying secularism, an antipathy to ideas of history and nation, or particular ideas about creation and world-order. It does employ a more-or-less common language for the proper relationship between humans and God, but does not have a distinct or shared understanding of that relationship, and it all speaks readily of wisdom in general terms, but has varied ideas about the acquisition of that wisdom, and the role of instruction. Only some of the literature is specifically concerned with behaviour, and the advice that it offers betrays no very distinctive ideas about human character.

Within these various negative results, however, it is possible to discern something more positive, which accords with the one area in which we did find a striking degree of correspondence between the texts – their presentation of God. That presentation is not unique to wisdom literature, and there are some grounds to suppose that it is geared not to the promotion of a particular ideology, but to the facilitation of theological discourse in a particular area. It seems possible to regard other characteristics in a similar light: wisdom literature in general presumes the importance of fearing God, for example, and is concerned with matters like human wisdom or divine judgement, but it employs the relevant language and categories without obviously having a common view of the content.

In that case, it may be quite wrong to think of wisdom literature as the embodiment of a specific ideology, when it may be something closer to a discourse played out according to a particular set of concerns and assumptions. These need not individually be specific to that literature, or even each be shared by every instance of wisdom writing, but in combination they provide a distinctive framework. There would be some analogy to this, perhaps, in the formal aspects of the literature, where we find strong associations with certain styles and genres, but also the exercise of considerable freedom in their use. Without pushing the point too far before we look at some other key considerations in the final chapter, it does seem possible that we should be thinking of our texts not as the reflections of a particular tradition of thought, but as the products of a particular mode of discourse – rather in the same way that an academic discipline offers certain formats and imposes certain concerns, conventions, and rules of engagement, without demanding specific views or conclusions.

Chapter 7

The Origins and Place of Wisdom Literature

The vast majority of people in the ancient world were illiterate, and very few people would have had the skills necessary to compose written texts. In Egypt and Mesopotamia, the scripts used for writing were complicated enough to require considerable teaching and practice, and the production of literature was essentially confined to the educated scribal classes. Even in Greek and Roman society, where the scripts were less daunting, the proportion of literate individuals was never high, and most would have belonged to particular groups or social strata. Recent studies of the evidence have generally suggested that much the same was true in Israel and Judah (see Young 1998), and although the social make-up of the group which returned from exile in Babylon means that it may have had an unusually high proportion of literate members, the numbers in post-exilic society as a whole probably remained low.

Correspondingly, ancient literature is overwhelmingly the product of quite a small class, within which the majority of individuals would have learned to read and write because those skills were expected in their professional lives, or at their level of society. Some texts may have originated in the writing down of oral compositions, prophetic oracles, or suchlike, but that does not make the texts themselves any less the product and possession of this literate class. Consequently, we sometimes need to distinguish between the origins and purposes of books and those of their contents: for instance, one of the demotic Egyptian instructions, *Ankhsheshonq*, contains sayings on agriculture which may have originated amongst farmers (although they did not necessarily do so) – that does not mean that the instruction itself, however, was written by or for farmers. In that example, the need for a distinction is obvious, since Egyptian farmers certainly did not produce books. It can be more difficult to recognize the problem when the content does actually correspond to the potential concerns of the literate class, but it is no less true that, say, the existence of sayings about kings in Proverbs does not by itself make Proverbs itself a product of the royal court (or even of the monarchic period), whatever the origin of those individual sayings.

Because few ancient Near Eastern compositions are kind enough to describe for us explicitly or accurately the circumstances in which they were composed, it is generally difficult to specify more precisely who it was within the literate class that produced them, and for whom they were written. Moreover, even where matters are not complicated by the inclusion of materials with a separate origin, the few clues which sometimes are available can be open to misinterpretation. As we saw earlier, for example, the father-son setting of instructions is a literary convention, which says little or nothing about the actual circumstances in which any particular instruction was composed. We can be misled in less obvious ways, however, as when Qohelet advises his readers to sow their seed in the morning and evening (Eccl. 11.6): this is a figurative expression, as we noted earlier, and Ecclesiastes was no more written for the farming community than was *Ankhsheshonq*. Establishing the origins of ancient literary texts on the basis of their content alone can be a hazardous business.

The wisdom literature, furthermore, cannot be assessed straightforwardly using form criticism, an approach commonly favoured in biblical scholarship for determining origin: form criticism looks to the constraints within a context which shaped the underlying conventions used in composition, but there is almost universal agreement that the advice literature, at least, has been adopted by Israel from abroad, or at least strongly influenced by foreign prototypes, so any such constraints lay outside Israel, and related to the needs of an earlier, foreign context. In any case, form criticism is intended to address the development of oral formulations, and, although it may incorporate folk proverbs or other oral material, wisdom literature is essentially a literary phenomenon.

When dealing with the biblical wisdom books, therefore, which offer very little internal evidence of date or origin, scholars have usually placed great emphasis on external and circumstantial evidence. We shall begin this chapter by assessing briefly the usefulness of that evidence, and the strength of the hypotheses which have been based upon it. By specifying a very particular origin for the texts, however, those hypotheses have created an issue around the relationship between wisdom literature and other forms of composition, which itself offers potential insights into the character of our materials. Our discussion of that relationship will take us back to some of the questions raised in the last chapter, and enable us to attempt a more definite description of this literature's character and role.

1. Social location of the literature

Perhaps surprisingly, given the very varied content of wisdom literature, theories about its origin have been dominated by attempts to link it with the royal bureaucracy and with formal education, and those attempts have been linked in particular to certain understandings of advice literature in Egypt. Neither association is clearly indicated by the internal evidence of the texts themselves: it is hard to find anything in Job, for example, which betrays governmental or educational concerns, and even Proverbs has only a very restricted amount of material which might be considered especially appropriate to such contexts. The evidence which we need to consider, therefore, comes mostly from outside our texts.

a. Wise men

As we saw at the beginning of this introduction, 'wisdom' can be used of skills more specific than the skill of life, and one can be 'wise' without being a Solomon, Job, or Qohelet. Even when somebody is described as wise in a general way (e.g. 2 Sam. 13.3), it does not have to mean that they possess wisdom in the sense that the wisdom literature characteristically understands the term. It may, however, have something of this sense (e.g. 2 Sam. 14.20; Isa. 19.12), and we find some interesting references to wisdom outside the wisdom literature itself. Deuteronomy 4.6, for example, says that Israel will be perceived as wise because of its possession of the Torah – an idea that may have been influential on the association of wisdom with Torah in Proverbs 1–9 and Ben Sira – while Jer. 8.8-9 apparently contradicts a claim to wisdom on that basis, suggesting that the Torah has been corrupted by the scribes.

Amidst the many and varied uses of 'wise', numerous scholars have tried to identify a specific group who called themselves 'the wise', and to associate the description in particular with a class of royal advisors. This is a difficult identification to sustain, however. There were undoubtedly individuals who were considered wise (e.g. Isa. 29.14), or even called themselves wise (e.g. Isa. 5.21; Jer. 9.22 ET 9.23), and some of these are associated with the offering of advice (e.g. Isa. 19.11; Jer. 18.18). This is not surprising, since 'wisdom' can certainly be used of skill in governance and political judgement (e.g. Deut. 1.13; 1 Kgs 3.9-12). The biblical sources, however, contain numerous lists of important groups (e.g. 2 Kgs 24.10-16), which nowhere include 'the wise', and, curiously, no official royal counsellor is ever actually called 'wise'. Even were there such a group, though, it is far from clear that we could automatically associate them with wisdom literature, which clearly owns no exclusive rights to the terminology of wisdom. Some biblical writers or traditions occasionally seem to think in terms of a sort of 'super wisdom', which means that the wisdom granted Solomon to rule Israel (1 Kgs 3.9-12) translates into extraordinary judgement (1 Kgs 3.16-28), the ability to create sayings, songs and fables (1 Kgs 5.9-14 ET 4.29-34), and ultimately a knowledge of everything (1 Kgs 10.1-10). That hardly gives us permission, though, to link every use of 'wise' with every other use of 'wise', and so tie wisdom literature specifically to some hypothetical group of counsellors.

b. Scribes and 'scribal' literature

Although it is difficult to identify in the biblical sources some particular group of royal scribes responsible for wisdom literature, it is common to describe the literature itself as 'scribal', and, in one sense, probably not improper to do so. There is, however, considerable scope for confusion here. As we noted above, literacy in the ancient Near East was largely confined in each culture to a particular class, which is commonly known as the 'scribal class', or 'scribal élite'. These classes arose in response to governmental requirements, and were originally connected to the concerns of the royal court. Their members filled administrative posts, but might also serve variously as priests, or in many other capacities: the scribal classes of Egypt and Mesopotamia came rapidly to be social classes into which members were born, more than merely professions. Members of these classes were trained in reading and writing, although they commonly also received a broader education, in a curriculum which passed on values and traditions. Since all the literature within Egypt, say, was produced by members of this class, all Egyptian literature is 'scribal', and much of it was used in the context of that education. Something similar could be said of Mesopotamia, and of the various regions or city-states influenced by Mesopotamian practices.

If we speak of the literate classes in Israel and Judah as the 'scribal classes', then, similarly, we must describe all the literature as 'scribal', by definition. Unlike Egyptologists or Assyriologists, however, biblical scholars have not generally been accustomed to speak in terms of an overarching 'scribal class', but have assigned literature to more precise social contexts, which are perceived as distinct from each other. When biblical scholars are dealing with Egyptian literature, therefore, descriptions of that literature as 'scribal' take on a very different sense, and the perception that 'scribal' Egyptian instructions have influenced biblical wisdom literature has contributed strongly to an idea that wisdom literature must therefore be the provenance of a particular professional 'scribal' context, just as Leviticus belongs to a 'priestly' context, or Jeremiah to a 'prophetic' one. What is a very general, almost redundant description in Egyptology becomes a very precise one in biblical studies.

We run into other difficulties if, instead of using Egyptological terminology within biblical studies, we try to apply categories from biblical scholarship to the foreign texts. A number of the Egyptian instructions, for example, are attributed to priests (who were, of course, members of the scribal class), but it makes no sense to separate them off from other instructions, and class them instead with hymns or prayers. If we use form or content as a criterion, rather than attribution, then it is unclear how we should deal with instructions that contain hymns, or (in Mesopotamia) hymns that appear to include precepts for behaviour. Confusions over terminology aside, it is simply not possible to identify, within the scribal classes of other states, some specific and distinct social or professional class which produced advice literature or other compositions resembling our wisdom literature. Even if we could do so, it would be wrong to presume that Israel or Judah must have had some matching class to produce its own wisdom literature.

The scribal origin of the foreign literature, then, does not itself constitute circumstantial evidence that biblical wisdom literature must have emerged in a specific scribal group or groups. There is rather more scope, perhaps, for arguing that we can determine the location of the Jewish literature from the concerns of its foreign counterparts. Some of the Egyptian instructions, in particular, are strongly oriented to the particular needs of the scribal class, and it is reasonable to suggest that such literature would only have been imitated by some group with similar needs. Of course, however, there remains a danger of category confusion within such an argument: the needs addressed within the foreign literature are not simply those of senior administrators (matters of that sort, indeed, are rarely addressed), but those of the literate class as a whole. Correspondingly, *Ptahhotep*, for instance, attempts to address the needs of readers who find themselves in many different positions. It would be difficult to claim either that only royal officials in Israel or Judah would have been interested enough in this literature to have borrowed it, or that much of the literature would have been particularly suited to their needs. Those scholars who pursue this line are obliged to suppose (entirely hypothetically) that the Jewish literature began as something much more concerned with professional needs, and only later took its present, very different shape. Even if they are right, and this was the way in which advice literature first reached Israel, then the acknowledged changes hardly oblige us to suppose that it remained confined to administrative circles.

c. The borrowing of foreign literature

Whatever the problems involved in calling the literature 'scribal', there is a quite separate argument based around the fact of borrowing literature from abroad, rather than the motivation for doing so. If Jewish wisdom literature shows extensive dependence on foreign literature, then the wisdom writers must have had access to a considerable range of foreign texts, written in foreign languages. The circles most likely to have obtained such access, it is argued, were those in which foreign languages would have been learned, and members of foreign scribal classes encountered, for diplomatic reasons. That is, again, circles involved in a particular aspect of royal administration.

There are some overgeneralizations involved in this argument. It is very difficult to see why, for instance, any professional diplomat would have learned Sumerian or Middle Egyptian, which were both archaic long before there were any Israelite administrators, but many of the texts often cited as sources for biblical literature would have been inaccessible without such knowledge. In practical terms, indeed, it is difficult to understand why any diplomat would have learned Egyptian even in its later forms, since Akkadian was used in diplomatic correspondence with Egypt before the time of Israel, and Aramaic would probably have served for diplomatic negotiations with both Egypt and Mesopotamia from at least the 8th century BCE (see 2 Kgs 18.26). To be sure, Israel may have had its linguists and scholars, but it is hard to see why we must identify them closely with the royal service.

The more significant point, though, is that we really do not know which foreign texts (apart from *Amenemope*) were known to Jewish writers, at what date they became available, and in what form they might have been found. A case can be made for Egyptian texts having entered Palestine in the period of the pre-Israelite city states, which were in the Egyptian sphere of influence (so Fox 2000: 19), but they could equally well have been encountered for the first time only many centuries later, when Jewish communities were established in Egypt, and there is virtually no period that can be excluded. They may have been known in Egyptian, in translation, or solely through adaptations: apart from *Ahiqar*, we know little or nothing about more local (and presumably much more accessible) traditions of composition, which may have acted as vehicles for Egyptian or Mesopotamian influence. We are hardly even in a position to speculate, furthermore, about the extent to which sayings may have spread orally or texts been acquired privately through trade. With so many unknown factors, it is really not possible to base any argument for origins on the relationship between Jewish and foreign texts, without heaping hypothesis upon hypothesis.

d. Schools

The association made by many scholars between wisdom literature and the royal administration is commonly linked to speculation that wisdom literature was composed for use in schools, and writers have often looked to the use of literature in scribal training abroad as a way of understanding the origin and function of the texts. The issues are basically distinct, though, and it is possible to argue for an educational background without presuming that the students were training to be administrators.

Here the evidence is partly internal, and the didactic tone of Proverbs has done much to persuade scholars that it was designed to be used in teaching. Proverbs does not present any part of itself as a school text, however, and its references to teaching are largely references to the instruction of children by their parents. Job is not explicitly educational at all, of course, and the reference to Qohelet's teaching in the epilogue of Ecclesiastes (12.9) is in the context of his literary activity. Only as late as Ben Sira do we find any possible mention of schooling, when he invites the untaught to his 'house of study', but this may be no more than an echo of wisdom's invitation in Prov. 9. His grandson, in the prologue to the Greek translation, portrays Ben Sira as passing on his learning through his writing, not through direct teaching. The internal evidence for an educational function really consists only, therefore, of a perception that the didactic and exhortatory tone of some wisdom literature might be suited to a school setting.

Since, furthermore, we know little or nothing about educational practices in Israel or Judah, the idea that schools may have existed at all is little more than conjecture (Weeks 1994: 132–56; cf. Crenshaw 1998). The various biblical references and inscriptions that have been adduced show nothing more than that reading and writing were taught somehow. Again, therefore, scholars have tended to appeal to foreign literature and practices, and especially to the Egyptian instructions. That instructions were used in Egyptian education is undeniable (many of them are preserved in copies by students), and it seems apparent also that they were intended to pass on values important to the scribal élite. It seems a short step to suppose that their Jewish counterparts played a similar role, but the matter is actually more complicated.

Egyptian education (not all of which took place in formal school settings) certainly employed textbooks specially created for use in education, and these included, amongst other things, works that commonly describe themselves as 'instructions in letter-writing'. Such works gather together a wide range of material designed for exercises in copying and composition, including items like model letters or passages extracted from literary texts. Although they sometimes use material taken from more conventional instructions, and occasionally even present themselves as 'instructions', these texts are very different from the usual members of the genre, and scholars normally describe them as 'miscellanies' (Gardiner 1937). Apart from such specialized teaching materials, however, Egyptian students also read and copied classic works of Egyptian literature, as we saw above, including a range of narrative and poetic works, and it seems to be in this category of reading that instructions proper belonged, with some of them continuing to be copied for many centuries after their composition. As we observed earlier, they tend to be poetic works, and some were probably difficult to read even from the outset: for later generations, their complicated style and archaic language would have presented a considerable challenge, and it is hard to see them as textbooks, designed to pass on information lucidly, or to provide stylistic models for imitation. Rather, alongside other texts, they formed a part of the shared cultural knowledge expected of an educated Egyptian. In a late poem praising ancient writers, the authors or protagonists of instructions dominate the list of classics (Papyrus Chester Beatty IV; see Lichtheim 1976: 175–8).

Their use in schools, then, does not set instructions apart from other Egyptian literature, and they were probably read outside educational contexts also (so far as we can judge from the extant copies). It is interesting, of course, to wonder how far a great deal of Egyptian literature might have been written with a view to passing on the values of the country's scribal élite to future generations (cf. Assmann 1999), but it would be at best simplistic to employ the secondary use of texts in schools as way of understanding their purpose. Egyptian instructions were no schoolbooks, and we cannot argue by analogy, therefore, that their Hebrew counterparts were schoolbooks. Even if we could, furthermore, it would be a considerable leap from there to supposing that the non-instructional sections of Proverbs, let alone the rest of the wisdom literature, must also have been schoolbooks.

e. Conclusions

Attempts to connect wisdom literature with royal administrators and with education are based on a lot of speculation and a certain amount of misunderstanding: we can hardly regard the case as proven. That is not to say, however, that the issues raised by discussion in this area are uninteresting and unimportant, or, indeed, that we ought to be looking for some quite different historical context in which to place wisdom literature. One thing that does emerge clearly, is that we need to think carefully about just what we are looking for when we seek a context.

For all that it is possible to align certain types of composition with the interests of certain groups within the literate stratum of a society, not all literature is so easily placed, and such groups are rarely watertight compartments within their society. In Egypt, it would be very difficult to separate out from the general scribal class some particular group involved in the composition of advice literature, and all scribes appear to have regarded classic instances of that literature as a part of their social and cultural heritage. In Mesopotamia, there is some evidence for scribal specialization within the transmission of literature, but scribes who copied sayings collections, for example, did not enjoy exclusive possession of those collections. In our own modern, literate cultures, we readily accept the coexistence of different interests, approaches, and opinions even within the curricula used to educate our children, and whilst we can recognize the different intellectual assumptions and priorities of, say, a science graduate and a classicist, we do not presuppose some fundamental distinction, or even antagonism between them. Without good reason, we should not impose a greater intellectual tribalism on the scribal élites of the ancient world, let alone tie that simplistically to different literary genres or fields of enquiry.

The grounds for linking biblical wisdom literature to any identifiable and distinct social context within the scribal élite are slender, at best, but it is not clear anyway that such a link would imply a significant degree of disconnection from other biblical literature or thought. If we found stronger evidence for a group of scribes at the heart of government, who largely disdained the literary and intellectual culture around them in favour of particular texts selected from the literature of other countries, this would not answer all our questions about wisdom literature, but merely pose a different, more difficult question: how could such a group, without parallel in the surrounding scribal cultures, have emerged and sustained its distinctiveness? The answer to such a question would surely have to be sought in the literary products of such a group, and so we would be back again to assessing the literature itself.

It would seem more valuable, or at least practical, to see the scribal character of wisdom literature as something associative, rather than dissociative: it is a basic characteristic that links all or most of the biblical literature within a broader cultural context. In many respects, that context is difficult for us to discern, and it is doubtful that we can envisage quite the same degree of coherence within the early Jewish élites as within, say, the Egyptian scribal class. It is important, nevertheless, for us to recognize that what members of the literate class held in common may have been at least as important as the differences between them. We have already observed numerous places where the wisdom books seem to draw on themes, styles, or ideas found in other biblical literature, and at this stage we can usefully look at the other side of this coin – those points at which other books draw on things we would more naturally associate with wisdom texts.

2. Wisdom in the Hebrew Bible

a. Wisdom 'influence'

Scholarship in this area, unfortunately, has become very tangled, with connections made between wisdom and other literature on a number of different levels, and using various criteria. We have already seen, at the beginning of chapter 5, the problems of classification that can arise when other texts appear to contain significant proportions of material that looks as though it would more properly belong in a wisdom composition. Those problems are really only the tip of an iceberg, however: especially during the 1960s, scholars identified reasons to associate a very high proportion of the biblical literature with wisdom literature, using a variety of criteria. In some cases, this association was described in terms of wisdom influence on other texts, but it was not uncommon for scholars to view whole compositions as wisdom compositions, and this understanding has been applied to, for example, the primeval history in Gen. 1–11, the story of Joseph in Gen. 37–50, the story of King David in 2 Samuel and 1 Kgs 1–2, the book of Esther, and even the historical books as a whole (McKenzie 1967; for the other claims, see Crenshaw 1969 and Morgan 1981). Beyond the narrative texts, Moshe Weinfeld (most fully in Weinfeld 1972) has argued for 'wisdom substrata' in Deuteronomy (see the critique of this position in Brekelmans 1979), and Jean Malfroy (1965) for that book's close links with Proverbs, while James Boston (1968) has identified wisdom influence even on the Song of Moses in Deut. 32. Various prophetic works have been identified as showing wisdom influence, most notably Isaiah (Fichtner 1949; Whedbee 1971; Vermeylen 1979; cf. the sensible evaluation in Williamson 1995) and Amos (Terrien 1962; Wolff 1964: 24–30; cf. Soggin 1995). The grounds adopted have varied with the particular claims made, but scholars have commonly pointed to the presence of words and expressions usually associated with wisdom literature, to assumptions about, for example, the character of divine action, to supposed wisdom concerns, or, most often, to a combination of these. In some discussions, much has been made of theories about the origin of wisdom literature: it is taken as significant, for instance, that Isaiah was a scribe and Joseph a royal advisor.

Observing the plethora of such theories, James Crenshaw called in a famous article for a tighter methodological constraint on such comparisons, which included 'exaggerated claims supported by dubious arguments and assumptions' (1969: 129), and in particular for a greater appreciation of the different views and meanings which might lie behind similar themes or expressions in wisdom and other literature. The extent to which his methodology might be applied, however, has been seriously constrained by a lack of consensus about just such views and meanings in wisdom literature. While wisdom thought remains a somewhat nebulous concept, as we saw in the last chapter, it is hard to use it as a criterion for identifying correspondences that are more than superficial. Vocabulary and forms of expression are little better as a guide, since it is notoriously difficult to identify some wisdom lexicon that is not merely a product of the literature's subject matter. So whilst recent years have seen much less enthusiasm for the pursuit of wisdom influence, this may be as much because there are so few candidate texts left to nominate, as because any clearer constraints have been established.

It would be impractical to address each of the proposals here – although it should be noted that some seem more plausible than others – but it is interesting to observe certain tendencies. In particular, the great majority of commentators have argued that wisdom is the source and not the recipient of influence, even though much of the biblical wisdom literature cited would commonly be dated later than the work with which it is being compared. A lot of historical assumptions about the character and place of wisdom literature are clearly at play, moreover, and it is common to create a quasi-historical explanation. Fichtner (1949), for example, spins from references scattered across the book, a complicated story about Isaiah belonging to the guild of the wise, but becoming disillusioned by their self-reliance and refusal to recognize proper wisdom from God. Despite the many difficulties, it would be hard to deny that much of this work has established formal and thematic overlaps between the wisdom literature and many other biblical texts. When it comes to evaluating the significance of those overlaps, however, we tend to be offered unhelpful vagueness or implausible precision.

Samuel Terrien's 1962 study of Amos offers an interesting exception. The argument for wisdom influence which he offers is not itself especially compelling, and rests on a variety of stylistic or terminological points of contact with wisdom literature, along with a slightly desperate suggestion that Amos might have been influenced by the famously wise inhabitants of Edom, since his home town of Tekoa was not far from there. His conclusion, however, is worth citing in full (Terrien 1962: 115):

> Such a hypothesis should not be construed as meaning that the prophet was not primarily steeped in the covenant theology of Israel. It rather tends to prevent the overstressing of the separation of classes among the leaders of the eighth century B.C. That various groups, such as priests, prophets, and wisemen existed should not be denied. At the same time, such groups were not alien one from the others, and they lived in a common and mutually interacting environment.

The point is an important one: common ground between wisdom and other types of literature can only be explained up to a point by presuming special circumstances in each case. If we find a lot of common ground with a lot of texts, then it becomes more reasonable to explain this in terms of a shared cultural context, and to lower the barriers between different types of author.

b. Wisdom as tradition or framework

Norman Whybray (1974) famously drew from this state of affairs the conclusion that wisdom must be conceived of as an intellectual tradition, rather than the property of a single group: his own terminological enquiry uncovered 'wisdom vocabulary' across a significant proportion of the Hebrew Bible, often corresponding to places where wisdom influence had already been perceived. On this understanding, wisdom literature is not the product of a particular group, but the wisdom books are individually products of a broader heritage, which simultaneously underpinned other compositions. This is an important and attractive theory, which explains both the lack of coherence at many levels between the wisdom books themselves, and the many points of contact that they have with other texts. It further dispenses with the need for a specific group of 'wise men', along with the historical problems attached to that issue, and, although Whybray does not explore the comparison in depth himself, it offers a situation which is much more analogous to that of Egypt, in particular.

Whybray has been criticized rightly on grounds of method, and it is true both that his arguments against a class of wise men are sometimes weak (however sound his conclusions), and that the criterion of shared vocabulary which he uses is open to attack on grounds of method (as he acknowledges himself). The case he makes, perhaps, is stronger than the way he makes it. Without further qualification, however, Whybray's approach is not without its own problems. For all that it is difficult to define the wisdom books closely, they nevertheless do have shared interests and a distinctive approach which makes it no less difficult to treat them as, essentially, miscellaneous products of an underlying intellectual tradition. Whybray (1974: 70) speaks of an 'informal' continuity between the wisdom books, derived from the familiarity of educated writers with earlier works, and goes no further than to allow that they may represent 'a distinct intellectual strand'. Although it may be perfectly proper, however, to reject the idea of 'wisdom circles' as a way to unite the different wisdom books, it is not improper to suggest that they share something more specific than this in common.

Another way of looking at the problem has been offered by Gerald Sheppard (1980), who does not attempt, however, so comprehensive an explanation. His starting point is not in the question of origins, but in the way that the Torah has been absorbed into the didactic framework of later wisdom texts like Ben Sira. For Sheppard, we are dealing with what he calls a 'hermeneutical construct', in which wisdom becomes a method of interpreting other traditions in the nascent biblical canon, and he reads that process back into secondary, editorial touches in several of the biblical books. At least a small proportion of the common ground between wisdom and other literature, in other words, stems from the progressive incorporation of literature into a body of texts at a time when wisdom literature had furnished a dominant style of presentation and discourse. Again, there may be more than a little truth in this, especially when we are dealing with passages like the end of Hosea (14.10 ET 14.9). When we look at the Qumran materials, indeed, it is easy to suspect that Sheppard has undersold his idea: later writers were clearly able to adapt the framework of instruction and wisdom to incorporate not only biblical traditions, but such concepts as the 'mystery to be'.

c. Wisdom and law

Not all the links between wisdom books and other literature need be explained, then, in terms either of specific influence or of shared origin, and some may reflect simply the ability of wisdom literature to provide a familiar structure, or the origin of all our texts in the shared elements of scribal culture. The issues become more complicated, though, when a relationship is perceived not simply between wisdom literature and individual other texts, but between broader traditions of thought and composition. In particular, scholars have tended to suggest that such relationships exist with law and law codes, on the one hand, and with apocalyptic literature on the other. The reasons are different, and we shall look briefly at them each separately.

Clearly, the explicit association of wisdom with Torah in Ben Sira and other late literature is important for our understanding of Judaism in that period and beyond. Voicing a conventional view, Blenkinsopp (1983: 130) speaks of 'wisdom and law as two great rivers which eventually flow together and find their outlet in rabbinic writings and early Christian theology.' If we are right to suspect such an association in Proverbs 1–9, of course, then this confluence must be placed earlier, but the whole image may anyway be misleading: it is difficult to see the links between wisdom literature and law entirely in terms of convergence.

One of the issues which tends to complicate form-critical analysis of the wisdom literature is the virtual identity between what we would call 'admonitions' in a wisdom context, and 'laws' in a legal context. This is true both for the so-called 'apodeictic' laws (e.g. Exod. 20.13), which present an absolute command – 'You shall (not) . . .!' – and for 'casuistic' laws, which present a situation and the appropriate response (e.g. Deut. 22.6). Proverbs is replete with sayings that match each of those types in form, and there are sometimes striking similarities of content as well – compare Deut. 19.14, for instance, with Prov. 22.28. The identity of texts does not reside in their individual components, so these resemblances do not mean that we need to start categorizing law codes as wisdom literature or sayings collections as law. They do point, however, to a degree of overlap that may be significant for the way in which we understand the nature and development of biblical law.

One approach to this (cf. Jackson 2006) involves looking beyond the collections themselves to the use of proverbs within society. As we noted much earlier, authority is attached to such sayings, and in some cultures they can play an important role as evidence in judicial proceedings or disputes: it is possible to understand the early development of laws and law codes in such terms. Approaching the matter from another direction, it is also possible to argue from foreign analogies that ancient law codes were composed to embody moral advice rooted in the values and concerns of the scribal élite (e.g. Fitzpatrick-McKinley 1999); that would, of course, give them much in common with the wisdom literature. In either case, we should have to understand a relationship with wisdom literature that is far more basic than suggested by the traditional image of a late confluence in Ben Sira, even if the narrative contexts in which the law codes have been placed draw them into a rather different realm of covenant theology.

This is not the place to go into the complicated issues surrounding the origins of biblical law, but it is hardly controversial to suggest that the apodeictic laws, at least, owe as much to idealism and moral exhortation as to any legal system, and some broad relationship with the advice literature seems likely on any reckoning. It is less clear that this can be expressed meaningfully as a relationship between law and wisdom literature more generally. The laws and some wisdom literature may have been created out of some of the same components, be they values, turns of phrase, or proverbial sayings, and such similarities may have made it easier for wisdom to become associated with Torah subsequently. To say that law and wisdom are related on those grounds, however, is in itself no more than like saying that a cake is related to *sauce béchamel* because they both have flour and butter in them. Equally, it is clear that obedience to the Torah may be perceived as effectively equivalent to wisdom (Deut. 4.6), which again enables later association of the two. It is much harder, however, to establish any precise way in which the law codes themselves correspond to the actual interests and assumptions of the wisdom literature as a whole.

d. Wisdom and apocalyptic

The case of apocalyptic literature is rather different. Here there is an apparent correspondence with the concerns of the wisdom literature, in that much apocalyptic is concerned with understanding the world in order to survive, with ideas of divine judgement, and even with instruction and the acquisition of knowledge. The God of apocalyptic, moreover, is in certain respects the God of wisdom literature: universal, supreme, and powerfully engaged with the running of his creation. It is little wonder either that some of the wisdom texts from Qumran may have been able to absorb apocalyptic elements, or that wisdom itself becomes a concern in some apocalyptic literature.

There are significant differences, however, perhaps especially in the focus of apocalyptic on revealed secrets: the biblical wisdom literature, at least, does not regard wisdom in terms of esoteric knowledge. It also lacks the eschatological concerns and the interest in the supernatural so characteristic of apocalyptic. Apocalyptic literature, on the other hand, commonly lacks the focus on individuals that is so much a hallmark of wisdom, and tends to understand problems in the world as the consequence of supernatural or structural issues. Although the two types of literature share certain concerns, then, they characteristically address them in very different ways. More formally, the mediation of knowledge through famous protagonists is certainly a point of contact at the compositional level, and apocalyptic can both share a testamentary quality with instructional literature and include instructional exhortations (the classic example is the 'Epistle of Enoch' in 1 Enoch 91–104). It would not usually be easy to mistake one for the other, however, and it is doubtful that we should read too much into the link: apocalyptic writers are familiar with wisdom writings, and employ their ideas or modes of expression, but they fit them into a very different worldview. As was the case with law codes, then, it is not difficult to see how connections were formed between the two types of literature, but those connections in no way imply a substantial identity.

On the face of it, therefore, it seems astonishing that some scholars, most notably Gerhard von Rad (1972: 263–83 and elsewhere) and Hans-Peter Müller (1972), have suggested that apocalyptic could trace its roots back into wisdom. This idea, however, has its own roots in an idea of wisdom that stretches rather further than the wisdom literature itself. On the one hand, wisdom thought is seen to embrace a general erudition and a particular interest in nature and the world, which is comparable to the quasi-scientific interests of some apocalyptic literature. On the other, it is noted that there are links between apocalyptic and divination, especially through dream interpretation, and also between divination and wisdom, since diviners may be described as 'wise men' (e.g. Dan. 2.12). Here, therefore, we seem to be trespassing into areas of 'wisdom' that have little to do either with wisdom literature or with the usual understandings of wisdom in wisdom literature. The claim might better be re-stated in terms of an apocalyptic origin within concerns and interests that related to education and certain specialist skills, and it is important not to make 'wisdom' here an artificial bridge between apocalyptic and wisdom literature, by making a lazy assumption that all wisdom is essentially one phenomenon. We must also be wary of presuming that influence can only run in one direction: von Rad makes much of a perception that certain wisdom literature seems aware of an 'end time', and concerned with the divine determination of history – but the examples he cites are largely from the later books, which are probably no less aware of apocalyptic literature's claims in this respect. The later wisdom texts very probably grow from much the same soil as apocalyptic texts, and to some extent the two are entwined together (see, for example, Collins 2005 on the indirect influence of apocalyptic motifs on Wisdom of Solomon). It is pushing far beyond the evidence to suggest, however, that they share a single root.

e. Concluding remarks

The enthusiasm of a certain generation for finding connections between wisdom and other literature may have been inspired by perceptions of the wisdom literature as historically and ideologically distinct – perceptions which have naturally been called into question as a consequence of the many links suggested. Whatever its roots, though, we have no comparable enterprise with which to compare this quest, and it is interesting to wonder what might have turned up if scholars had devoted so much energy to identifying connections between other types of literature. It seems likely that any such investigations would only tend to affirm the broad interconnectedness of biblical literature, which, for all its individual interests and ideas, arose within the context of a relatively small literate class, much of it across a period of just a few centuries.

The problems of method involved in assessing wisdom literature's own connections are significant, but they arguably derive more from the vagueness of the questions being posed and the categories being used than from anything else. It is not difficult to determine potential links between two individual compositions; we could, for instance, look without too much difficulty at the connections between Job and Genesis, or, maybe less productively, Ecclesiastes and Jonah. To do so usefully, however, we should need to have both a clear understanding of each text, and some criteria for determining what we should take to be a significant connection. The task becomes much more difficult when we start to try comparing wisdom literature as a whole with other texts, both because we have already had to make such a set of judgements to establish the connections between the wisdom books, and because it is harder to evaluate the significance of any connection which we find.

The real problems arise, however, if we start to say either that a connection with one wisdom book is equivalent to a connection with them all, or that components used in wisdom composition are themselves somehow 'wisdom'. Both confusions are common in the discussion of wisdom influence, and both result from a more general confusion between parts and wholes. The first is surely obvious: not every form, expression, or idea in each wisdom book is shared by every wisdom book, and so a link with, say, a particular passage in Proverbs does not constitute a link with wisdom literature as a whole. Indeed, a link with advice literature more generally need still not be a 'wisdom' link: however many admonitions a text employs, or however many proverbs, it may still have nothing in common with Job, and precious little with Ecclesiastes.

The second issue is similar, and is again most clearly illustrated with reference to Proverbs. Much of that book consists, as we saw earlier, of sayings which originated as proverbs, or at least imitate the style of proverbs. That does not mean, however, that it is useful to describe proverbs themselves as 'wisdom', if we take the term to imply that individual sayings somehow embody all the assumptions and concerns of wisdom literature. If we want to talk about proverbs as 'folk wisdom' or somesuch, then there is nothing to stop us, but we must again guard against any idea that people using proverbs are doing or thinking the same as people writing wisdom books, or that they naturally belong within some single category. Sometimes the term 'wisdom' is transferred even beyond the building blocks of the literature to supposed contexts, so that scribal circles become 'wisdom circles' and schools become 'wisdom schools' almost by default, and therefore anything scribal or educational becomes 'wisdom' as well. With so much Israelite discourse rendered 'wise' almost by definition, we must begin to suspect that 'wisdom' has become more of a liability than an asset in our discussions, and that debates about origin and influence would do well to retire the term.

For all the confusion, however, it is possible to extract some useful points. Firstly, and most obviously, wisdom literature draws to some extent on a common pool of terms and expressions: other writers use not only much of the vocabulary typical of wisdom discourse, but also various types of sayings and admonitions found frequently in advice literature. Since all of these were presumably in use by much of the population, this is hardly surprising. Writers may place expressions in contexts that differentiate them from common or other usage, which is how legal and instructional admonitions, for instance, come to be read differently, but they are not thereby laying claim to them as a private possession, and common usage persists alongside. The wisdom books also clearly draw at times on other literature, and other literature on wisdom writings, so that we may reasonably speak of an active literary culture within which traditions of composition may have been more or less distinct, but were not isolated. At the level of ideas, it is difficult to find anything in the wisdom literature as a whole which is not found elsewhere as well, and its concerns with knowledge, creation, and the relationship between humans and God are all echoed also in, for instance, the early chapters of Genesis, where they take, however, a very different form.

3. Placing and defining wisdom

From our review of the texts themselves, it is obvious that we cannot just use their form or style to define wisdom literature more broadly. In the last chapter, it became clear also that what they have in common theologically or intellectually is far from a straightforward set of clear and distinct ideas. In this chapter, we looked outside the texts to questions of social context and the relationships with other literature, again finding nothing that would offer us a firm basis for distinguishing and defining wisdom literature. It is not a corpus that lends itself to simple classification using criteria which are either intrinsic or extrinsic, and if we attempt to apply such a classification, we must either make the criteria hopelessly vague, or adjust the contents of the corpus. So, for example, when Katharine Dell attempts to define wisdom literature by form, content, and context, even a fairly generous treatment of each leads her effectively to eject Job: while it '. . . essentially springs from the same intellectual and spiritual quest as other wisdom books and must be seen as such on a broad definition . . . we need to have some profound reservations about simply assuming that Job is "wisdom literature", as narrowly defined' (Dell 2000: 43). If we trim the corpus to fit our definition, however, it is not clear just what we are left to define: wisdom literature is our category, not one bequeathed to us by the biblical writers themselves, and if we are to justify its use, then we need a description that corresponds to such use, not a definition of some separate grouping owned by no one.

An alternative way forward is offered by James Crenshaw (1982: 19):

> . . . formally, wisdom consists of proverbial sentence or instruction, debate, intellectual reflection; thematically, wisdom comprises self-evident intuitions about mastering life for human betterment, groping after life's secrets with regard to

innocent suffering, grappling with finitude, and quest for truth concealed in the created order and manifested in Dame Wisdom. When a marriage between form and content exists, there is wisdom literature. Lacking such oneness, a given text participates in biblical wisdom to a greater or lesser extent.

Now, clearly this sort of list might be considered cheating by the purist: if we include all the major themes and forms of all the wisdom books (and permit them to be so vague as 'intellectual reflection'), then it is not surprising that the definition can embrace all those books. The point, though, is that Crenshaw is starting from the reality of the corpus, and expressing wisdom not as a checklist, but in terms of two separate dimensions. If we think of a graph with 'formal' and 'thematic' axes, then any other text can be assigned coordinates which place it in relation to the area where our wisdom books cluster. However thematically similar, that text will never be wisdom literature without the right form to place it near that zone, and however formally similar, a different theme will still pull it to one edge. This is clever and pragmatic, even if it is only really a way of encapsulating the problem of definition, rather than of solving it. It raises the interesting question, though, of just what sort of phenomenon we must be looking at, that might require such multidimensional description.

In the last chapter, we spoke of wisdom composition as a mode of discourse, and if there is a lesson to be learned from the material covered in this chapter, it is that such discourse existed within a complicated and interconnected literary culture, where other texts could certainly share aspects of that discourse whilst retaining a strong attachment to other types and traditions of writing. In passing, I compared the way in which a modern academic discipline functions, and that is an analogy which could be pushed a little further in the light of our subsequent investigations. Viewed in itself, such a discipline appears broadly coherent: we find an established body of concerns, traditional ways of approaching those concerns, and perhaps a broadly technical vocabulary which has evolved to discuss them. There are also accepted forms of composition – monographs, articles, etc – which are widely used, but which offer scope for adaptation, or even supplementation (a few biblical scholars, even, have tried their hand at more creative forms of expression). No less importantly, we might find similar concerns addressed outside the discipline, and different concerns addressed in similar ways, while the boundaries of the discipline itself are far from clearcut.

Wisdom literature is not dry-as-dust academic work, but strongly poetic in character, so none of this is to say that it arose as the products of an academic discipline *per se*. The point, rather, is that we need not look far afield to find the same sort of phenomenon, in which a recognizable kinship between texts defies precise delimitation, and for which criteria of style or theme cannot be applied in isolation. What shapes and characterizes such things is the participation of writers who employ a repertoire of genres to address a particular area of concern, with an awareness of assumptions and conventions applied by other writers to the same issue. Crenshaw's 'marriage between form and content' is not, therefore, such a very unusual type of relationship, and if it is an accurate description of wisdom literature, then it potentially places that literature in a recognizable context of composition. Giving a label to this is more difficult, however, since we do not tend to classify our literature in the same way that we classify our academic work: wisdom is not specifically a genre, a movement, or a school of thought. Since it is far from clear, moreover, that the wisdom texts were identified as a distinct corpus by contemporary readers, we should probably not strive too hard to identify some classification that the writers might themselves have used. Perhaps we can do no better than to speak of their works loosely as products of a wisdom tradition, which drew on long-established genres linked to exhortation or disputation, was marked by a characteristic style of discourse, and focused on particular problems surrounding individual human life.

If this tradition was fostered by some particular group within the literate scribal class, then we have no secure information about that group, while its reliance on established conventions means that we must be wary both of assigning historical significance to the differences between individual texts, and of taking the general focus of the literature to reflect positive opposition to works with a different focus. Since individual sayings did not necessarily originate within the literature itself, moreover, it is difficult for us to establish the historical context of the texts on internal evidence. Beyond the probable fact that it originated within the literate élite, therefore, the wisdom literature remains something of a mystery in socio-historic terms – but that is true of much ancient literature. What we can say, more positively, is that the wisdom books seem not to have been cut off from other literature, in terms either of their dependencies or of their influence.

It is beyond doubt that some wisdom texts came to be very significant for the subsequent development of Jewish literature and thought more generally, with Proverbs 1–9 in particular pointing the way for advice literature to become a key vehicle for the Torah in later literature. If other texts were less obviously important in that respect, then we should remember that Job and Ecclesiastes have both continued nevertheless to attract considerable attention from readers and commentators for more than two thousand years. Although it has sometimes been marginalized in scholarship, therefore, there is nothing inherently marginal about wisdom literature.

Further Reading

With many different assumptions and approaches to be found in current scholarship on wisdom literature, no single book can give an adequate impression of the subject area as a whole. Correspondingly, it is a good idea to look at several of the many surveys, general studies and introductions available. Amongst older works, Rankin's 1936 lectures on wisdom literature as 'humanism' still offer an interesting perspective, and von Rad (1972) remains a classic, although many of its historical assumptions would now be questioned. Crenshaw (1981, available also in the form of a revised edition, published in 1998), and Murphy (1996) are of particular value among the more modern introductions, each offering many insights, but possessing distinct approaches. Crenshaw's collected essays on wisdom (1995) also include several surveys both of the literature and of scholarship at that time.

Chapter 1: Wisdom literature and its foreign counterparts

With so much written about the foreign literature, it is helpful to read the original texts without applying to them the sort of templates and filters often found in biblical scholarship's approach to them. The Sumerian texts discussed here are conveniently available in translation online, in the Electronic Text Corpus of Sumerian Literature (http://etcsl.orinst.ox.ac.uk/), and the Akkadian ones can mostly be found in Lambert (1960). Miriam Lichtheim's volumes of translated Egyptian texts (1973, 1976, 1980) include most of those mentioned, but discussions of origin and date have moved on since they were published, and for the earlier instructions, at least, it is easier to get a sense of context from Parkinson (1997, a paperback edition of which was published by OUP in 1999).

Chapter 2: The book of Proverbs

The finest commentary available in English at present is by Michael Fox (2000, 2009), although Bruce Waltke's work (2004, 2005), from a more conservative perspective, is also helpful, and Murphy (1998) often useful. My own works on Proverbs (Weeks 1994, 2007) discuss many of the questions addressed here in more detail, and present a range of other opinions. For a very different approach to the book, see Whybray (1972), but Norman Whybray also produced a valuable overview of scholarship on the book (1995). Martin (1995) continues to serve as an excellent short introduction, although it is becoming dated.

Chapter 3: The book of Job

There is much written on Job, from a wide variety of perspectives. David Clines' commentary (1989, 2006, 2010) is exceptionally valuable in its discussion of the text, and provides a very full bibliography, although his ideas about the book as a whole are presented more accessibly in his many articles on the subject (see especially Clines 1990). Carol Newsom offers a rather different perspective in her important study (Newsom 2003), and she has written a very helpful overview of recent research (2007). Good (1990) may be of particular interest to readers interested in the literary aspects of the book, and the problems of its translation.

Chapter 4: Ecclesiastes

The vast literature on Ecclesiastes reflects not only the many particular problems raised by the book, but also a basic lack of consensus about its nature and message: no single work can begin to reflect the diversity of opinion. Of the many English language commentaries available, those by Fox (1989, 1999), Crenshaw (1987), and Seow (1997) are currently the best, although Gordis (1968) is still of much value. For a very different approach, see Lohfink (2003). Eric Christianson (2007) has provided a survey of the book's reception history which is both important and enjoyable.

Chapter 5: Other Jewish wisdom literature

On wisdom psalms, see Weeks (2005), with the literature cited there. For the later wisdom literature generally, see especially the excellent survey by John Collins (1998). There are no entirely satisfactory commentaries on Ben Sira, but Skehan and Di Lella (1987) is useful. The finest commentary on Wisdom of Solomon is in French (Larcher 1983–5), but Winston (1979) is valuable, and Grabbe (1997) provides a very useful introduction; Winston (2005) offers an overview of recent scholarship, and is in a volume (Passaro and Bellia 2005) which has several important essays. On the Qumran texts, see especially Harrington (1996) for the main texts in translation with a useful account of each, and Goff (2007) for detailed discussion and a thorough coverage of the extensive scholarly literature. The principal editions of the texts are found in various volumes of the DJD series, but see conveniently Parry and Tov (2004). There is an important collection of essays in Hempel *et al.* (2002), and an accessible (though now rather dated) survey in van der Woude (1995).

Chapter 6: Wisdom thought

Questions of thought are touched on in most introductions to the literature (and see especially von Rad 1972), but detailed studies have been rare in recent scholarship. On the place of wisdom literature in many of the modern attempts to formulate a biblical theology, see the critiques of each in Barr (1999), *passim*. For a detailed discussion of theology in Proverbs in particular, although the conclusions are of more general relevance, see the excellent Boström (1990). This includes a critical assessment of earlier ideas about creation and order. Creation, understood in a rather different way, underpins Leo Perdue's attempts (1994, 2007) to characterize wisdom thought more generally, although the studies are, I think, beset by a lack of definitional clarity. The idea is also important in Walter Brueggemann's work (recently 2008: 179–87), alongside an emphasis on the human focus in wisdom literature (see especially Brueggemann 1972).

Chapter 7: The origins and place of wisdom literature

Older theories about the emergence of wisdom literature in an administrative, educational context are addressed in Weeks (1994). Recent scholarship has tended to be more cautious, but there is still a tendency in some literature to link elements of these theories with other ideas to create highly speculative reconstructions; see, for instance, the interesting and provocative Perdue (2008), which relies on a great many problematic assumptions. With regard to the broader scribal context of Jewish literature, see especially Carr (2005). Katharine Dell (2006) has recently sought to place Proverbs, more specifically, in a wider intellectual context, and has affirmed its close relationship with other Jewish literature.

Notes

Chapter 1

1 Sumerian was the language of the Sumerian culture in southern Mesopotamia. It was replaced as the spoken language of the region by Akkadian around the early Second Millennium, but continued to be learned, spoken, and used by scribes for many centuries as a classical language (see Woods 2006).

2 Egyptian history is conventionally divided into a series of named periods, corresponding to particular ruling dynasties. There are some disputes over the precise dates of certain dynasties, but more importantly over which dynasties should be included in certain periods, so different sources will sometimes give different dates. The Old Kingdom lasted from around the mid-3rd millennium until the 22nd century BCE, when there was a collapse of centralized power. This was reasserted around a century later, ushering in the Middle Kingdom, widely regarded by later Egyptians as a golden age. Under the 13th dynasty, which ruled from the end of the 18th to the middle of the 17th century BCE, Egypt became divided again, with parts of the country coming under foreign rule. The New Kingdom saw the country reunited once more, between the mid-16th and 11th centuries.

Chapter 4

1 The quotation is from his essay 'Self-Reliance', first published in 1841.

Bibliography

Albright, W. F. 1920. 'The Goddess of Life and Wisdom', *AJSL* 36: 258–94.

Aletti, J-N. 1977. 'Séduction et parole en Proverbes I-IX', *VT* 27: 129–44.

Alster, B. 1974. *The Instructions of Suruppak: A Sumerian Proverb Collection*, Mesopotamia, 2. Copenhagen: Akademisk Forlag.

——1997. *Proverbs of Ancient Sumer: The World's Earliest Proverb Collections*, 2 vols. Bethesda, Md.: CDL Press.

Assmann, J. 1979. 'Weisheit, Loyalismus und Frömmigkeit', in E. Hornung and O. Keel (eds), *Studien zu altägyptischen Lebenslehren*, OBO, 28. Freiburg, Sw.: Universitätsverlag; Göttingen: Vandenhoeck & Ruprecht: 11–72.

——1983. 'Schrift, Tod und Identität: Das Grab als Vorschule der Literatur im alten Ägypten', in A. Assmann *et al.* (eds), *Schrift und Gedächtnis, Beitrage zur Archäologie der literarischen Kommunikation*. Munich: W. Fink: 64–93.

——1999. 'Cultural and Literary Texts', in G. Moers (ed.), *Definitely: Egyptian Literature. Proceedings of the Symposium "Ancient Egyptian Literature: History and Forms", Los Angeles March 24–26, 1995*, Lingua Aegyptiaca Studia Monographica, 2. Göttingen: Seminar für Ägyptologie und Koptologie: 1–15. German version: 'Kulturelle und literarische Texte', in A. Loprieno (ed.), *Ancient Egyptian Literature. History and Forms*, Probleme der Ägyptologie, 10. Leiden, New York, Cologne: Brill, 1996: 59–82. The English version was written earlier, but published later.

——2006. *Ma'at: Gerechtigkeit und Unsterblichkeit im alten Ägypten*, 2nd ed, Munich: Beck.

Baines, J. 1991. 'Society, Morality, and Religious Practice', in B. E. Schafer (ed.), *Religion in Ancient Egypt. Gods, Myths, and Personal Practice*. London: Routledge: 123–200.

Barr, J. 1994. *Biblical Faith and Natural Theology: The Gifford Lectures for 1991: Delivered in the University of Edinburgh*. Oxford: Oxford University Press.

——1999. *The Concept of Biblical Theology: An Old Testament Perspective. Based on the Cadbury Lectures delivered at Birmingham University in 1968*. London: SCM.

Baumann, G. 1996. *Die Weisheitsgestalt in Proverbien 1–9: traditionsgeschichtliche und theologische Studien*, FAT, 16. Tübingen: Mohr-Siebeck.

Becker, J. 1965. *Gottesfurcht im alten Testament*, Analecta Biblica, 25. Rome: Pontifical Biblical Institute.

Blenkinsopp, J. 1983. *Wisdom and Law in the Old Testament: The Ordering of Life in Israel and early Judaism*, Oxford Bible Series. Oxford: Oxford University Press.

Boston, J. R. 1968. 'The Wisdom Influence upon the Song of Moses', *JBL* 88: 196–202.

Boström, L. 1990. *The God of the Sages: The Portrayal of God in the Book of Proverbs*, ConBOT, 29. Stockholm: Almquist & Wiksell.

Brekelmans, C. 1979. 'Wisdom Influence in Deuteronomy', in Gilbert 1979: 28–38.

Broyde, M. J. 1995. 'Defilement of the Hands, Canonization of the Bible, and the Special Status of Esther, Ecclesiastes, and Song of Songs', *Judaism* 44: 65–79.

Brueggemann, W. 1972. *In Man We Trust: The Neglected Side of Biblical Faith*. Richmond: John Knox Press.

——2008. *Old Testament Theology: An Introduction*. Library of Biblical Theology. Nashville: Abingdon Press.

Burke, D. G. 1982. *The Poetry of Baruch: A Reconstruction and Analysis of the Original Hebrew Text of Baruch 3:9–5:9*, Septuagint and Cognate Studies, 10. Chico: Scholars Press.

Camp, C. 1985. *Wisdom and the Feminine in the Book of Proverbs*, Bible and Literature Series, 11. Sheffield: Almond Press.

Carr, D. 2005. *Writing on the Tablet of the Heart: Origins of Scripture and Literature*. New York: Oxford University Press.

Christianson, E. S. 2007. *Ecclesiastes Through the Centuries*, Blackwell Bible Commentaries. Malden, Oxford, & Carlton: Blackwell.

Clines, D. J. A. 1989. *Job 1–20*, WBC, 17. Dallas: Word Books.

——1990. 'Deconstructing the Book of Job', in *What Does Eve do to Help? And Other Readerly Questions to the Old Testament*, JSOTSup, 94. Sheffield: Sheffield Academic Press: 106–23.

——1998. 'The Arguments of Job's Three Friends', in *On the Way to the Postmodern: Old Testament Essays 1967–1998*, JSOTSup, 292, 2 vols. Sheffield: Sheffield Academic Press: vol 2, pp. 719–34.

——2006. *Job 21–37*, WBC, 18A. Nashville: Thomas Nelson.

——2010. *Job 38–42*, WBC, 18B. Nashville: Thomas Nelson.

Collins, J. J. 1977. 'The Biblical Precedent for Natural Theology (Abstract)', *JAAR* 45: 70.

——1998. *Jewish Wisdom in the Hellenistic Age*, Louisville: Westminster John Knox Press. Edinburgh: T&T Clark.

——2005. 'The Reinterpretation of Apocalyptic Traditions in the Wisdom of Solomon', in Passaro and Bellia 2005: 143–55.

Conybeare, F. C., Rendel Harris, J., and Smith Lewis, A. 1913. *The Story of Aḥikar: From the Aramaic, Syriac, Arabic, Armenian, Ethiopic, Old Turkish, Greek and Slavonic Versions*, 2nd edn. Cambridge: Cambridge University Press.

Corley, J. 2005. 'An Intertextual Study of Proverbs and Ben Sira', in Jeremy Corley and Vincent Skemp (eds.), *Intertextual Studies in Ben Sira and Tobit: Essays in Honor of Alexander A. Di Lella, O.F.M.*, CBQMS, 38. Washington: The Catholic Biblical Association of America: 155–82.

Crenshaw, J. 1981. *Old Testament Wisdom: An Introduction*. Atlanta: John Knox Press.

——1987. *Ecclesiastes: A Commentary*, Old Testament Library. Philadelphia: Westminster Press.

——1995. *Urgent Advice and Probing Questions: Collected Writings on Old Testament Wisdom*. Macon: Mercer University Press.

——1998. *Education in Ancient Israel: Across the Deadening Silence*, Anchor Bible Reference Library. New York: Doubleday.

Day, J., Robert G., and Hugh G. M. Williamson (eds.) 1995. *Wisdom in Ancient Israel: Essays in Honour of J.A. Emerton*. Cambridge: Cambridge University Press.

Dell, K. J. 1991. *The Book of Job as Sceptical Literature*, BZAW, 197. Berlin & New York: de Gruyter.

——2000. *"Get Wisdom, Get Insight": An Introduction to Israel's Wisdom Literature*. London: Darton Longman & Todd.

——2005. 'Does the Song of Songs have any Connections to Wisdom?', in A. C. Hagedorn (ed.), *Perspectives on the Song of Songs*, BZAW, 346. Berlin: de Gruyter: 8–26.

——2006. *The Book of Proverbs in Social and Theological Context*. Cambridge & New York: Cambridge University Press.

Derousseaux, L. 1970. *La Crainte de Dieu dans l'Ancien Testament. Royauté, Alliance, Sagesses dans les royaumes d'Isra'l et de Juda: Recherches sur la racine yârê'*, Lectio Divina, 63. Paris: Cerf.

Emerton, J. A. 2001. 'The Teaching of Amenemope and Proverbs XXII 17–XXIV 22: Further Reflections on a Long-Standing Problem', *VT* 51: 431–64.

Erman, A. 1924. 'Eine ägyptische Quelle der "Sprüche Salomos"', *SPAW* 15: 86–93, tab. VI–VII.

Fichtner, J. 1949. 'Jesaja unter den Weisen', *TLZ* 74: 76–80.

Fischer, S. 1999. *Die Aufforderung zur Lebensfreude im Buch Kohelet und seine Rezeption der ägyptischen Harfnerlieder*, Wiener alttestamentliche Studien, 2. Frankfurt am Main: Peter Lang.

Fitzpatrick-McKinley, A. 1999. *The Transformation of Torah from Scribal Advice to Law*, JSOT Sup, 287. Sheffield: Sheffield Academic Press.

Fontaine, C. R. 1982. *Traditional Sayings in the Old Testament: A Contextual Study*, Bible and Literature Series, 5. Sheffield: Almond Press.

Fox, M. V. 1977. 'Frame-Narrative and Composition in the Book of Qohelet', *HUCA* 48: 83–106.

——1986. 'The Meaning of Hebel for Qohelet', *JBL* 105: 409–27.

——1988. 'Aging and Death in Qohelet 12', *JSOT* 13: 55–77.

——1989. *Qohelet and his Contradictions*, JSOTSup, 71, Bible and Literature Series, 18. Sheffield: Almond Press.

——1995. 'World Order and Ma'at: A Crooked Parallel', *JANESCU* 23: 37–48.

——1997. 'Who Can Learn? A Dispute in Ancient Pedagogy', in M.L. Barré (ed.), *Wisdom, You Are My Sister: Studies in Honor of Roland E. Murphy, O.Carm., on the Occasion of his Eightieth Birthday*, CBQMS, 29. Washington: Catholic Biblical Association of America: 62–77.

——1999. *A Time To Tear Down And A Time To Build Up: A Rereading Of Ecclesiastes*. Grand Rapids and Cambridge: Eerdmans.

——2000. *Proverbs 1–9: A New Translation with Introduction and Commentary*, AB, 18A. New York: Doubleday.

——2009. *Proverbs 10–31: A New Translation with Introduction and Commentary*, AB, 18B. New York: Doubleday.

Fredericks, D. C. 1988. *Qoheleth's Language: Re-evaluating its Nature and Date*, Ancient Near Eastern Texts and Studies, 3. Lewiston, Queenston, Lampeter: Edwin Mellen Press.

Freedman, D. N. 1990. 'The Book of Job', in W.H. Propp, B. Halpern, and D.N. Freedman (eds.), *The Hebrew Bible and its Interpreters*, Biblical and Judaic Studies from the University of California, San Diego, 1. Winona Lake: Eisenbrauns: 33–51.

Galling, K. 1969. 'Der Prediger',in Ernst Würthwein, Kurt Galling, and Otto Plöger, *Die fünf Megilloth*, 2nd edn; Handbuch zum alten Testament, 1/18. Tübingen: J. C. B. Mohr [Paul Siebeck]: 73–125.

Gardiner, A. H. 1937. *Late-Egyptian Miscellanies*, Bibliotheca Aegyptiaca, 7. Brussels: Édition de la Fondation égyptologique reine Elizabeth.

Gese, H. 1958. *Lehre und Wirklichkeit in der alten Weisheit: Studien zu den Sprüchen Salomos und zu dem Buche Hiob*. Tübingen: Mohr.

Gilbert, M. (ed.) 1979. *La Sagesse de l'Ancien Testament*, BETL, 51. Gembloux: J. Duculot; Leuven: Leuven University Press.

Goff, M. J. 2007. *Discerning Wisdom: The Sapiential Literature of the Dead Sea Scrolls*, VTSup, 116. Leiden & Boston: Brill.

Golka, F. 1993. *The Leopard's Spots: Biblical and African Wisdom in Proverbs*. Edinburgh: T&T Clark. German version: *Die Flecken des Leoparden: biblische und afrikanische Weisheit im Sprichwort*, Arbeiten zur Theologie, 78. Stuttgart: Calwer, 1994.

Good, E. M. 1990. *In Turns of Tempest: A Reading of Job with a Translation*. Stanford: Stanford University Press.

Goodman, M. 1990. 'Sacred Scripture and "Defiling the Hands"', *JTS* 41: 99–107.

Gordis, R. 1968. *Koheleth – The Man and His World: A Study of Ecclesiastes*, 3rd edn. New York: Schocken.

Grabbe, L. L. 1997. *Wisdom of Solomon*, Guides to Apocrypha and Pseudepigrapha. Sheffield: Sheffield Academic Press.

Gruber, M. I. 1990. 'Fear, Anxiety and Reverence in Akkadian, Biblical Hebrew and other North-West Semitic Languages', *VT* 40: 411–22.

Gunkel, H., and Begrich, J. 1933. *Einleitung in die Psalmen: die Gattungen der religiösen Lyrik Israels* Göttinger Handkommentar zum alten Testament; Göttingen: Vandenhoeck & Ruprecht. Translated by J. D. Nogalski as *Introduction to Psalms: The Genres of the Religious Lyric of Israel* (Macon: Mercer University Press, 1998).

Habel, N. 1972. 'The Symbolism of Wisdom in Proverbs 1–9', *Interpretation* 26: 131–56.

Hadley, J. M. 1995. 'Wisdom and the Goddess', in Day *et al.* 1995: 234–43.

Harrington, D. J. 1996. *Wisdom Texts from Qumran*, The Literature of the Dead Sea Scrolls. London & New York: Routledge.

Heim, G. 2001. *Like Grapes of Gold Set in Silver: An Interpretation of Proverbial Clusters in Proverbs 10:1–22:16*, BZAW, 273. Berlin & New York: de Gruyter.

Hempel, C., Lange, A. and Lichtenberger, H. (eds.) 2002. *The Wisdom Texts from Qumran and the Development of Sapiential Thought*, BETL, 159. Leuven: Leuven University Press & Peeters.

Hirshman, M. 2001. 'Qohelet's Reception and Interpretation in Early Rabbinic Literature', in James L. Kugel (ed.), *Studies in Ancient Midrash*. Cambridge, Mass.: Harvard University Center for Jewish Studies: 87–99.

Horbury, W. 1995. 'The Christian Use and the Jewish Origins of the Wisdom of Solomon', in Day *et al.* 1995: 182–96.

Hornung, E. 1982. *Conceptions of God in Ancient Egypt: The One and the Many*. Translated by J. Baines from *Der Eine und die Vielen: Ägyptische Gottesvorstellung* (Darmstadt: Wissenschaftliche Buchgesellschaft, 1971). Ithaca: Cornell University Press; London: Routledge & Kegan Paul.

Hurowitz, V. A. 2007. 'The Wisdom of Šūpê-amēlī – A Deathbed Debate Between a Father and Son', in Richard J. Clifford (ed.), *Wisdom Literature in Mesopotamia and Israel*, SBL Symposium Series, 36. Atlanta: SBL: 37–51.

Jackson, B. 2006. *Wisdom-Laws: A Study of the Mishpatim of Exodus 21:1–22:16*. Oxford & New York: Oxford University Press.

Janzen, J. G. 2009. *At the Scent of Water: The Ground of Hope in the Book of Job*. Grand Rapids & Cambridge: Eerdmans.

Kayatz, C. 1966. *Studien zu Proverbien 1–9: Eine form- und motivgeschichtliche Untersuchung unter Einbeziehung ägyptischen Vergleichsmaterials*, WMANT, 22. Neukirchen-Vluyn: Neukirchener Verlag.

Knox, W. L. 1937. 'The Divine Wisdom', *JTS* 38: 230–37.

Koch, K. 1955. 'Gibt es ein Vergeltungsdogma im alten Testament?', *ZTK* 52: 1–42. An abbreviated ET by Thomas Trapp appeared as 'Is there a Doctrine of Retribution in the Old Testament?', in James Crenshaw (ed.), *Theodicy in the Old Testament*, Issues in Religion and Theology, 4. Philadelphia: Fortress Press: 57–87.

Küchler, M. 1979. *Fruhjudische Weisheitstraditionen: zum Fortgang weisheitlichen Denkens im Bereich des fruhjudischen Jahweglaubens*, OBO, 26. Freiburg, Sw.: Universitatsverlag.

Lambert, W. G. 1960. *Babylonian Wisdom Literature*. Oxford: Clarendon Press.

——1995. 'Some New Babylonian Wisdom Literature', in Day *et al.* 1995: 30–42.

Lang, B. 1986. *Wisdom and the Book of Proverbs: A Hebrew Goddess Redefined*. New York: Pilgrim Press.

Larcher, C. 1985. *Le Livre de la Sagesse ou la Sagesse de Salomon*, 3 vols, Etudes Bibliques n.s., 1. Paris: Gabalda.

Levy, L. 1912. *Das Buch Qoheleth: Ein Beitrag zur Geschichte des Sadduzäismus: Kritisch untersucht, übersetzt und erklärt*. Leipzig: J.C. Hinrichs.

Lichtheim, M. 1973. *Ancient Egyptian Literature: A Book of Readings. Volume 1: The Old and Middle Kingdoms*. Berkeley, CA, Los Angeles, CA, & London: University of California Press.

——1976. *Ancient Egyptian Literature: A Book of Readings. Volume 2: The New Kingdom*. Berkeley, CA, Los Angeles, CA, & London: University of California Press.

——1980, *Ancient Egyptian Literature: A Book of Readings. Volume 3: The Late Period*. Berkeley, CA, Los Angeles, CA, & London: University of California Press.

——1983. *Late Egyptian Wisdom Literature in the International Context: A Study of Demotic Instructions*, OBO, 52. Freiburg, Sw.: Universitätsverlag; Göttingen: Vandenhoeck & Ruprecht.

Lindenberger, J. M. 1983. *The Aramaic Proverbs of Ahiqar*, Johns Hopkins Near Eastern Studies. Baltimore and London: Johns Hopkins University Press.

Lo, A. 2003. *Job 28 as Rhetoric: An Analysis of Job 28 in the Context of Job 22–31*, VTSup 97. Leiden & Boston: Brill; Atlanta: SBL.

Lohfink, N. 2003. *Qoheleth: A Continental Commentary*. Translated by S. McEvenue from *Kohelet* (Die neue Echter Bibel; Würzburg: Echter Verlag, 1980). Minneapolis: Fortress Press.

Longman III, T. 1991. *Fictional Akkadian Biography*. Winona Lake: Eisenbrauns.

——1998. *The Book of Ecclesiastes*, NICOT. Grand Rapids and Cambridge: Eerdmans.

Loretz, O. 1964. *Qohelet und der alte Orient. Untersuchungen zu Stil und theologischer Thematik des Buches Qohelet*. Freiburg im Breisgau, Basel, & Wien: Herder.

McGlynn, M. 2001. *Divine Judgement and Divine Benevolence in the Book of Wisdom*, WUNT, 139. Tübingen: Mohr Siebeck.

McKane, W. 1970. *Proverbs: A New Approach*, Old Testament Library. London: SCM.

McKenzie, J. L. 1967. 'Reflections on Wisdom', *JBL* 86: 1–9.

Malfroy, J. 1965. 'Sagesse et loi dans le Deutéronome', *VT* 15: 49–65.

Martin, J. D. 1995. *Proverbs*, Old Testament Guides. Sheffield: Sheffield Academic Press.

Meinhold, A. 1991. *Die Sprüche. Teil 1: Sprüche Kapitel 1–15*, Zürcher Bibelkommentare, 16.1. Zürich: Theologischer Verlag.

Miller, D. B. 2002. *Symbol and Rhetoric in Ecclesiastes: The Place of Hebel in Qohelet's Work*, SBL Academia Biblica, 2. Atlanta: SBL.

Moran, W. L. 1983. 'Notes on the Hymn to Marduk in Ludlul Bēl Nēmeqi', *JAOS* 103: 255–60.

Morgan, D. F. 1981. *Wisdom in the Old Testament Traditions*. Atlanta: John Knox Press; Oxford: Blackwell.

Müller, H. -P. 1969. 'Magisch-mantische Weisheit und die Gestalt Daniels', *UF* 1: 79–94.

Muraoka, T. 1979. 'Sir. 51, 13–30: An Erotic Hymn to Wisdom?', *JSJ* 10: 166–78.

Murphy, R. E. 1978. 'Wisdom – Theses and Hypotheses', in J. G. Gammie *et al.* (eds.), *Israelite Wisdom: Theological and Literary Essays in Honor of Samuel Terrien*. Missoula: Scholars Press for Union Theological Seminary: 35–42.

——1987. 'Religious Dimensions of Israelite Wisdom', in P. D. Miller *et al.* (eds.), *Ancient Israelite Religion: Essays in Honor of Frank Moore Cross*. Philadelphia: Fortress Press: 449–58.

——1996, *The Tree of Life: An Exploration of Biblical Wisdom Literature*, 2nd edn. Grand Rapids: Eerdmans.

——1998, *Proverbs*, WBC, 22. Nashville: Thomas Nelson.

Newsom, C. A. 2002. 'The Book of Job as Polyphonic Text', *JSOT* 97: 87–108.

——2003. *The Book of Job: A Contest of Moral Imaginations*. New York: Oxford University Press.

——2007, 'Re-considering Job', *CBR* 5: 155–82.

Nougayrol, J., *et al.* (eds.) 1968. *Ugaritica V*, Mission de Ras Shamra, 16, Bibliothèque archéologique et historique Institut français d'archéologie de Beyrouth, 80. Paris: P. Geuthner.

Parkinson, R. B. 1997. *The Tale of Sinuhe and other Ancient Egyptian Poems 1940–1640 BC*. Oxford: Clarendon Press.

——2002. *Poetry and Culture in Middle Kingdom Egypt: A Dark Side to Perfection*. London & New York: Continuum.

Parry, D. W., and Tov, E. (eds.) 2004. *The Dead Sea Scrolls Reader. Part 4: Calendrical and Sapiential Texts*. Leiden & Boston: Brill.

Passaro, A., and Bellia, G. 2005. *Yearbook 2005. The Book of Wisdom in Modern Research: Studies on Tradition, Redaction, and Theology. With an Introduction by John J. Collins*, Deuterocanonical and Cognate Literature. Berlin & New York: de Gruyter.

Perdue, L. 1994. *Wisdom & Creation: The Theology of Wisdom Literature*. Nashville: Abingdon Press.

——2007. *Wisdom Literature: A Theological History*. Louisville & London: Westminster John Knox Press.

——2008. *The Sword and the Stylus: An Introduction to Wisdom in the Age of Empires*. Grand Rapids & Cambridge: Eerdmans.

Perry, T. A. 1993. *Dialogues with Kohelet: The Book of Ecclesiastes: Translation and Commentary*. University Park, PA: Pennsylvania State University Press.

Plath, S. 1963. *Furcht Gottes. Der Begriff יִרְאָה im Alten Testament*, Arbeiten zur Theologie, 2.2. Stuttgart: Calwer.

Posener, G. 1956. *Littérature et politique dans l'Égypte de la XIIe dynastie*, Bibliothèque de l'École des hautes études, 307. Paris: H. Champion.

Rad, G. von. 1972. *Wisdom in Israel*. Translated by J. D. Martin from *Weisheit in Israel* (Neukirchen-Vluyn: Neukirchener Verlag, 1970). London: SCM.

Rankin, O. S. 1936. *Israel's Wisdom Literature: Its Bearing on Theology and the History* of Religion: The Kerr lectures delivered in Trinity College, Glasgow, 1933–36. Edinburgh: T&T Clark.

Reese, J. M. 1970. Hellenistic Influence on the Book of Wisdom and its Consequences, Analecta Biblica, 41; Rome: Biblical Institute Press.

Sanders, J. T. 1983. Ben Sira and Demotic Wisdom, SBL Monograph Series, 28. Chico: Scholars Press.

Schmid, H. H. 1966. Wesen und Geschichte der Weisheit: eine Untersuchung zur Altorientalischen und Israelitischen Weisheitsliteratur, BZAW, 101. Berlin: Töpelmann.

——1968. Gerechtigkeit als Weltordnung: Hintergrund und Geschichte der alttestamentlichen Gerechtigkeitsbegriffes, Beiträge zur historischen Theologie, 40. Tübingen: Mohr [Siebeck].

Schroer, S. 2000. Wisdom Has Built Her House: Studies on the Figure of Sophia in the Bible. Translated by L. M. Maloney and W. McDonough from Die Weisheit hat ihr Haus gebaut. Studien zur Gestalt der Sophia in den biblischen Schriften (Mainz: M. Grünewald, 1996). Collegeville: Liturgical Press.

Seow, C. -L. 1997. Ecclesiastes: A New Translation with Introduction and Commentary, AB, 18C. New York: Doubleday.

Sheppard, G. T. 1980. Wisdom as a Hermeneutical Construct: A Study in the Sapientalizing of the Old Testament, BZAW, 151. Berlin: de Gruyter.

Shields, M. 2006. The End of Wisdom: A Reappraisal of the Historical and Canonical Function of Ecclesiastes. Winona Lake: Eisenbrauns.

Shupak, N. 2005. 'The Instruction of Amenemope and Proverbs 22.17–24.22 from the Perspective of Contemporary Research', in Ronald L. Troxel et al. (eds.), Seeking out the Wisdom of the Ancients: Essays offered to Honor Michael V. Fox on the Occasion of his Sixty-fifth Birthday. Winona Lake: Eisenbrauns: 203–20.

Skehan, P. W. and di Lella, A. 1987. The Wisdom of Ben Sira: A New Translation with Notes by Patrick W. Skehan: Introduction and Commentary by Alexander di Lella, AB, 39. New York: Doubleday.

Soggin, J. A. 1995. 'Amos and Wisdom', in Day et al. 1995: 119–23.

Terrien, S. 1962. 'Amos and Wisdom', in B.W. Anderson and W. Harrelson (eds.), Israel's Prophetic Heritage: Essays in Honor of James Muilenburg. New York: Harper; London: SCM: 108–15.

Uehlinger, C. 1997. 'Qohelet im Horizont mesopotamischer, levantinischer und ägyptischer Weisheitsliteratur der persischen und hellenistischen Zeit', in L. Schwienhorst-Schönberger (ed.), Das Buch Kohelet. Studien zur Struktur, Geschichte, Rezeption und Theologie, BZAW, 254. Berlin & New York: de Gruyter: 155–247.

Veldhuis, N. 2000. 'Sumerian Proverbs in their Curricular Context' (review of Alster 1997), JAOS 120: 383–399.

Vermeylen, J. 1979. 'Le Proto-Isaïe et la Sagesse d'Israël', in Gilbert 1979: 39–58.

Waltke, B. K. 2004. The Book of Proverbs: Chapters 1–15, NICOT. Grand Rapids: Eerdmans.

——2005. The Book of Proverbs: Chapters 15–31, NICOT. Grand Rapids: Eerdmans.

Weeks, S. 1994. Early Israelite Wisdom, Oxford Theological Monographs. Oxford: Clarendon Press. Corrected paperback edition: Oxford: Oxford University Press, 1999.

——2005. 'Wisdom Psalms', in John Day (ed.), Temple and Worship in Biblical Israel. London & New York: T&T Clark: 292–307.

——2006. 'The Context and Meaning of Proverbs 8.30a', JBL 125: 433–42.

——2007. Instruction and Imagery in Proverbs 1–9. Oxford: Oxford University Press.

Weinfeld, M. 1972. *Deuteronomy and the Deuteronomic School*. Oxford: Clarendon
    Press.
Westermann, C. 1995. *Roots of Wisdom: The Oldest Proverbs of Israel and Other
    Peoples*. Translated by J.D. Charles from *Wurzeln der Weisheit: die ältesten
    Sprüche Israels und anderer Völker* (Göttingen: Vandenhoeck & Ruprecht, 1990).
    Edinburgh: T&T Clark.
Whedbee, J. W. 1971. *Isaiah and Wisdom*. Nashville: Abingdon Press.
Whybray, R. N. 1972. *The Book of Proverbs*, Cambridge Bible Commentary. Cambridge:
    Cambridge University Press.
——1974. *The Intellectual Tradition in the Old Testament*, BZAW, 135. Berlin: de
    Gruyter.
——1979. 'Yahweh-sayings and their Contexts in Proverbs, 10,1–22,16', in Gilbert
    1979: 153–65.
——1981. 'The Identification and Use of Quotations in Ecclesiastes', in J. A. Emerton
    (ed.), *Congress Volume, Vienna, 1980*, VTSup, 32; Leiden: Brill: 435–51.
——1994a. *The Composition of the Book of Proverbs*, JSOTSup, 168. Sheffield: JSOT
    Press.
——1994b. 'The Structure and Composition of Proverbs 22.17–24.22', in S. E. Porter *et
    al.* (eds.), *Crossing the Boundaries: Essays in Biblical Interpretation in Honour of
    Michael D. Goulder*, Biblical Interpretation Series, 8. Leiden: Brill: 83–96.
——1995. *The Book of Proverbs: A Survey of Modern Study*, History of Biblical
    Interpretation Series, 1. Leiden: Brill.
Williamson, H. G. M. 1995. 'Isaiah and the Wise', in Day *et al.* 1995: 133–41.
Wilson, W. T. 1994. *The Mysteries of Righteousness: The Literary Composition and
    Genre of the Sentences of Pseudo-Phocylides*, Texte und Studien zum antiken
    Judentum, 40. Tübingen: Mohr.
——2005. *The Sentences of Pseudo-Phocylides*, Commentaries on Early Jewish Literature.
    Berlin & New York: de Gruyter.
Winston, D. 1979. *The Wisdom of Solomon: A New Translation with Introduction and
    Commentary*, AB, 43. Garden City, NY: Doubleday.
——2005. 'A Century of Research on the Book of Wisdom', in Passaro and Bellia 2005:
    1–18.
Wolff, H. W. 1964. *Amos' Geistige Heimat* WMANT, 18; Neukirchen-Vluyn:
    Neukirchener Verlag. Translated by F. R. McCurley as *Amos, the Prophet: The
    Man and his Background* (Philadelphia: Fortress Press, 1973).
Wolters, A. 2001. *The Song of the Valiant Woman: Studies in the Interpretation of
    Proverbs 31: 10–31*. London, Atlanta, & Hyderabad: Paternoster.
Woods, C. 2006. 'Bilingualism, Scribal Learning, and the Death of Sumerian', in Seth L.
    Sanders (ed.), *Margins of Writing, Origins of Cultures*, Oriental Institute Seminars,
    2. Chicago: The Oriental Institute of the University of Chicago: 95–124.
Woude, A.S. van der. 1995. 'Wisdom at Qumran', in Day *et al.* 1995: 244–56.
Yoder, C. R. 2001. *Wisdom as a Woman of Substance: A Socioeconomic Reading of
    Proverbs 1–9 and 31:10–31*, BZAW, 304. Berlin & New York: de Gruyter.
Young, I. 1998. 'Israelite Literacy: Interpreting the Evidence', *VT* 48: 239–53, 408–22.

General Index

Index of Authors

Select Index of Passages Cited
and Discussed